OXFORD STUDIES IN EPISTEMOLOGY

OXFORD STUDIES IN EPISTEMOLOGY

OXFORD STUDIES IN EPISTEMOLOGY

Volume 2

Edited by

Tamar Szabó Gendler and John Hawthorne

OXFORD
UNIVERSITY PRESS

OXFORD
UNIVERSITY PRESS

Great Clarendon Street, Oxford OX2 6DP

Oxford University Press is a department of the University of Oxford.
It furthers the University's objective of excellence in research, scholarship,
and education by publishing worldwide in

Oxford New York

Auckland Cape Town Dar es Salaam Hong Kong Karachi
Kuala Lumpur Madrid Melbourne Mexico City Nairobi
New Delhi Shanghai Taipei Toronto

With offices in

Argentina Austria Brazil Chile Czech Republic France Greece
Guatemala Hungary Italy Japan Poland Portugal Singapore
South Korea Switzerland Thailand Turkey Ukraine Vietnam

Published in the United States
by Oxford University Press Inc., New York

First published 2007

British Library Cataloguing in Publication Data
Data available

Library of Congress Cataloging in Publication Data
Data available

Typeset by Laserwords Private Ltd., Chennai, India
Printed in Great Britain
on acid-free paper by
Biddles Ltd, King's Lynn, Norfolk

ISBN 978–0–19–923706–7
ISBN 978–0–19–923707–4 (pbk)

1 3 5 7 9 10 8 6 4 2

EDITORS' PREFACE

It is with great pleasure that we introduce the second issue of *Oxford Studies in Epistemology*, inaugurated in 2005 as a member of Oxford's expanded collection of *Oxford Studies* serials. The diverse set of essays that appear here represent some of the most interesting epistemological work going on in the English-speaking world today, providing the reader with a glimpse into an active and vibrant area of philosophical investigation.

Published biennially under the guidance of a distinguished editorial board, each issue of *Oxford Studies in Epistemology* seeks to include an assortment of exemplary papers in epistemology, broadly construed. *OSE* aims to publish not only traditional works in epistemology, but also work that brings new perspectives to traditional epistemological questions, and that opens new avenues of investigation.

These commitments are evident in the contents of the second issue. The papers that appear here are diverse in their foci, but uniform in their quality. Two are concerned with the question of how the challenge of radical skepticism can be met, with Richard Fumerton raising challenges for one line of thought in "Epistemic Conservatism: Theft or Honest Toil" and Nico Silins providing a defense of another in "Basic Justification and the Moorean Response to the Skeptic." Two others explore tensions that surround the idea of epistemic rationality: David Christensen's "Does Murphy's Law Apply in Epistemology? Self-Doubt and Rational Ideals" and Allan Gibbard's "Rational Credence and the Value of Truth." Gibbard's paper serves as a target for responses by Frank Arntzenius in "Rationality and Self-Confidence" and Eric Swanson in "A Note on Gibbard's Rational Credence and the Value of Truth," with a reply by Gibbard in "Aiming at Truth over Time: Reply to Arntzenius and Swanson." Finally, two essays reflect the journal's ongoing commitment to bringing work on epistemology in related fields to the attention of philosophers: linguist Kai von Fintel and philosopher Anthony Gillies's "An Opinionated Guide to Epistemic

Modality'' and primatologist Laurie Santos's ''The Evolution of Irrationality: Insights from Non-human Primates.''

As in the past, some of the papers that appear here were brought to our attention by members of the editorial board, others were solicited directly from authors; all were refereed by the members of our Editorial Advisory Board, to whom we are grateful. Thanks are due to all of its members: Stewart Cohen (Arizona State University), Keith DeRose (Yale University), Richard Fumerton (University of Iowa), Alvin Goldman (Rutgers University), Alan Hájek (Australian National University), Gil Harman (Princeton University), Frank Jackson (Australian National University and Princeton University), Jim Joyce (University of Michigan), Scott Sturgeon (Birkbeck College London), Jonathan Vogel (University of California at Davis), and Tim Williamson (University of Oxford) We are also indebted to our outstanding managing editor Roald Nashi, for his superb editorial assistance, and to Peter Momtchiloff, for his continuing support of this project.

Tamar Szabó Gendler, Yale University
John Hawthorne, Oxford University

CONTENTS

List of Figures viii
List of Contributors ix

PAPERS

1 Does Murphy's Law Apply in Epistemology? Self-Doubt and Rational Ideals 3
David Christensen

2 An Opinionated Guide to Epistemic Modality 32
Kai von Fintel and Anthony S. Gillies

3 Epistemic Conservatism: Theft or Honest Toil? 63
Richard Fumerton

4 The Evolution of Irrationality: Insights from Non-Human Primates 87
Laurie R. Santos

5 Basic Justification and the Moorean Response to the Skeptic 108
Nicholas Silins

SYMPOSIUM

6 Rational Credence and the Value of Truth 143
Allan Gibbard

7 Rationality and Self-Confidence 165
Frank Arntzenius

8 A Note on Gibbard's "Rational Credence and the Value of Truth" 179
Eric Swanson

9 Aiming at Truth Over Time: Reply to Arntzenius and Swanson 190
Allan Gibbard

Index 205

LIST OF FIGURES

2.1. Willet's taxonomy of evidentials 39

4.1. Depiction of the Trading Situation 97

5.1. The key positions 117

6.1. Pairs of functions generated by various functions h 153

8.1. The report relation for $g_1(x) = 1 - (1 - x)^3, g_0(x) = 1 - x^3$ 183

LIST OF CONTRIBUTORS

Frank Arntzenius
UNIVERISTY OF OXFORD

David Christensen
BROWN UNIVERSITY

Kai von Fintel
MASSACHUSETTS INSTITUTE OF TECHNOLOGY

Richard Fumerton
UNIVERSITY OF IOWA

Allan Gibbard
UNIVERSITY OF MICHIGAN

Anthony Gillies
UNIVERSITY OF MICHIGAN

Laurie Santos
YALE UNIVERSITY

Nicholas Silins
CORNELL UNIVERSITY

Eric Swanson
UNIVERSITY OF MICHIGAN

PAPERS

1. Does Murphy's Law Apply in Epistemology? Self-Doubt and Rational Ideals

David Christensen

Formally inclined epistemologists often theorize about ideally rational agents—agents who exemplify rational ideals, such as probabilistic coherence, that human beings could never fully realize. This approach can be defended against the well-known worry that abstracting from human cognitive imperfections deprives the approach of interest. But a different worry arises when we ask what an ideal agent should *believe* about her own cognitive perfection (even an agent who is in fact cognitively perfect might, it would seem, be uncertain of this fact). Consideration of this question reveals an interesting feature of the structure of our epistemic ideals: for agents with limited information, our epistemic ideals turn out to conflict with one another. This suggests that we must revise the way we see ideal agents in epistemic theorizing.

1. IDEAL VERSUS HUMAN-CENTRIC RATIONALITY

What would an ideally rational agent believe? Of course, the answer depends on just what kind of ideally rational agent is in question. But when epistemologists consider this question, they don't simply answer "everything true". Rationality, after all, involves reacting correctly to the evidence one has, but does not seem to require having all possible evidence about everything. Thus, if we seek to

Thanks to Don Fallis, Hilary Kornblith, Michelle Kosch, Don Loeb, Mark Moyer, Roald Nashi, Derk Pereboom, Tomoji Shogenji, Nico Silins, and Peter Sutton for helpful discussions and/or comments on earlier drafts. Special thanks to Louis deRosset and Jonathan Vogel, who each provided extensive and incisive written comments. Versions of this paper were read at NYU, Cornell, UMass, and Brown, and I thank the participants for valuable discussion.

understand rationality by constructing a model of ideally rational belief, we will not concentrate on an omniscient being. Instead, we'll consider a non-omniscient thinker who nevertheless is in certain respects cognitively perfect. We might, for example, stipulate the following kinds of things about such an ideally rational agent's beliefs. They would not be based in wishful thinking. They would be independent of the agent's likes and dislikes. They would respect whatever evidence the agent had. And they would respect the logical relations among claims the agent had beliefs about. Let us call a non-omniscient agent who nevertheless is ideally rational an IRA.[1]

This general approach to theorizing about rationality dovetails nicely with the tradition which relates rationality to thinking logically, and then characterizes rational belief with the aid of formal logic. Those who see belief as a binary, all-or-nothing, kind of state have thus often taken logical consistency and logical closure to be rational ideals. And those who conceive of beliefs as coming in degrees have taken conditions based on probabilistic coherence—which can be seen as little more than applying standard deductive logic to graded beliefs—as ideals.[2]

Of course, this whole formal approach to thinking about rationality has been criticized. The main line of criticism takes off from the fact that ideals such as logical consistency or probabilistic coherence are very clearly far beyond the capacities of any human to achieve—even more so than complete freedom from prejudice or wishful thinking. Such ideals require, for instance, that an agent believe (or, in the case of coherence conditions, be completely certain of) every logical truth. Why then, it is asked, should rules that might apply to a peculiar sort of imaginary beings—ideal thinkers with limited information—have any bearing on us? The fact that we

[1] For a sense of how widespread this approach is, see the following *Stanford Encyclopedia* entries: James Joyce on Bayes' Theorem, Sven Ove Hansson on Logic of Belief Revision, James Hawthorne on Inductive Logic, Robert Koons on Defeasible Reasoning, and William Talbott on Bayesian Epistemology. Books in this tradition include Savage (1954), Ellis (1979), Horwich (1982), Maher (1993), and Levi (1997).

[2] By "conditions based on probabilistic coherence," I mean not only conditions requiring agents to have precise real-valued degrees of confidence satisfying the laws of probability, but also less restrictive conditions modeling rational degrees of belief by sets of probability functions, or qualitative probabilities. For convenience, I'll use the term "probabilistic coherence" to refer to this whole family of conditions.

humans have the particular limitations we do, it is urged, is not just some trivial footnote to epistemology; it's a central aspect of our epistemic predicament. Interesting epistemology—epistemology for humans—must take account of this fact.[3]

I think that this line of criticism should be resisted. While there are certainly some projects in epistemology that must take careful account of human limitations, they do not exhaust interesting epistemology.[4] For example, if one's epistemological project were to characterize our ordinary, casual way of using the words "rational" and "irrational" to apply to people, then it might be hard to see how humanly unattainable ideals would play an important role: everyone fails to live up to humanly unattainable ideals, but we obviously don't call everyone "irrational". But there's little reason to think that epistemology should be restricted to such a thin notion of rationality. (Similarly, ethics should not be restricted to studying moral ideals that are perfectly attained by the ordinary people we'd hesitate to call "immoral".)

A related point applies to the project of developing a notion of rationality that's closely linked to an "ought"-implies-"can" notion of epistemic responsibility. Clearly, we don't want to blame anyone for failing to live up to an unattainable ideal. But there are certainly evaluative notions that are not subject to "ought"-implies-"can". I would argue that our ordinary notion of rationality is one of them: when we call a paranoid schizophrenic "irrational", we in no sense imply that he has the ability to do better.[5]

Another epistemic enterprise in which the importance of highly idealized models might be questioned is the so-called "meliorative project"—epistemology aimed at our cognitive improvement. Some have claimed that any interesting epistemology must be aimed at providing us with guidance to help ourselves (or perhaps others) to think better. I personally doubt that philosophers are particularly well-equipped for this sort of endeavor. But even putting that doubt aside, I see no reason to think that the sole point

[3] For some representative instances of this line of criticism, see Hacking (1967), Cherniak (1986), Goldman (1986), Kitcher (1992), and Foley (1993).

[4] I cannot make the case for this claim here in full. What follows is a brief sketch, with references to more sustained discussions.

[5] See Feldman and Conee (1985), Alston (1985), and Christensen (2004: 6.4) for more discussion of this point.

of epistemology should be the production of manuals for cognitive self-help.[6]

What projects are there, then, which make manifestly unattainable epistemic ideals worth studying? One such project is that of assessing us as a species. After all, there is no reason to suppose—even if we are the cognitive cream of the mammalian crop—that we're the be-all and end-all of any evaluative epistemic notion we come up with. Indexing epistemic perfection to the cognitive capacities of *homo sapiens* clearly begs some interesting questions.

But the most important reason for resisting the impatience some express about idealized models of rationality does not depend on the interest of evaluating humans as a species. It is clear that our ordinary rationality judgments are based in assessments of people's levels of performance along certain dimensions of epistemic functioning. And these dimensions may well be ones whose extremes are beyond human reach. Freedom from wishful thinking is a plausible example. Predicting consequences of social policies in a way that's untainted by self-interest is another. More examples include evaluating other people's behavior and character without prejudice from emotional ties, or from bigotry based on race or sexual orientation. And a natural candidate for this list is having beliefs that do not violate logic.

If rationality consists (at least partly) in good performance along this sort of dimension, then one natural approach to understanding rationality more clearly is to study candidates for rationality-making qualities by abstracting away from human cognitive limitations, and considering idealized agents who can perfectly exemplify the qualities under consideration. Is logical consistency of all-or-nothing belief a rational desideratum? What about probabilistic coherence of degrees of confidence? How should agents update their beliefs when presented with new evidence? It seems that questions like these may be approached, at least in part, by asking ourselves, "What would an IRA believe?"

Now it is important to see that the suggestion here is not that questions about rational ideals *reduce to* questions about what ideal agents would believe. Any such reduction would likely run afoul of immediate counterexamples involving, for example, beliefs about

[6] See Christensen (2004: 6.5) for further references and discussion.

the existence of ideally rational agents.[7] It might be the case that any ideally rational agent would be quite confident that there were conscious beings who could not remember making any cognitive errors; this does nothing to show that such a belief is rationally mandatory in general. But this sort of problem does not, I think, undermine the usefulness of IRAs in studying rationality. It's just that one has to be alert to the distinction between those aspects of an IRA's beliefs which help make it ideally rational, and those that are mere side-effects of the idealization.

It might be insisted that we must still connect considerations about IRAs with claims about us non-ideal agents. However, there are simple, plausible ways of doing this. For example, one attractive thought is that if the constraints that apply to IRAs describe the endpoint of a spectrum, then the closer an actual agent's beliefs are to that end of the spectrum, the better (presumably, ceteris paribus). Efficiency in cars is a nice analogue here: perfect efficiency is impossible, but (ceteris paribus) the more closely one approaches this end, the better. Moral principles also might work this way: I am undoubtedly psychologically incapable of being perfectly fair or generous; but the more closely I approximate perfect fairness and generosity, ceteris paribus, the better.[8]

To my mind, some of the most promising applications of highly idealized theorizing about rationality involve taking probabilistic coherence as a constraint on degrees of belief. Considerations along the lines rehearsed above, I think, show that some of the most common objections to idealizations involving probabilistic coherence, on the grounds that they abstract so far from human limitations, are misguided. I would like, then, to say something like: "Well, of course none of us can be probabilistically coherent, but that's no big deal. We can see that coherence is an ideal in part by showing that IRAs have coherent credences. And as far as my own beliefs are concerned, the closer I can come to having coherent credences, the more rational my beliefs will be."[9]

[7] Williamson (2000: 209–10) makes essentially this point.

[8] Zynda (1996) argues along these lines; see also Christensen (2004: 6.5).

[9] This thought presupposes that we can make sense of one's beliefs coming closer to coherence. Zynda (1996) develops a way of making sense of this notion in order to give normative force to the unrealizable ideal of coherence.

Unfortunately, I now think that the claim that IRAs are coherent is probably false, and that the claim about the rationality of approaching coherence in my own beliefs is at least problematic. The reasons for this are related to, but ultimately quite different from, the worries about idealization described above. They raise what seems to me an interestingly different difficulty for the standard way of using ideal agents in theorizing about rationality, a difficulty flowing from the structure of our epistemic ideals.

2. IDEAL RATIONALITY MEETS POSSIBLE COGNITIVE IMPERFECTION

The problem I would like to examine involves a very different way in which cognitive imperfection poses an obstacle to taking probabilistic coherence as a rational ideal. The problem arises from an agent's apparently rational reflection on her own beliefs. Let us begin by thinking about a case involving a clearly non-ideal agent:

Suppose I prove a somewhat complex theorem of logic. I've checked the proof several times, and I'm extremely confident about it. Still, it might seem quite reasonable for me to be somewhat less than 100 percent confident. I should not, for example, bet my house against a nickel that the proof is correct. After all, balancing my checkbook has shown me quite clearly that my going over a demonstrative argument, even repeatedly, is not sure proof against error. Given my thorough checking, my being in error this time may be highly unlikely; nevertheless, it is hard to deny that I should give it some nonzero credence. Let us call the theorem I've proved T. And let us use M to denote the claim that, in believing T, I've come to believe a false claim due to a cognitive mistake. The question now arises: given this sort of doubt, how strongly—ideally speaking—should I believe T?

It seems that my giving some slight credence to M is required by my recognition that I may sometimes exhibit cognitive imperfection. And to the extent that I have any rational credence at all in M, I must have some rational credence in the negation of T (since M obviously entails ~T). So my confidence in T should fall short of absolute certainty; in probabilistic terms, it should be less than 1.

But if something like this is correct, it seems to raise an obstacle to taking coherence as a rational ideal for me—an obstacle quite different from that raised by the fact that coherence is humanly unattainable. For according to this argument, it would not be *rational* for me to have full confidence in T, a truth of logic. In fact, if I did manage to have the coherence-mandated attitude toward T, the argument would urge me to back away from it. So the problem is not the usual one cited in connection with human cognitive limitations. It's not that I *can't* achieve the probabilistically correct attitude toward T—in this case, I may well be perfectly capable of that. The problem is that, in the present case, it seems that my beliefs would be worse—less rational—if I were to adopt the attitude toward T that's mandated by probabilistic coherence.

It is worth pointing out that the problem is not just about having maximal belief in logical truths. To see this, suppose I give some positive credence to ~T. Now consider what credence I should give to (~T v C), for some ordinary contingent claim C. If it is different from my credence in C, then my credence in these two contingent claims will violate the principle that logically equivalent claims get equal credence. On the other hand, if my credence in (~T v C) is equal to my credence in C, then I will violate the principle that my credence in a disjunction of logically incompatible disjuncts should be the sum of my credences in the disjuncts.

The basic problem is that coherence puts constraints on my credences based on the logical relations among all the claims in which I have credences—including contingent claims. To the extent that I have doubts about whether certain logical relations hold, and to the extent that those doubts are reflected in my credences, coherence may be violated—even when explicit consideration of logical truths is not involved. For another example, suppose that contingent claim P logically entails contingent claim Q, but I am not absolutely certain of this. In at least some such cases, it would seem that I should then have somewhat higher credence in P than in (P & Q). But if I do, then again I have given logically equivalent contingent claims different levels of credence.

Clearly, this problem should be disconcerting to those of us who would advocate coherence—either the simple version, or one of the standard generalizations—as a component of ideal rationality. To my mind, the threat it poses is significantly deeper than that posed by the fact that probabilistic perfection is not humanly possible. Thus it's worthwhile seeing whether the one might resist the claim that it would be irrational for me to be coherent.

3. CAN I RATIONALLY BE CERTAIN OF T?

Suppose one were to argue as follows:

Certainty Argument: Granted, I must give ~T at least as much credence as I give to M. But I have the strongest possible kind of justification for full confidence in T—I've proved it demonstratively. So I should give it full confidence, and should give ~T, and thus M, zero credence. (After all, my proof of T serves as a proof of not-M!) I may not be a perfect being, but I have the best possible reason for believing T, and thus the best possible reasons for being certain that I haven't come to believe a false claim due to a cognitive mistake.

I think that this argument should not tempt us. To see why, suppose that I work out my proof of T after having coffee with my friend Jocko. Palms sweaty with the excitement of logical progress, I check my work several times, and decide that the proof is good. But then a trusted colleague walks in and tells me that Jocko has been surreptitiously slipping a reason-distorting drug into people's coffee—a drug whose effects include a strong propensity to reasoning errors in 99 percent of those who have been dosed (1 percent of the population happen to be immune). He tells me that those who have been impaired do not notice any difficulties with their own cognition—they just make mistakes; indeed, the only change most of them notice is unusually sweaty palms. Here, my reason for doubting my proof, and the truth of T, is much stronger. It seems clear that in the presence of these strong reasons for doubt, it would be highly irrational for me to maintain absolute confidence in T. Yet the certainty argument would, if sound, seem to apply equally to such extreme cases.

Could this verdict possibly be resisted? Could one argue that, initial appearances to the contrary, we actually can embrace the certainty argument, even in the strong doubt case? One way of attempting this would capitalize on distinguishing carefully between two sorts of cases: the bad ones, where the drug has impaired my reasoning and my proof is defective, and the good ones, in which I'm one of the lucky 1 percent who is immune to the drug's effects and my proof is correct. It might be pointed out that we cannot assume that what would be irrational for the person in the bad case would be irrational for someone in the good case. After all, those in the good case have constructed flawless sound proofs of T, and those in the bad case have made errors in reasoning. To say that what holds for one must hold for the other would be to conflate having a correct proof with seeming to oneself to have a correct proof. So it might be argued, that although it would be clearly wrong for most people who find out that they've been dosed to dismiss the resulting doubts, at least if I am in the good case, I am in a different epistemic position, and I may rationally dismiss the doubts.[10]

Now I think that there is something to this point. I would not claim that the epistemic situations of the drug-sensitive person and the immune person are fully symmetrical. After all, the drug-sensitive person in the envisioned type of situation makes a mistake in reasoning even before she finds out about the drug, and the drug-immune person does not. But granting the existence of an asymmetry here does not mean that it is rational for the drug-immune person to disregard the evidence suggesting that he has made an error. And it seems clear—especially when one keeps in mind that those who are affected by the drug don't notice any impairment in their reasoning—that, given the evidence suggesting I've made a mistake, it would be irrational for me to maintain full confidence in my reasoning, even if I happen to be in the good case.[11]

Thus we cannot exploit the real epistemic asymmetry between the drug-sensitive and drug-immune people to argue that the latter may after all avail themselves of the certainty argument. And if this is

[10] The envisioned argument is inspired by a point Thomas Kelly (2005) makes in a different context, though he should not be saddled with it here.

[11] See Feldman (manuscript) and Christensen (2007) for discussion of parallel points relating to the epistemology of disagreement.

correct, it is hard to see how we can support applying the Certainty Argument even to the original cases involving mild self-doubts raised by memories of misadventures in checkbook balancing. Nothing in the Certainty Argument hinged on the mildness of the doubt about my proof. In fact, it does not seem that even the weak positive reasons for doubt provided by the checkbook-balancing memories are needed to prove the point. Suppose I've never made a mistake in balancing my checkbook or in any other demonstrative reasoning. Surely that doesn't license me in being certain that such mistakes are impossible. And as long as such mistakes are possible, it is hard to see how I can be *certain* that they have not occurred. Even if my reason for doubt is slight, and, so to speak, metaphysical—so slight that in ordinary cases, I wouldn't bother to think about it—still, it would seem irrational to be absolutely certain that I had not come to believe a false claim due to a cognitive mistake. And thus it would seem irrational for me to be absolutely certain of T.

If this is right, it underlies a troubling result for those of us who see coherence as a rational ideal. For the only way I can live up to the ideal of coherence here would seem to be by irrationally dismissing the possibility that a cognitive mistake led me to believe T falsely. Being certain of logical truths seems not only to be something that I can't always do—it seems like something I often shouldn't do. And that makes it hard to see what kind of an epistemic ideal probabilistic coherence could be.

4. WOULD AN IDEALLY RATIONAL AGENT BE CERTAIN OF HER OWN IDEALITY?

The troubling result flows from the fact that I must believe myself to be epistemically fallible. But if rational ideals can be thought of as those that would make an *ideal agent's* beliefs rational, perhaps this is not the right way to think about the issue. Perhaps an IRA would not only never make a cognitive error, but would also (rationally) be certain of her own cognitive perfection. If that were so, then we could at least hold that an IRA would have probabilistically coherent beliefs. And this might help explain a sense in which coherence was, after all, an epistemic ideal. The idea would be something like this: my self-doubts, which prevent me from rationally being certain of T, are a distracting byproduct of my fallen epistemic state. Consideration of IRAs, who are unaffected by such problems, allows us to see what ideally rational beliefs would be like.[12]

It has been claimed that ideal agents have this sort of self-confidence. Jordan Howard Sobel (1987) argues that what he calls "ideal intellects" not only are probabilistically coherent, but display a number of other features as well: They are always absolutely certain, and correct, about their own credences. They have the sort of trust in their future credences that is embodied in van Fraassen's Principle of Reflection. And they are absolutely certain that they are probabilistically coherent. Thus an ideal intellect would not only be absolutely certain of T—she'd also have the sort of high intellectual self-opinion that would seem to be needed to be rationally certain that ~M.

Sobel defends this conception of an ideal intellect as embodying a kind of full integration and self-possession. He also notes that violation of the ideals can leave an agent open to guaranteed betting losses similar to those that figure in standard Dutch Book arguments. For example, suppose an agent doubts (however slightly) that she's perfectly coherent. If the agent's doubt is realized—that is, if she is actually incoherent—then she is of course susceptible to a classic Dutch Book. But suppose that the agent is actually coherent; she just isn't completely confident that she is. Such an agent will accept a bet in which she will pay the bookie some amount—say $X—if she's coherent, as long as the bookie agrees to pay her enough if she's incoherent. The agent will lose $X on this bet, and the bookie can determine this fact merely by consulting the agent's credences. Thus, as in the standard Dutch Book argument, the bookie can take advantage of the agent by knowing nothing except the agent's credences.[13]

[12] I should note that would not solve the whole problem. We would still need to say something about how ideals that apply to such imaginary agents would relate to rationality assessments for humans. Clearly, this task is complicated if we acknowledge that an ideal for the imaginary agent is one which, at least in some cases, it would be worse for a human agent to approach. I'll return to this issue below.

[13] Although Sobel points out the betting vulnerabilities associated with violating his ideals, he sees the main ground for the ideals as lying in our conception of a fully integrated and self-possessed agent (1997: 72).

Should we, then, hold that IRAs would have the sort of confidence in their own rational perfection that would preclude the sort of worries that seem to undermine rational certainty in T for human beings? It seems to me that reflection on the motivation behind theorizing about IRAs should make us wary of such a move. As noted above, an IRA, as usually conceived of in theorizing about rationality, is quite different from an omniscient god. The IRA reasons perfectly, and is thus logically omniscient (or at least logically infallible),[14] but the IRA is not assumed to be factually omniscient. This conception of an IRA carries with it no obvious presumption that an IRA would *know* that she was ideally rational. For such an agent to be rationally confident that she was ideally rational, it would seem that some sort of warrant would be required. But while it seems likely that many IRAs would have excellent evidence of their rational prowess, it also seems unlikely that all of them (or perhaps any of them) could be *rationally certain* of their own rational ideality.

If an IRA had been around for a long time, and if she had a good memory, she might well have evidence that she possessed an excellent epistemic track record. Unlike most of us, she would never have been corrected for a cognitive error. But it's hard to see how even a very long and distinguished epistemic history could justify the sort of absolute self-confidence at issue here. For it's clearly possible for an agent to think flawlessly up until time t, and then to make a mistake. Clearly, a spotless record up until time t does nothing to tell against this particular possibility.

It's also difficult to see how an agent could be introspectively aware of her own cognitive perfection—or, more precisely, it's hard to see how any sort of introspective awareness could justify absolute self-confidence. Anyone who has experienced some of the common states of consciousness involving diminished cognitive capacities knows that, in some cases, it's pretty easy to tell introspectively that one is epistemically impaired. But not all impairments are evident

[14] Many use "logically omniscient" to describe the IRA. As Zynda (1996) points out, one might well not want to require full omniscience (i.e. being certain of every logical truth), but rather infallibility (being certain of all logical truths *about which the agent has any opinion at all*). This distinction will not affect the substance of the discussion below.

in this way (and even if they were, there's no reason to think that all possible impairments would be). So the fact that an agent seems to herself to be thinking with perfect lucidity could hardly justify absolute epistemic self-confidence.

It might also be held that some sort of first-person presumption of rationality must exist which is independent of any reliance on introspection, or on the sort of evidence one might use in making third-person assessments of rationality. Such a presumption might be argued not to need justification by anything else. I do not aim to dispute this sort of claim here. I would only insist that any such presumption would have to fall far short of rendering rational an agent's absolute confidence that she was absolutely logically inerrant.

What should we think about the argument showing that an agent who doubts her own coherence is vulnerable to guaranteed betting losses? I think that on closer inspection, it turns out to be unpersuasive. Note that in the standard Dutch Book arguments, the bookie offers the agent a set of bets with two properties: (1) the agent finds each bet in the set fair, and (2) the set of bets taken together is logically guaranteed to result in a net loss (for the agent's side of the bets). The existence of a set of bets with these two properties is the crux of the argument; the imagined bookie adds only entertainment value. In the present argument, if the agent is actually coherent but is not fully confident of this fact, the set of bets the bookie would offer pays the bookie only because it includes a bet which pays him if the agent is coherent. Although the agent would indeed lose money on this set of bets in the actual world—since she is in fact coherent—it is not a set of bets which is logically guaranteed to result in a loss for the agent. The bookie can know that the agent will lose only because the bookie knows the contingent fact that the agent has coherent credences. So it seems that this guaranteed betting loss is more an artifact of the betting situation than an indication of any rational defect on the agent's part.

For all of these reasons, it seems unlikely that an IRA would be rationally certain of her own cognitive perfection. And these considerations also raise an obstacle to arguing that extreme self-confidence flows from a sort of ideal integration or self-possession that characterizes ideally rational intellects. Even if one found this line persuasive in isolation, the considerations above suggest that such extreme self-confidence would be inconsistent with what is clearly central to our conception of an IRA: not having irrationally held beliefs.

5. CAN AN IDEALLY RATIONAL AGENT BE CERTAIN OF T?

It might be objected, however, that the whole line of argument in the previous section is misdirected. After all, what's directly at issue in our example is just whether the IRA can rationally be certain of ~M. The broader claim discussed above, which concerns the agent's own general rational perfection, is clearly a logically contingent proposition. But ~M follows from T—it's a truth of logic! So the fact that the IRA can't rationally be certain that she *never* makes logical errors is simply irrelevant. The IRA has solid a priori reason to be certain that *in believing that T*, she doesn't believe a falsehood. No reliance on track records or introspection is required.

Although this argument rightly points out a disanalogy between ~M and general epistemic self-confidence, it seems to me that the disanalogy will not suffice for the use to which the argument would put it. We should first note in general that the fact that an agent has a priori justification for some belief does not render her justification immune to undermining or rebutting by a posteriori considerations. If it did then, even in the case where Jocko tells me that he drugged my coffee, I would be justified in continuing to believe T. But given that even a priori justifications are vulnerable in this way, it's not clear why the IRA's justification for being absolutely confident in T wouldn't be undermined by any general uncertainty she had about her own cognitive perfection.

We can see this point from a different angle by supposing, as the objection urges, that the IRA may be uncertain of her own logical prowess, while nevertheless being fully certain of both T and ~M. To begin with, let's consider a case in which the IRA, though actually cognitively perfect, doesn't have much confidence at all that she is ultra-reliable when she becomes certain of apparent theorems—let's say she has never checked her theorem-detection by consulting external sources, or even by reconsidering the apparent theorems she has come to believe. Suppose that this moderate self-assessment is rational. Can such an agent nevertheless be rationally certain of T and ~M?

It seems to me unlikely that this will be rational. If the agent can be rationally certain of T and ~M, she presumably can perform similar feats a great many times—there is nothing special about T. So for all of the apparent theorems (say $T_1 - T_{10,000}$) the agent considers, she may rationally be certain of the corresponding propositions ($\sim M_1 - \sim M_{10,000}$), each denying that she has mistakenly come to believe a falsehood. Assuming that the agent can keep track of what theorems she has become certain of, she would then seem to have excellent reason to think that she has become certain of 10,000 theorems in a row, without once accepting a false one due to cognitive error. But for the IRA to accomplish this feat without having extraordinary theorem-recognition abilities, something else extraordinary would have to be true. She would have to be extremely lucky (avoiding cognitive errors by sheer luck, or only making cognitive errors that happened not to result in believing false claims), or perhaps be guided by some other force which did have extraordinary powers of theorem-recognition. However, it is hard to see how the fact that an agent is an IRA—the fact that she never makes a logical mistake—would make it rational for the agent to be at all sure that, insofar as her theorem-recognition abilities might have fallen short, extraordinary luck or guidance resulted in her correctly assessing 10,000 theorems in a row. So it's hard to see why we should think that an IRA could be rationally certain of $\sim M_1 - \sim M_{10,000}$ while being only moderately confident in her own theorem-recognition ability.

Could the agent's confidence in $T_1 - T_{10,000}$ *make it rational* for the agent to have a high degree of confidence that she had extraordinary theorem-proving power? I don't think so. This would be like an agent consulting the gas gauge in her car to determine both the level of fuel and what the gas gauge read, and using the resulting beliefs to rationalize confidence that the gauge was accurate; or looking at a series of colored squares to determine both what color the squares were and how they looked, and using that to make rational her confidence that her color vision was accurate. If the agent begins with a rational moderate degree of confidence in her theorem-recognition abilities, it seems clear that she cannot make higher confidence rational in the manner envisaged.[15]

Would our verdict change if the agent's confidence in her own cognitive perfection were short of certainty, but very high rather than moderate? I think not. For the question is whether the agent can rationally be *absolutely certain* of the results of her theorem-consideration. Once we see how rational confidence in T is undermined by an agent's moderate views about her own cognitive perfection, it seems clear that even very small doubts about her own cognitive perfection should have some effect in limiting the confidence that it is rational for that agent to have in T.

The problem is just a reflection of the basic fact that lies behind all of the examples we've looked at: that the rationality of first-order beliefs cannot in general be divorced from the rationality of certain second-order beliefs that bear on the epistemic status of those first-order beliefs. This is the reason that, in the case of an ordinary person who has proved a theorem, empirical evidence about being drugged in certain ways can undermine a belief whose justification was purely logical. Thinking about $\sim M_1 - \sim M_{10,000}$ is simply a way of amplifying a point that applied to the original ~M: that insofar as an agent is not absolutely confident in her own logical faculties, it is likely to be irrational for her to be absolutely confident in particular beliefs delivered by those faculties.[16]

Does this point apply to even the most simple and obviously self-evident-seeming beliefs? If not, there may be a different way to

[15] This argument is adapted from arguments given in a different context by Richard Fumerton (1995: 173–81), Jonathan Vogel (2000), and Stewart Cohen (2002). I should note that the argument does not presuppose that the IRA could not get any track-record-type evidence of her own reliability. It's just that any such evidence would depend on some way of checking the IRA's proofs. So if others checked the proofs and agreed with them, or if the IRA found theorems she had proved listed in a logic book, or even if the IRA made multiple attempts to prove the same sentences and got consistent results, that would count for something—after all, there would be some possibility that the IRA could get something other than confirming evidence. The problem with the procedure envisioned is that it completely begs the question of the IRA's theorem-proving accuracy.

[16] This suggests that even if one doesn't harbor doubts about distinguishing logical truths from factual ones, there will still be a sense in which our knowledge of logical truths gets ensnared—via reflection on cognitive fallibility—in the web of belief about ordinary factual matters.

argue that the IRA would have full confidence in $\sim M_1 - \sim M_{10,000}$. Consider a logical truth that, to us, is maximally obvious—say,

(T′) Everything is self-identical.

Even if it were granted that we would be irrational to place full confidence in complex logical theorems, it might be claimed that we should at least be able to be absolutely confident in claims such as T′. And if so, we ought to be able to have full rational confidence in the negation of

(M′) In believing that everything is self-identical, I'm believing a false claim due to a cognitive mistake.

But the IRA, it might well be argued, would experience all logical truths, including $T_1 - T_{10,000}$, as being just as self-evident as T′. So it would, after all, be rational for such a being to be completely certain of $\sim M_1 - \sim M_{10,000}$. The apparent problem arises only if we're misled by ignoring the IRA's superior ability to see clearly and distinctly in cases where we cannot.

It seems to me that this strategy for supporting the IRA's certainty about $\sim M_1 - \sim M_{10,000}$ will not work. For even if we grant that all theorems are as simple and obviously self-evident to her as T′ is to us, I doubt that the obviousness or self-evidence of T′ licenses us in being absolutely certain of $\sim$ M′. Even if there were some special way of seeing clearly and distinctly that occurs when I contemplate claims like T′, I don't think I can rationally be absolutely certain that no drug or demon could make it seem to me that I'm seeing clearly and distinctly when in fact I'm contemplating a falsity. And to the extent that I cannot absolutely preclude that possibility of M′, I fall short of rational absolute certainty in T′. For similar reasons, even if all logical truths strike the IRA the way T′ strikes me, she cannot absolutely preclude the possibility that her cognitive process has misfired or been interfered with in a way that allows some falsehoods to seem self-evidently true. Thus it seems to me that the IRA cannot rationally be absolutely certain of $\sim M_1 - \sim M_{10,000}$, and thus she cannot rationally be absolutely certain of $T_1 - T_{10,000}$.

If the argument of the last two sections is right, then, we are faced with the following sort of problem: given that an agent has the sort of limited evidence IRAs have typically been taken to have, it turns out that there is a tension among three prima facie appealing (though, admittedly, loosely formulated) rational ideals.

(1) LOGIC: An agent's beliefs must respect logic by satisfying (some version of) probabilistic coherence.
(2) EVIDENCE: An agent's beliefs (at least about logically contingent matters) must be proportioned to the agent's evidence.
(3) INTEGRATION: An agent's object-level beliefs must reflect the agent's meta-level beliefs about the reliability of the cognitive processes underlying her object-level beliefs.

The problem we saw was that if a standard IRA satisfied (LOGIC) with respect to her beliefs about theorems, and (EVIDENCE) with respect to her beliefs about the reliability of her own cognitive processes, she could not respect (INTEGRATION) with respect to the connections between these two kinds of beliefs.

There are several different reactions possible here. One could of course take the problem as showing that there's something wrong with at least one of the purported rational ideals—at least, in the ways I've been interpreting them. Since I find each of them quite attractive, though, I'd like to explore two other options. The first is to trace the problem to the peculiarities of the standard kind of IRA that I've been discussing, and to avoid the problem by considering a different kind of ideally rational agent. The second is to develop a revised understanding of the use of ideal agents in theorizing about rationality. I'll discuss these in the next two sections.

6. CAN VARIANT IDEAL AGENTS AVOID THE TENSION?

If the conflict among the three principles arises only because we are taking our IRA to have incomplete evidence, might we avoid the whole problem by simply dropping this assumption? After all, God, on some standard conceptions, is an agent who is not only perfectly rational, but also perfectly informed. It can be hard to understand how God knows things—it would seem that nothing like our ordinary sources of empirical evidence would be necessary (or, really, of any use at all) for God's omniscience. For my part, I'm not at all sure that it finally makes sense that God could be *rationally* certain of all truths. But perhaps it does, and if there were such a being, we've seen no reason to think that she would have trouble simultaneously satisfying our three principles.

Now I don't want to explore the tenability of supposing that an omniscient being could rationally be certain of her own rational perfection. For in any case, it seems to me that we cannot simply sidestep our problem by investigating ideal rationality with reference to the beliefs of such a being. A central component of epistemic rationality is having beliefs appropriate to incomplete information. A godlike agent's credences would presumably simply mirror the facts—the agent would be certain of all the truths, have zero confidence in all falsities, and have no intermediate degrees of belief at all.[17] Thus such a model would tell us nothing about a central component of epistemic rationality—the sort of component that's in part captured by something like (EVIDENCE). A useful model of epistemic rationality cannot simply collapse rational belief into truth.

Might there be a non-omniscient ideal agent who could yet be sufficiently free of rational self-doubt to satisfy the three principles? If not, we'd have an argument that rational perfection required factual omniscience. This would, I think, be quite a surprising result. As noted at the outset, rationality seems to be a notion designed in part to abstract from well-informedness. We certainly don't see ordinary cases in which a person lacks information as constituting any sort of lapse in rationality. So it would be surprising that, although each of our rational principles seems to be aimed at capturing some aspect of thinking well, and not at some aspect of being well-informed, the three principles together required factual omniscience for their joint satisfaction. On the surface, though, what would be required to satisfy the principles would not be omniscience. We've seen that the agent would need to be absolutely certain that she had not been led by cognitive mishaps to err in believing any of $T_1 - T_{10,000}$, but this does not obviously imply anything about the agent's confidence about, for example, the number of stars in the Milky Way. So it is not clear to me that only an omniscient being could satisfy the three principles.

[17] At least in propositions that have truth-values. If e.g. certain propositions about the future don't have truth-values, then even God can't know them.

Nevertheless, it is also not clear that there is any reasonably neat way of describing an agent whose epistemic powers are less than an omniscient god's, yet who could rationally completely dismiss the sort of doubts about herself that would undermine rational absolute confidence in the theorems she accepted. Without some clear conception of the epistemic resources such a being would have to have, it's not clear whether she would serve as a useful model for studying principles of rationality. At this point, then, I don't see a way of using a superknowledgeable variant of the standard IRA to study rational ideals in a context where they don't conflict.

Another way of altering the standard IRA to avoid the tension among the three principles would be to think of an IRA who had no self-doubts because she was completely devoid of beliefs about herself—or, at least, about her own beliefs. After all, it is only when the agent begins to reflect on the possibility of her own epistemic imperfection that the problem seems to arise. Perhaps, instead of imagining an IRA who rationally rejects possibilities of her own error, we could conceive of an IRA who simply never entertains them in the first place.

Again, the question that naturally arises is whether such an agent could be ideally rational. After all, it is not in general rational for an agent to ignore empirical possibilities that bear on the truth of her beliefs. Consider, for example, an ordinary agent who is absolutely certain that it's four o'clock, because her watch reads four o'clock and she hasn't ever considered the possibility that her watch is inaccurate. In this case, it's clear that her absolute confidence betrays a rational failing. Perhaps a closer analogy to our case would be an agent who completely trusted her visual perception, and ignored the possibility that things weren't quite as they appeared. Even an agent who had never seen a mirage would not be rational in having absolute confidence that the world was just the way it looked. We might well think that such an agent was by default entitled to believe that the world was the way it looked, but not that she was entitled to absolute certainty.

Moreover, it's doubtful that an agent who had no concept of herself having a mistaken belief, or no inclination or capacity to reflect critically on her own beliefs at all, could correctly be categorized as ideally rational. There may be some relatively thin sense of rationality that abstracts away from second-order reflection on an agent's beliefs.[18] But critical reflection on one's beliefs is not just something peripheral to rational belief-management—it seems to be a central component of what it is to believe rationally in the fullest sense. And even if we should hesitate to require much in the way of actual second-order reflection, it would seem that if an agent did not reflect on her beliefs at all, and if her beliefs were such that they would be undermined if she did reflect, the agent's beliefs would not be ideally rational. If that's right, then it would seem that ideally rational beliefs would be sensitive to second-order considerations of the sort we've been discussing. So I don't think that the tension among our principles can be avoided by positing unselfconscious but ideally rational agents.

I won't take a stand here on whether the three principles are, in the end, jointly satisfiable, either by an omniscient God or by some lesser being who falls short of complete omniscience. But at this point, I don't see a way of imagining an idealized agent who satisfies the principles and also can serve as a useful model for studying the question of how non-extreme degrees of belief should be constrained by logical structure. So I'd like to turn now to examine the following question: supposing that there is no useful model of an ideally rational agent who satisfies the three principles, what implications does this have for the study of formal constraints on rationality?

7. RATIONAL IDEALS WITHOUT IRAS

The suggestion that rationality might require violating coherence raises a question about what we should say about the agent—perhaps an imaginary agent with unlimited cognitive powers but limited evidence—who *does* take self-doubt into account appropriately, and thus violates probabilistic coherence? There seem to be two possibilities. First, one could say that, since such an agent's beliefs would not completely respect logic, the agent

[18] A proposal along somewhat similar lines, applied to knowledge rather than rationality, is made by Ernest Sosa (1997). Sosa distinguishes "animal knowledge", which does not require any reflection on an agent's beliefs, from a better kind, "reflective knowledge", which does.

would not be ideally rational. On this view, ideal rationality simply could not in general be achieved by an agent who reacted to limited evidence in the best possible way (though perhaps it could be achieved by God). A second option would be to say that, insofar as such an agent achieved the best possible beliefs given her evidence, the agent would be ideally rational. On this view, one would acknowledge that an ideally rational agent might be probabilistically incoherent.

Now I'm not sure that the difference between these two views is much more than verbal. One may see "ideal rationality" as forming the best possible beliefs given one's evidence; or one may see it as perfectly exemplifying all rational ideals. But it is important to see that even if one calls the incoherent agent ideally rational, one is not thereby denying that coherence is a rational ideal. We're quite familiar with other ideals that operate as values to be maximized, yet whose maximization must in certain cases be balanced against, or otherwise constrained by, other values. In scientific theory choice, simplicity and fit with the data are plausible examples of balancing. In ethics, promoting well-being and respecting rights may illustrate a different sort of way in which one ideal constrains another. And tension between ideals has been advocated in epistemology, by those who think we should choose our beliefs (in the all-or-nothing sense) so as to maximize true beliefs while also minimizing false ones.[19] In all of these cases, the fact that ideals can be in tension with one another does not undermine their status as ideals. So we can still see (LOGIC) as a rational ideal once we see how it is to be constrained by (EVIDENCE) and (INTEGRATION).

Because of the particular way in which these three ideals interact, there turns out to be a strange way in which the mere possibility of epistemic misadventure implies an actual epistemic imperfection. The (INTEGRATION)-mandated interaction between our first-order beliefs about logic and our second-order beliefs about ourselves results in something that might be called Murphy's Law for epistemology. The usual version of Murphy's Law states that, if it's possible for something to go wrong, it will. The epistemic cousin says that if it's possible that something has gone epistemically wrong (more specifically, if it's possible that I've made a

[19] Thanks to Don Fallis for reminding me of this example.

mistake in thinking about some theorem T), then something has actually gone epistemically wrong (my belief about T falls short of some rational ideal). For either I'm certain of T, in which case my belief fails to reflect appropriately the possibility that I've made a cognitive error, or I'm uncertain about T, in which case my belief fails to respect logic.

What implications does this have for our theorizing about formal conditions on rational belief? If we agree that all the rational ideals cannot be simultaneously realized by a non-omniscient agent, can we still use idealized agents in thinking about how logic should constrain rational belief? If so, will the standard arguments supporting formal conditions on rational belief be affected?

I think that we may continue to use idealized agents in studying formal conditions on rational belief. One way to do this is simply to ignore the fact we've been focusing on: that the standard idealized agent is violating certain strictures about taking self-doubt into account. We could also, more self-consciously, suppose that an agent was cognitively unlimited, in the sense that she could achieve probabilistic coherence, but then stipulate that either (*a*) she didn't have any second-order beliefs, or (*b*) she was certain that she was ideally rational, or (*c*) she didn't take the possibility of her rational imperfection as a reason to be less than fully confident of logical theorems. Having conceived of our agent in any of these ways, we could then consider arguments that such an agent should have probabilistically coherent beliefs. In one of these ways, it seems to me that we could still run standard arguments based on rational constraints on preferences, or based on invulnerability to Dutch Books.

If we do this, we will have to understand what we are doing in a way that departs from the standard way in which people have thought about the idealized agents they've imagined. We cannot, in these cases, think of the imaginary agent as ideally rational. For the agent would be irrationally ignoring or rejecting epistemically relevant possibilities, or failing to take them into account rationally in adjusting her beliefs. Nevertheless, the fact that one is not considering the agent as ideally rational does not, I think, undermine the agent's value as a device to help think about a particular dimension of rationality: how logical structure should constrain degrees of belief.

This can be seen by reflecting on the purpose of imagining idealized agents. The purpose of the idealization is in part to abstract away from certain human cognitive limitations, and thus to open up the possibility—which is closed off for agents such as us—of satisfying conditions such as probabilistic coherence. And the idealization should also abstract away from other interfering factors. For example, a Dutch Book argument may assume that the imagined agent values money linearly, and exclusively. The point of this assumption is not that it's particularly rational to value money this way—the purpose is just to isolate one central way in which beliefs and preferences relate to one another. Now, if I'm right, it turns out that one thing that can interfere with an agent's beliefs respecting logic completely is the sort of (rational) self-doubt we've been examining. In stipulating away considerations of (even rational) self-doubt, we create a situation in which the logical constraint on belief can be studied in isolation.

It is important to remember that considerations about the beliefs of ideal thinkers should not anyway be thought of as providing a reductive analysis of the concept of a rational ideal. The idea is not that we take a condition to be a rational ideal in virtue of the fact that the condition would be satisfied by an ideally rational agent. So if it turns out that rational ideals are in tension with one another (at least for agents with limited information) we may reasonably allow one rational ideal to be violated in order to study another under limited-information conditions. So the interest of the idealized-agent-based arguments would not be vitiated by acknowledging that the agents involved were not, after all, ideally rational. If coherence can be supported by arguments based on this sort of model agent, that tells in favor of taking it as a rational ideal.

But how could the envisioned sort of ideal have the right sort of evaluative implications for humans? Once we admit that our coherent idealized agent is not actually ideally rational, doesn't the whole exercise lose its epistemic significance?

I think that once we see the structure of epistemic ideals in the way I've been urging, we can see that this is not a problem. It's always been clear that the sort of evaluative principle in question—for example, the more coherent an agent's beliefs are, the better—must be understood as subject to a ceteris paribus clause rooted in the limitations of an agent's cognitive system. For example, if improving coherence precluded gathering evidence, or required becoming a paranoid schizophrenic, then ceteris wouldn't be paribus, and the agent's beliefs would be less rational if she took the more coherent option.[20] What the above discussion makes clear is that the ceteris paribus conditions must be understood to encompass another dimension. It's not just that our human fleshly limitations might happen to impose epistemic costs on maximizing certain epistemic desiderata. Conflict among epistemic desiderata turns out to flow as well from something much more general: it turns out that our very status as beings with limited information places some epistemic desiderata at odds with others.

So even for us, it still makes sense to say that the more coherent our beliefs are, the better, ceteris paribus. But the ceteris paribus conditions make reference to other epistemic ideals. And if the only way of achieving the probabilistically correct attitude toward some claim T would involve embracing irrational beliefs about my own logical invincibility, or violating the principle that my object-level beliefs should cohere with my meta-level beliefs about the reliability of the cognitive processes behind those object-level beliefs, then adopting the coherent attitude toward T might well render my beliefs less rational.

So: if all this is right, then the tension among epistemic ideals, at least for agents with limited information, requires us to reconceptualize the sorts of ideal agents often considered in studying formal constraints on degrees of belief, but it doesn't undermine their usefulness. And the fact that the ideal of probabilistic coherence may be constrained by other epistemic ideals, and not just by human limitations, doesn't undermine its status as an epistemic ideal.

However, I do worry that other aspects of formal epistemology might not be left undisturbed by the problem I've been discussing. The classic Bayesian view combines a probabilistic coherence requirement with a claim about how beliefs are informed by evidence. Conditionalization, and Jeffrey's generalization of it, are the two standard formal accounts of how evidence bears on belief. Both of these accounts presuppose probabilistic coherence.

[20] Zynda (1996) defends probabilistic coherence as an ideal which imposes prima facie obligations on us.

One might, of course, study these formal accounts of accommodating evidence by the method I've just recommended for studying formal constraints on an agent's simultaneous beliefs: one might employ probabilistically coherent idealized agents, acknowledging that such agents should not be thought of as ideally rational. And I think that this might well be very useful for studying many cases of evidence bearing on belief. It might even allow us to model cases where some evidential sources undermine others. So a probabilistically coherent ideal agent who employed conditionalization might allow one to model how strongly I should believe that it's four o'clock, given that my watch says it is, and given information about my watch's unreliability.

But I don't yet see how this would allow us to model the way my belief in T should be affected by evidence that Jocko has drugged my coffee. Stipulating probabilistic coherence gives the wrong result: the probability of T, conditional on any evidence at all, will still be 1. The strategy of abstracting away from the conditions imposed by (EVIDENCE) and (INTEGRATION) will not work here, since those conditions are centrally important in determining how evidence about my being drugged affects the level of credence in T it is rational for me to have. So it seems to me that the tension among our epistemic ideals does pose a problem for traditional formal ways of characterizing how evidence bears on rational belief.

I think that this problem might turn out to be difficult to solve, especially formally. This is because the solution would seem to have to respect all three of the principles; and, as we've seen, the principles are in some tension with one another. And the correct way of balancing or constraining one ideal by another is likely to prove difficult to capture in a formal system.

I don't want to argue that this problem can't be solved. One might, for example, try the sort of tactic Dan Garber (1983) proposed for handling one version of the old evidence problem. Garber thought the problem stemmed from the assumption of logical omniscience, and so to relax that assumption, he treated certain logical implications metalinguistically, and allowed ideal agents to be less than certain of them. So one might try saying that the credence I should have that T is the probability that the sentence "T" is true, given that I seem to have a proof of it and that I know I have been drugged in a certain way.

This might seem to give the right result in a circumscribed local way. But even this type of model presupposes that the agent is probabilistically coherent over a large range of claims—this is needed for the conditionalization-based mechanism to apply. Garber's particular version assumes that the agent is certain of at least all truth-functional tautologies. But I see no reason to think that proofs of truth-functional tautologies should be exempt from the effects of Jocko's drugs.

Moreover, I suspect that this sort of approach—at least in a simple form—would end up divorcing rational belief too sharply from logic. Even if we restrict our attention to T, and suppose that it's not a truth-functional tautology, the envisioned mechanism would seem to render irrelevant the actual cogency of the agent's reasoning in proving T. Her proof would enter into determining the rationality of her degree of credence in T only as an apparent proof. The fact that T really is a logical truth would have no direct impact on the question of how much rational confidence it merited. Whether certain inferences were logically correct would have no direct impact on the rationality of beliefs supported by those inferences.

The problem with this is especially clear if we think about cases of much milder reasons for doubt. Suppose that Cherry is an excellent reasoner, while Kelly is a poor reasoner, and that the two are separately thinking about some matter. Cherry, through her usual flawless reasoning, becomes highly confident that P. Kelly, through her usual logical blunders, also becomes highly confident that P. It seems to me that we need to count Cherry's confidence in P as more rational than Kelly's. And this remains true even if we add that Cherry's and Kelly's reasons for self-doubt are equivalent (perhaps neither has been given much feedback on her cognitive performance—they both happen to have discovered a few checkbook-balancing errors) and they have the same generally positive assessment of their own reasoning abilities. While the rationality of an agent's belief does depend on the agent's second-order assessment of her reliability, it also depends on other things, including the first-order reasoning on which the belief is based.

Of course, these worries are only preliminary, and it remains to be seen how difficult a problem we're left with. But if the arguments we've been looking at are correct, whatever account we end up giving of the way beliefs should be informed by evidence will have to take into account the interaction among epistemic ideals that we've been examining—in particular, the way that what is rational for an agent to believe in general is constrained by what is rational for an agent to believe about herself.

REFERENCES

Alston, William P. (1985) 'Concepts of Epistemic Justification', in *Epistemic Justification: Essays in the Theory of Knowledge* (Ithaca, NY).

Cherniak, Christopher (1986) *Minimal Rationality* (Cambridge).

Christensen, David (2004) *Putting Logic in its Place: Formal Constraints on Rational Belief* (New York).

—— (2007) 'Epistemology of Disagreement: The Good News', *Philosophical Review*, 116: 187–217

Cohen, Stewart (2002) 'Basic Knowledge and the Problem of Easy Knowledge', *Philosophy and Phenomenological Research*, 65: 309–29.

Ellis, Brian (1979) *Rational Belief Systems* (Totowa, NJ).

Feldman, Richard (manuscript) 'Reasonable Disagreements'.

—— and Earl Conee (1985) 'Evidentialism', *Philosophical Studies*, 48: 15–34.

Foley, Richard (1993) *Working without a Net* (New York).

Fumerton, Richard (1995) *Metaepistemology and Skepticism* (Lanham, Md.).

Goldman, Alvin (1986) *Epistemology and Cognition* (Cambridge).

Garber, Daniel (1983) 'Old Evidence and Logical Omniscience in Bayesian Confirmation Theory', in John Earman (ed.), *Testing Scientific Theories (Minnesota Studies in the Philosophy of Science*, 10 (Minneapolis): 99–132.

Hacking, Ian (1967) 'Slightly More Realistic Personal Probability', *Philosophy of Science*, 34: 311–25.

Horwich, Paul (1982) *Probability and Evidence* (New York).

Kelly, Thomas (2005) 'The Epistemic Significance of Disagreement', *Oxford Studies in Epistemology*, 1: 167–96.

Kitcher, Philip (1992) 'The Naturalists Return', *Philosophical Review*, 101: 53–114.

Levi, Isaac (1997) *The Covenant of Reason* (New York).

Maher, Patrick (1993) *Betting on Theories* (New York).

Savage, Leonard J. (1954) *The Foundations of Statistics* (New York).

Sobel, Jordan Howard (1987) 'Self-Doubts and Dutch Strategies', *Australasian Journal of Philosophy*, 65: 56–81.

Sosa, Ernest (1997) 'Reflective Knowledge in the Best Circles', *Journal of Philosophy*, 94: 410–30.

Vogel, Jonathan (2000) 'Reliabilism Leveled', *Journal of Philosophy*, 97: 602–23.

Williamson, Timothy (2000) *Knowledge and its Limits* (Oxford).

Zynda, Lyle (1996) 'Coherence as an Ideal of Rationality', *Synthèse*, 109: 175–216.

2. An Opinionated Guide to Epistemic Modality

Kai von Fintel and Anthony S. Gillies

INTRODUCTION

Epistemic modals are interesting in part because their semantics is bound up both with our information about the world and with how that information changes as we share what we know. Given that epistemic modals are dependent in some way on the information available in the contexts in which they are used, it's not surprising that there is a minor but growing industry of work in semantics and the philosophy of language concerned with the precise nature of the context-dependency of epistemically modalized sentences. Take, for instance, an epistemic *might*-claim like

(1) Jimbo might go to the party.

This sentence is true iff Jimbo's party-going is compatible with some (relevant) body of information. But that is where agreement ends. Whose information counts? Maybe it is just the knowledge of the speaker that is relevant. Maybe it is the knowledge of the speaker plus her conversational partners. Maybe it is information in some looser sense than *knowledge* that is relevant, or maybe epistemic modals require some more delicate way of aggregating that information. These strategies are all ways of exploring the extent to which epistemic modals are context-dependent. But maybe it isn't even information available in the context of utterance that is primarily relevant in the first place. That would make the

This is the paper formerly known as "Epistemic Modality for Dummies". The paper grew out of our presentations in an informational session at the annual meeting of the APA Eastern Division, 30 Dec. 2005. We would like to thank Frank Jackson and Timothy Williamson for their comments. We thank Josh Dever and the rest of the M&E reading group at the University of Texas at Austin, whose comments Josh relayed to us. We also thank Chris Potts and Timothy Sundell for comments.

truth-conditions of modals relative to bodies of information not provided by the context at all.[1]

In this paper, we will not directly contribute or even comment on that debate. Instead, we will present some of the background, linguistic and semantic, that we feel is necessary to be able to follow and contribute to ongoing work. We will also point to a number of open problems that the current upsurge in work has not yet attended to. We hope that a fuller picture of the properties of epistemic modals can help to broaden and deepen our understanding of this fascinating area.

This paper is structured as follows. After situating epistemic modals within the general setting of modality in natural language, we sketch the standard formal semantic approach to epistemic modality, which is a context-dependent possible worlds semantics. Then, we discuss two ways in which this semantics has to be refined or replaced: epistemic modals are evidential markers signaling the presence of an (indirect) inference or deduction and epistemically modalized sentences give rise to speech acts beyond just the assertion of the possible worlds proposition they express. We present two ways of approaching the second issue, one involving a bit of handwaving about multiple speech acts associated with one utterance and the other employing a dynamic semantic perspective on epistemic modals, which departs from the standard static semantics in interesting ways.[2]

1. MULTIPLICITY OF MODAL MEANINGS

Expressions of epistemic modality mark the necessity/possibility of an underlying proposition, traditionally called the PREJACENT,

[1] We have dubbed such "relativist" semantics *CIA theories* (von Fintel and Gillies, 2006) since in our general reformulation of them they propose that truth values are relative to contexts, indices, and (points of) assessment. It is hard to keep up with the flood of papers on the topic. It started with MacFarlane (2003) and Egan *et al.* (2005). Then came Egan (2005), Yalcin (2005), Stephenson (2005), and Swanson (2005). More recently, work on the topic was presented at a conference at the Australian National University and many relevant papers are slated to appear in a volume on the topic, among them MacFarlane (2006). We have our own take on the issue: we criticize the relativist approach in our "CIA Leaks" (2006) and we will present an alternative view in our "*Might* Made Right" (in progress).

[2] For a more general overview of modality in natural language, epistemic and other, see von Fintel and Gillies (2007).

relative to some body of evidence/knowledge. The stock examples use the English modal auxiliary verbs *must* and *might*:

(2) a. There must have been a power outage overnight.
b. There might have been a power outage overnight.

Other relevant expressions include further modal auxiliaries such as *may, ought, should, can, could, have to, needn't* and adverbial expression such as *possibly, probably, certainly, apparently, supposedly, allegedly*.

Many of these expressions do not unambiguously express epistemic modality. In fact, many modals can express many different flavors of modality, depending on contextual factors. A spectacularly chameleonic modal is the English modal *have to*, as the following examples show (we use traditional labels to indicate the particular flavors of modality involved):

(3) a. *Given all those wet umbrellas,* it **has to** be raining. [epistemic]
b. *According to the hospital regulations,* visitors **have to** leave by six pm. [deontic]
c. *According to my wishes as your father,* you **have to** go to bed in ten minutes. [bouletic]
d. Excuse me. *Given the current state of my nose,* I **have to** sneeze. [circumstantial]
e. *Given the choices of modes of transportation and their speeds,* to get home in time, you **have to** take a taxi. [teleological]

The variability continues even within a given type of meaning, as the following examples of different epistemic uses of *might* demonstrate:

(4) a. *As far as Bill knows,* John **might** be the thief.
b. *Given what we knew at the time,* John **might** have been the thief.
c. *Given the results of the DNA tests,* John **might** be the thief. But *if we take the eyewitness seriously,* John **can't** have been the thief.

When we encounter an unmodified modal on its own, as in (5), the context will have to help disambiguate:

(5) John has to be in New York.

(5) could be an epistemic claim or a deontic claim. If epistemic, it might be based on just the speaker's evidence or all available evidence or . . .

In sum, simple modal expressions (like *can, might, must, have to*) have a multitude of uses: different flavors of modality (epistemic, deontic, . . .) and different subflavors (what Bill knows, what we knew, what the DNA tests reveal).

Given this systematic multiplicity of meanings, a successful semantic analysis cannot simply divide and conquer, say by developing an analysis of deontic *ought* that shows no connection to a separate analysis of epistemic *ought*. Instead, we should combine a shared semantic core with mechanisms for modulating the core meaning in context.

2. A CONTEXT-DEPENDENT POSSIBLE WORLDS SEMANTICS

The semantics for modals proposed by Kratzer (1977, 1978, 1981, 1991), based on the seminal work by Kripke (1963), Hintikka (1962), and Copeland (2002), is designed to fulfill the two desiderata we just identified (a common semantic core supplemented by mechanisms for contextual modulation). The basic idea is that modals are quantifiers over possible worlds. Just what possible worlds a particular occurrence of a modal quantifies over is determined explicitly by restrictor phrases (*according to, given, based on*, etc.) or implicitly by the context. Kratzer proposed to make the interpretation of a modal relative to a contextual parameter, which she called the CONVERSATIONAL BACKGROUND.[3] Instead of saying that the parameter is of the type of an accessibility relation (a relation between worlds), she proposed that conversational backgrounds are functions from evaluation worlds to sets of propositions. Some example values for the parameter are *what is known*, which would map any world into

[3] Kratzer actually made the interpretation relative to *two* conversational backgrounds: the MODAL BASE, which provides the set of accessible worlds, and the ORDERING SOURCE, which induces an ordering on the worlds provided by the modal base. The complications ensuing from using an ordering are mostly irrelevant to our purposes here, although for a fuller treatment of epistemic modality and in particular for an understanding of weak necessity modals like *ought* and *should*, one would have to include the ordering in the semantics.

the set of propositions known in that world, or *what the hospital regulations require*, which would map any world into the propositions that need to be true according to the hospital regulations in that world.

For concreteness, we will assume that sentences with modals in them have a logical form that includes a silent "pronominal" of the type of a conversational background, whose value is determined by the context (just as the value of a free pronoun like *she* is determined by the context), possibly with the aid of restricting expressions (*judging by the DNA evidence, according to your father's wishes, in view of what the eyewitness told us,...*):

(6) *might* (B) (ϕ)

might (B) (ϕ) is true in w iff ϕ is true in *some* world that is B-accessible from w

B: the *conversational background* (Kratzer), a function from worlds to sets of propositions, or simpler to sets of worlds (i.e. an accessibility function of sorts)

ϕ: the prejacent proposition

The lexical entry for *must* would be analogous, treating it as a universal quantifier instead of as an existential quantifier like *might*.

Kratzer also proposes that *if*-clauses should be seen as restrictors of the contextual argument of the modal. In other words, *if*-clauses are used to temporarily (hypothetically) restrict attention to a subset of the B-accessible worlds. Consider a "conditional" sentence such as (7).

(7) If John is not in his office, he might be in the cafe.

In Kratzer's proposal, what happens is that the proposition that John is not in his office is (temporarily, hypothetically) added to the body of evidence that the modal *might* is sensitive to. The modal then claims that there are some worlds compatible with that body of evidence and with the proposition that John is not in the office in which he is in the cafe.

We will not really deal with conditionals in this paper, but would like to point out that based on Kratzer's proposal, any progress in the analysis of modals, epistemic or otherwise, will also contribute to the analysis of conditionals, since according to this story, *if*-clauses are simply devices to further modulate modal claims.

It should be noted that not all modals show maximal flexibility as to what kind of conversational background they tolerate. For example:

- English *might* doesn't have deontic uses;[4]
- German *sollen* can only be based on hearsay evidence;
- etc.

These idiosyncrasies can be modeled as selectional restrictions on the kind of conversational background a modal is willing to combine with. A related issue that, as we mentioned in the introduction, has received a lot attention recently is what bodies of evidence epistemic modals can be sensitive to. One might have expected that there is considerable contextual variability, ranging from solipsistic readings (*what the speaker knows*) to community-based readings (*what we know*) all the way to even more objective readings (*what the available evidence would indicate if anybody bothered to evaluate it*). Whether that is in fact what we find and whether we need new semantic mechanisms to deal with the facts about epistemic modals is the subject of an ongoing dispute, in which we will not engage here.[5]

We will now turn to two aspects in which the semantics we have sketched here is not quite adequate (yet).

3. EVIDENTIALITY

Imagine that we are seeing people coming into the building carrying wet umbrellas. It would be perfectly reasonable to say *It must be raining*. Our semantics as sketched above would support such a claim: in all of the worlds compatible with the available evidence (wet umbrellas, the absence of any other good explanation for the

[4] Tim Sundell (pc) points out to us that this is strictly speaking not obviously true. Consider examples such as the following:

(i) You might send your grandmother a thank you note for the present. After all, she cashed in her 401K to buy it for you.

While *might* here doesn't have the expected permission sense, it does seem to traffic in something like deontic advice rather than epistemic possibility. We leave the proper treatment of this use of *might* to someone else for now.

[5] See n. 1 for references to work in this debate.

wet umbrellas, ...), it is raining. But now imagine that we look out the window and see the pouring rain. In that case, it would be exceedingly strange to say *It must be raining*. In fact, what one should say in this scenario is the non-modalized sentence *It is raining*. Why would that be? Surely, in all of the worlds compatible with the available evidence (the fact that it is pouring outside, the absence of any indication that we are being deceived, ...), it is raining. So, the truth-conditions of the modal sentence appear to be satisfied.

Karttunen (1972) was one of the first authors to claim that such examples make it seem that an epistemic necessity modal actually makes a weaker claim than the corresponding non-modalized sentence, something not predicted by the standard possible worlds semantics. He considers the following pair of examples:

(8) a. John must have left.
 b. John has left.

He writes:

> Intuitively, (8a) makes a weaker claim than (8b). In general, one would use the epistemic *must* only in circumstances where it is not yet an established fact that John has left. In stating (8a), the speaker indicates that he has no first-hand evidence about John's departure, and neither has it been reported to him by trustworthy sources. Instead, (8a) seems to say that the truth of *John has left* in some way logically follows from other facts the speaker knows and some reasonable assumptions that he is willing to entertain. A man who has actually seen John leave or has read about it in the newspaper would not ordinarily assert (8a), since he is in the position to make the stronger claim in (8b). (1972: 12).

We have to dispute the claim that *must*-claims are weaker than unmodalized claims. Here is an example of an appropriate use of *must* in a case of a logical inference from given premises:

(9) The ball is in A or in B or in C.
 It is not in A. It is not in B.
 So, it must be in C.

There is clearly no sense at all of weakness in the conclusion in (9). What we would like to suggest is that epistemic modals signal the presence of an indirect inference or deduction rather than of a direct observation. This is independent of the strength of the claim being made.

Our proposal was in fact anticipated by Frege:

> What distinguishes the apodeictic from the assertoric judgment is that it indicates the existence of general judgments from which the proposition may be inferred—an indication that is absent in the assertoric judgment. (1879: 5)

In fact, Karttunen also cites this passage from Frege and continues

> so, the role of *must* in (8a) is to indicate that the complement proposition is inferred but not yet known to be true independently. The intuitive feeling that (8b) is a weaker assertion than (8b) is apparently based on some general conversational principle by which indirect knowledge—that is, knowledge based on logical inference—is valued less highly than 'direct' knowledge that involves no reasoning. (Karttunen, 1972: 13)

Our claim that epistemic modals signal the presence of an indirect inference or deduction rather than of a direct observation amounts to claiming that epistemic modals incorporate a kind of EVIDENTIAL meaning component. Evidential markers are expressions found in many languages that signal the source of evidence a speaker has for the prejacent claim. Evidentials often come in a system of related meanings. Figure 2.1 is a reproduction of Willet's (1988) taxonomy of evidentials. It appears that seen as evidentials, epistemic modals are markers of INDIRECT INFERENCE, that is the rightmost branch of Willet's system.[6] It should be noted that the literature on evidentials

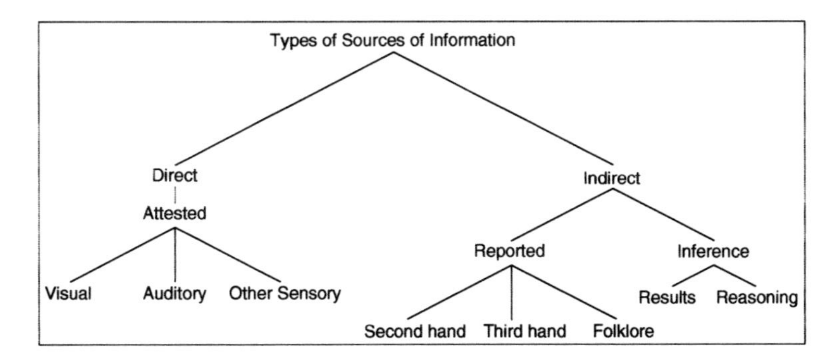

Figure 2.1. Willet's taxonomy of evidentials

[6] Note that epistemic modals do not cover the notion of indirect evidence derived from reports (the sister of indirect inference in Willet's system). Frank Jackson (pc) gave us a relevant scenario. When one reads in a book that the Battle of Hastings was

often makes a strict distinction between epistemic modality and evidentiality, but the facts we have discussed here indicate that this is too simplistic a position.[7]

It is an open problem how exactly to capture the evidential flavor of epistemic modals in the kind of possible worlds semantics we have assumed so far. There is a proposal by Kratzer (1991) according to which epistemic modals don't simply range over the worlds compatible with what is known; she suggests that in addition, they are sensitive to other less reliable sources of information. This again is meant to capture the apparent weakness of epistemic modals. We do not deny that one *can* use *must* in situations where one is drawing on assumptions that do not attain the status of confident knowledge. But when it comes to signaling weakness of an inference, it is often much more appropriate to use expressions like *ought* or *should*.[8] As we showed above, *must* is not an automatic carrier of a signal of weakness. In the absence of any other concrete proposal, we will leave the problem unresolved and hope that future research will find a solution.[9]

4. EPISTEMIC MODALITY IN THE SECOND DIMENSION

So far, we have assumed that modalized sentences express complex propositions with a possible worlds-based quantificational meaning

fought in 1066, one's evidence is indirect; one does not observe the battle or anything like that. But it would be wrong to say 'The Battle of Hastings must have been fought in 1066'.

[7] See also Blain and Déchaine (2007) and Matthewson *et al.* (2006) for cross-linguistic evidence for the close connection between epistemic modality and evidentiality.

[8] The compositional semantics of weak necessity modals like *ought* and *should* is explored by von Fintel and Iatridou (2006).

[9] Another proposal for handling Karttunen's problem appears in Veltman (1985). The basic idea is to assign truth-values based on an underying system of "states", where: (i) those states might be partial, not always determining the truth/falsity of the basic sentences; and (ii) the states are ordered by whether one state can "grow" into another. Then *must* says, at a state, that its prejacent is true in every state that can be gotten to from there. So, in general, *must* ϕ will not entail ϕ since the present state might not decide the fate of ϕ even though it is true at all the successor states. We are not sure whether this in fact solves the problem as we have characterized it, which is not so much a problem of unexpected weakness but a problem of finding the semantic source of the signal of indirect inference. We'll leave this to another occasion or other researchers.

built on top of a prejacent unmodalized proposition. While this is indeed the standard analysis in formal natural language semantics, it is not actually the standard assumption in descriptive and typological linguistics.

The most common analysis in descriptive work treats modality as an expression of the speaker's attitude towards the prejacent proposition, rather than giving rise to a complex proposition with its own distinct content. The prevalence of this conception can perhaps be traced back to the influence of Kant, who wrote in the *Critique of Pure Reason* that "the modality of judgments is a very special function thereof, which has the distinguishing feature that it does not contribute to the content of the judgment" (1781: 74). This idea seems to have influenced both practising linguists and a subset of logicians, including Frege, who wrote in the *Begriffsschrift* that "[b]y saying that a proposition is necessary I give a hint about the grounds for my judgment. But, since this does not affect the conceptual content of the judgment, the form of the apodictic judgment has no significance for us" (1879: 5).

Some prima-facie evidence that the speaker's comment analysis is not entirely crazy comes from considering exchanges like the one in (10):

(10) Q: Why isn't Louise coming to our meetings these days?
A: She might/must be too busy with her dissertation.

(We note that dialogues like this one are used by Simons in her recent work on parentheticals (2006). Here, we adapt her paradigm to the case of epistemic modals.) The crucial point is that what is proposed as the reason for Louise's absence is that she is too busy with her dissertation, not that it might or must be the case that she is too busy with her dissertation. In other words, the response in (10) offers the prejacent as the answer to the question and the epistemic modals seem to signal something like the speaker's assessment of the likelihood that this is the right answer.

If one wants to take this as evidence that modals do not contribute to the truth-conditional content of the sentence, one needs to develop an alternative semantics for them. Two possibilities are of particular interest. (i) Epistemic modals might be treated as "parentheticals", phrases that give side-remarks in a separate semantic dimension from the normal truth-conditional content. The recent treatment of such parentheticals by Potts (2005) might be thought to be adaptable to the analysis of epistemic modals. (ii) Epistemic modals might be treated as "speech act modifiers". While presenting an unmodalized sentence is interpreted as a straightforward assertion, adding an epistemic modal might indicate that a different kind of speech act (albeit with the same truth-conditional content) is performed. One might for example say that a sentence like *There might have been a mistake* expresses the speech act "I (hereby) advise you not to overlook the possibility that there has been a mistake" (cf. Eric Swanson's work in progress (2005)).

In either implementation, the speaker's comment analysis faces serious problems, most importantly the fact that epistemic modals can be embedded in yet more complex constructions. Consider for example the following sentence:

(11) If there might have been a mistake, the editor will have to reread the manuscript.
  a. $\neq$ If there has been a mistake, as is possible, the editor will have to reread the manuscript.
  b. $\neq$ If I advise you not to overlook the possibility that there has been a mistake, the editor will have to reread the manuscript.

As we can see, the attempted paraphrases in (11a) and (11b) do not come anywhere near what (11) means. It should be obvious that what the modalized sentence (*there might have been a mistake*) contributes to the truth-conditions of the entire complex is precisely the truth-conditions we had assumed it expresses: if the evidence is compatible with there having been a mistake, the editor will have to reread the manuscript.

There are many other cases in which an epistemic modal embeds felicitously and where it contributes modalized truth-conditions:[10]

[10] This is not to say that epistemic modals embed completely freely. For example, when we try to combine a deontic modal with an epistemic modal, we can do so in one way:

(i) It's midnight. These kids must be allowed to stay up really late. [epistemic over deontic]

But the other way (which would embed an epistemic modal under a deontic modal) is not possible:

(ii) They ought to have to be home. [Not: deontic over epistemic]

(ii) has no reading where it would say that there is an obligation for it to follow from the evidence that they are home.

(12) There can't have been a mistake. [Negation over modal]
(13) Bill thinks that there might have been a mistake. [Attitude predicate over modal]
(14) Where might you have put the keys? [Question over modal]
(15) The keys might have been in the drawer. [Past over modal]
(16) The editor reread the manuscript because there might have been a mistake. [Causal operator over modal][11]
(17) The detective interviewed every resident who (based on the time of the accident) might have seen the accident. [Quantifier over modal]

So, we find it unlikely that the speaker's comment analysis is correct in either of the two forms we have considered above, since they would not allow the contribution of epistemic modals to have compositional effects in embedded positions. We will look at two other possibilities. One is a semantically conservative proposal, according to which epistemic modals have exactly the kind of possible worlds semantics we have been assuming but sentences with epistemic modals are used to perform more than the speech act of asserting that possible worlds proposition. The other approach is to reconsider the entire semantic set-up and move to a more dynamic picture already at the semantic level.

5. MULTIPLE SPEECH ACTS?

In this section, we propose a conservative addition to the possible worlds semantics for epistemic modals. Our proposal is inspired

Another case that has received some attention is that epistemic modals seem to serve as some kind of barrier for quantifier raising, see von Fintel and Iatridou (2003).

We have nothing further to say here about why epistemic modals show these effects. The crucial point we're trying to make is that they *can* sometimes be embedded in complex constructions, not that they always can.

[11] Frank Jackson (pc) doubts that this is really a causal operator over a modal; rather, he would argue that this example involves a causal operator over a belief in an epistemic possibility. That is, (16) is best thought of as:

(i) The editor reread the manuscript because she believed there might have been a mistake.

That would be just fine with us, because it shows the epistemic modal embedded twice over.

by a similar proposal by Simons on other kinds of parentheticals (2006). Consider:

(18) Q: Why isn't Louise coming to our meetings these days?
A: I heard she is too busy with her dissertation.

Simons suggests that the answer in (18) achieves two simultaneous speech acts: an assertion that I heard that she is too busy with her dissertation *and* offering her dissertation work as an explanation of her absence. Crucially, while the second speech act is the *main point* of the utterance, the truth-conditional content of the assertive speech act is such that the putative "parenthetical" *I heard*... does in fact contribute to the truth-conditions of the sentence it occurs in.

We would like to say that epistemic modalized sentences similarly are used to effect two speech acts. Consider again:

(19) There might have been a mistake (in the calculation).

Our suggestion is that a sentence like (19) is used to make two speech acts: an assertion (?)[12] that it is compatible with the evidence that there has been a mistake, *and* proffering (with an explicit lack of conviction) that there has been a mistake *or* giving advice not to overlook the possibility that there has been a mistake.[13]

This picture would explain two properties of epistemically modalized sentences that create a conflict for the two-dimensional proposals we discussed in the previous section: (i) the main point of an epistemically modalized sentence often seems to be centered around the truth of the prejacent, while (ii) epistemically modalized sentences can be rather freely embedded and then seem to contribute the standard possible worlds meaning of epistemic possibility/necessity. The multiple speech acts analysis says that unembedded uses of epistemically modalized sentences are used to effect two speech acts, one of which is the putting forward of the prejacent, thus accounting for property (i); in embedded occurrences,

[12] Whether the speech act is really one of assertion proper is something that might have to be rethought. If the claim made by epistemic modals is relative to not just the speaker's evidence but to some more objective or communal body of evidence, then the speaker may not be in a position to really assert anything about that evidence, especially if we assume strong norms of assertion such as the knowledge-based norms defended by some. We will leave this question open here.

[13] We readily admit that one would have to sharpen the characterization of the proposed second speech act. After all, whenever one asserts ϕ, one would appear to be giving advice not to overlook the possibility that ϕ. What precisely is special about epistemic modals then? (Thanks to the Austin reading group for raising this issue.)

the epistemically modalized sentence is not used to (directly) effect a speech act at all and all it does is contribute its truth-conditional content, thus accounting for property (ii).[14]

Since there are two speech acts, one of which has as its content the modalized proposition and the other of which has as its content the prejacent, it is not too surprising to find evidence that both propositions can be at play in complex dialogues. Pascal and Mordecai are playing Mastermind. After some rounds where Mordecai gives Pascal hints about the solution, Pascal says

(20) There might be two reds.

Mordecai, knowing the solution, has a range of possible responses:

(21) a. That's right. There might be.
b. That's right. There are.
c. That's wrong. There can't be.
d. That's wrong. There aren't.

Clearly, Mordecai's response can target *either* the epistemic claim or the prejacent proposition. The possibility that in dialogue, the truth-conditions of the prejacent are saliently at issue should therefore not be taken as evidence that epistemic modals do not contribute to the truth-conditions of the sentence they occur in. (One should also not take such data as evidence that a non-standard semantics for the modal is needed.)

We would recommend that fans of a static possible worlds semantics explore the prospects for the multiple speech-act pragmatics we have sketched here. Pursuing this line means taking seriously the idea that epistemic modals are not, properly speaking, things that go in for assertion. Another way to go, though, is to say that it's all assertion, but that the effect of assertion is a bit more delicate than on the Stalnaker picture. And one way of cashing that out is to model those (dynamic) effects in the semantics proper. Pursuing this line means redrawing the border between semantics and pragmatics, capturing (some of) the effects successful assertions have on the context in the semantics proper. This is the place to move to an exposition of the dynamic semantic approach to epistemic modals, which is what the remaining sections of the paper are concerned with.

[14] Thanks to the Austin reading group for pressing us on the point discussed in this paragraph.

6. TWO SOURCES OF INSPIRATION FOR A DYNAMIC PERSPECTIVE

Two morals have emerged thus far. First, modals—and so epistemic modals—are context sensitive: they act as quantifiers over sets of worlds, just which sets being a function of context. And we have seen that there is good reason to explore the idea that epistemic modals involve a kind of non-propositional comment on their prejacents. (We'll set aside the problem of the evidential signal carried by epistemic modals.) One lesson to draw from this pair of morals is that understanding the interpretation of epistemic modals may well force us to rethink the division of labor between the semantics of these constructions and their pragmatics. We now turn to sketching a dynamic semantics for epistemic modals that does just that by assimilating some of the pragmatic effects of utterances into the semantic values assigned to them.[15]

Our goal here is not to present the most sophisticated or most comprehensive treatment of epistemic modals in a dynamic semantics. We intend to leave a lot of interesting questions unasked and unanswered. Instead, what we want to do is to motivate thinking about epistemic modals from a dynamic perspective, give some background for the uninitiated, and show how the framework—even in the most toyish scenarios—can be fruitful for exploring how our pair of morals impinges on the semantics for modals.

The kind of dynamic framework we sketch below draws inspiration from two sources: classic theories of the interplay between context and assertion, and the semantics of formal programming languages.

Begin with the familiar picture of assertion (Karttunen, 1974; Lewis, 1979; Stalnaker, 1978): An (assertive) utterance of a sentence ϕ in a well-run conversation takes place against a background context, the set of worlds compatible with what has been established up to that point. The proposition expressed by the speaker's utterance of ϕ is constrained by the context. And, finally, that proposition is

[15] We have drawn freely on some classic references (Groenendijk and Stokhof, 1991; Heim, 1982; Kamp, 1981; Veltman, 1996).

added to the context, changing it by reducing the uncertainty in it a bit.

Dynamic semantics takes this picture and pushes it further, focusing on the relation between the context prior to the utterance and the context posterior to the utterance. We thus swap the aim of trying to identify the CONTENT of bits of natural language—what proposition an utterance of them expresses—for the aim of trying to identify the CONTEXT CHANGE POTENTIAL of those bits—how utterances of them affect contexts.[16]

Similarly for the case of the semantics of programs. Begin with a simple propositional language and add to it the ability to represent actions such as **if** ϕ **then** α **else** β. To the stock of atomic sentences and boolean connectives we add a stock of atomic PROGRAMS and suitable program operators (sequencing, choice, test, and so on). We can then interpret such a language in a pretty simple extension of the standard possible worlds semantics for propositional modal logic (Harel *et al.*, 2000). It is clear enough what declarative sentences of such a language mean: their interpretations are just the set of states at which they are true. Programs, on the other hand, express *relations* between states: a pair $\langle u, v \rangle$ is in the interpretation of a program π just in case executing π in state u (possibly) terminates in state v. The intuition is that programs express their input–output relations. So the complex program **if** ϕ **then** α **else** β has as its denotation the set of pairs of states $\langle u, v \rangle$ such that either ϕ is true at u and v results from executing the program α in u or ϕ is not true at u and v results from executing the program β at u.

Dynamic semantics takes this picture and pushes it further, treating *all* sentences as programs for changing the context. They are instructions for updating it. Thus the semantic values of sentences are of the same kind associated with programs: relations between states (i.e. contexts), or, as they are more familiarly known, CONTEXT CHANGE POTENTIALS (CCPS).

So much for inspiration. We next sketch a pseudo-dynamic semantics for a simple propositional language and say in just

[16] There need not be anything sacrosanct about the context to be updated being identified with the common ground. It could be the hearer's information state, or what she takes the common ground to be, or what she takes the speaker to take the common ground to be. At the most abstract level, the issue is about how a body of information responds to the information a sentence carries.

what sense it is not quite dynamic. We then make it truly dynamic by adding epistemic modals into the mix. Finally we show how, even in this simple system, the dynamic perspective has something interesting to say about our two guiding morals.

7. ALMOST DYNAMIC SEMANTICS

Let's keep things simple. Suppose we have a small fragment of natural language that uses propositional logic—the closure of a set of atomic sentences under negation ($\neg$) and conjunction ($\wedge$)—as an intermediate language: expressions of natural language are mapped (via an isomorphism) to expressions of this intermediate formal language, which are then mapped (via homomorphism) to semantic values.[17] Since the semantics will treat sentences as programs for changing contexts, we need to settle on what kind of information is represented in those contexts. Our intermediate language is expressively pretty poor, so the chunks of information our semantics will traffic in will be pretty coarse: for now we will assume that it is the hearer's information about the world that undergoes change when she interprets bits of natural language, representing the information she has by the set of worlds compatible with it. Such information states—really not anything other than conversational backgrounds—will be our contexts.

Let us take worlds to be functions from atomic sentences to truth-values, information states to be sets of worlds, and the set of information states to be the powerset of the set W of worlds.[18] That leaves us with two special cases of information states. The MINIMAL information state is W itself, the state in which no world has yet been ruled out. At the other end of the spectrum lies the ABSURD information state $\emptyset$—we want to stay out of that one since it represents a broken context.

[17] This is the so-called "indirect method" of interpretation familiar from Montague's PTQ.

[18] Since the information we are trafficking in is coarse, we assume that worlds decide the truth-values of the atoms of our language and that two worlds are distinguishable just in case they differ over some atom. So, for our purposes here, we will assume that worlds are simply functions from atoms to truth-values. Nothing important is lost if we further assume that the set of atoms for our propositional language is finite, thus keeping the space of worlds finite.

The motivating intuition is that sentences express programs for changing information states, and so should have as denotations relations between information states. So, for example, interpreting an atom ϕ should take us to posterior states which have only the ϕ-worlds from the prior state in them. Thus $\langle s, s' \rangle$ should be in the interpretation assigned to ϕ just in case s' is just like s except we throw out the worlds in which ϕ is false. That would match the motivating idea pretty well: ϕ is a program for eliminating falsifying worlds from consideration.

We could proceed in this way giving the CCPs as relations between states, and certainly some proposals in dynamic semantics do (see, e.g. Beaver, 2001; Groenendijk and Stokhof, 1991). But with just a bit of sleight of hand we can express these relations between states as functions on the set of states, making things a little more manageable. So that is what we will do.

Here is a simple assignment of CCPs to sentences of our intermediate language as update-profiles. Where ϕ is some formula of our intermediate language, $[\![\phi]\!]^{ccp}$ denotes the function on information states that is ϕ's meaning.[19] Thus, given a context s as argument, $[\![\phi]\!]$ takes us to the posterior state we might write (using prefix notation for our function) $[\![\phi]\!](s)$. We instead follow the convention in dynamic semantics and write the functions using postfix notation:

(22) PSEUDO-DYNAMIC UPDATE SEMANTICS

(a) $s[\![p]\!] = \{w \in s : w(p) = 1\}$,

(b) $s[\![\neg\phi]\!] = s \setminus s[\![\phi]\!]$,

(c) $s[\![\phi \wedge \psi]\!] = s[\![\phi]\!][\![\psi]\!]$.

The atomic case is straightforward enough. Negation is set-subtraction: first figure the update induced on the input state by the embedded sentence; any world surviving this update is eliminated from the input state. And conjunction is functional composition, the output state to interpreting the first conjunct is the input for interpreting the second.

But assigning interpretations is only part of the job a semantic theory has to do. We also want it to predict entailments, patterns

[19] When there is no risk of confusing $[\![\cdot]\!]^{ccp}$ for the (static) context-invariant interpretation function $[\![\cdot]\!]^{classic}$ over our fragment, we will conserve the ink and omit the superscript.

of consistency, and the like. And for that we need to be able to say when a sentence is true—that is, true with respect to an information state. Once we take the plunge into the dynamic framework, there are—purely formally speaking—a number of entailment relations one might opt for.[20] We adopt a simple perspective, based on two simple intuitions:

(23) a. A sentence is true in a state iff the information it carries is already present in that state.

b. A sequence of sentences entails another sentence if adding the information of that sequence to any state yields a state in which the sentence is true.

The formal implementation of these is, in turn:

(24) a. ϕ is true in s, $s \models \phi$, iff $s[\![\phi]\!] = s$.

b. $\phi_1, \ldots, \phi_n$ entail ψ, $\phi_1, \ldots, \phi_n \models \psi$, iff for any s: $s[\![\phi_1]\!] \ldots [\![\phi_n]\!] \models \psi$.

Thus truth is a matter of seeing whether the relevant information state is a fixed-point of the CCP of the relevant sentence, and entailment is the natural generalization of this: to see if an entailment holds we add up the CCPs of the putative entailers and see if the putative entailee is true in the resulting context.[21]

8. THE LACK OF REAL DYNAMICS SO FAR

Sadly, we do not yet have anything particularly "dynamic" here. We began by noting that one inspiration for dynamic semantics is a picture of assertion whereby contexts evolve as conversations proceed by adding to them the contents of the sentences asserted. Perhaps all we have done so far is foster confusion by complicating this original—and rather pleasingly elegant—picture. But there is a point to our fostering. We will show, precisely, in what sense our update semantics for our toy fragment is not at all dynamic, thereby saying what we need to get some real dynamics. Adding epistemic

[20] See, e.g. van Benthem (1996) for a discussion of some of the menu of options.

[21] Two small notes: (i) we have opted for an "update-to-test" flavor of entailment; (ii) since in a dynamic set-up order of updates may well matter to what state we land in, and entailment is defined in terms of a sequence of updates, order may well matter to entailment as well.

modals on top of the system as it now stands will turn out to do the trick. From confusion comes enlightenment.

Whenever we have a space of information states (contexts), we can in general ask what it means to say that one state contains at least as much information as another. This may well impose some structure on the space of states, and often enough that structure is pretty well-behaved in that the relation *at least as much information as* partially orders the space of contexts and is such that every pair of contexts has a *join*—that is, if c and c' are two contexts, then there is a least informative context c'' that contains at least as much information as c and at least as much information as c'.[22] Now, an update function just amounts to a complicated way of doing something that should be simple if the following holds:

(25) Updating a context c with ϕ is the same as taking the join of c and the update of the *minimal* state with ϕ.

In that case, the context c is not contributing anything special to the interpretation, and CCPs can be replaced by intersecting classical propositions. That turns out to be exactly what is going on in our simple semantics.

Let's walk through why. We have a space of contexts (information states)—the set of subsets of W, call it I. Since an information state is just a set of worlds, one state contains at least as much information as another just in case the first is a subset of the second. It is easy to check that set intersection is a join operation for this space of states (remember that W is the minimal state): $s' \cap s = s'$ iff $s' \subseteq s$. Now, the claim is that our update function above offers nothing really new if the following holds:

(26) For any state s and formula ϕ: $s[\![\phi]\!] = s \cap W[\![\phi]\!]$.

And a simple inductive proof shows that (26) does hold. In fact, $W[\![\phi]\!]^{\text{ccp}}$ is just the (static) context-invariant propositional content $[\![\phi]\!]^{\text{classic}}$—the set of ϕ-worlds.

Given this reduction of our CCPs to mere adding of propositional contents, it is no surprise that our dynamified versions of truth and entailment similarly reduce. (26) straightaway entails that

[22] Equivalently: let $\circ$ be a binary operator over the space of contexts $\mathcal{C}$ with minimal element 0. The operator $\circ$ is a join iff it commutes, associates, and is such that for any context c: (i) $c \circ 0 = c$ and (ii) $c \circ c = c$. It then induces an order over $\mathcal{C}$: if $c \circ c' = c'$ then c' contains at least as much information as c does.

(27) a. $s \models \phi$ iff $s \subseteq [\![\phi]\!]^{\text{classic}}$.
b. $\phi_1, \ldots, \phi_n \models \psi$ iff, for any s: $s \cap [\![\phi_1]\!]^{\text{classic}} \cap \ldots \cap [\![\phi_n]\!]^{\text{classic}} \subseteq [\![\psi]\!]^{\text{classic}}$.

Consider (27a). Our definition has it that $s \models \phi$ iff $s[\![\phi]\!]^{\text{ccp}} = s$. But by (26), $s[\![\phi]\!]^{\text{ccp}} = s \cap W[\![\phi]\!]^{\text{ccp}} = s \cap [\![\phi]\!]^{\text{classic}}$. Thus we have that $s \models \phi$ iff $s \cap [\![\phi]\!]^{\text{classic}} = s$. But the latter is true iff $s \subseteq [\![\phi]\!]^{\text{classic}}$. A similar argument works for (27b).

The possibility of this kind of reduction of these CCPs follows from a general result: we can reduce a function on sets in this way exactly when that function is ELIMINATIVE and DISTRIBUTIVE.[23] For our CCPs these generic properties are the following:

(28) a. (ELIMINATIVITY) $s[\![\phi]\!] \subseteq s$.
b. (DISTRIBUTIVITY) $s[\![\phi]\!] = \bigcup_{w \in s} \{w\}[\![\phi]\!]$.

Eliminativity just says that contexts change by shrinking uncertainty—no backtracking or information loss allowed. And distributivity is the requirement that computing the changes to a state induced by a sentence can just as well be got by taking the worlds in that state one at a time, figuring the changes induced by the sentence to those singletons, and collecting up the results at the end. Distributive functions thus only care about very local matters of fact since the sets they operate on can be replaced with singletons of the elements that make up those sets. Our update function satisfies both constraints, and that is what underlies the possibility of reducing the CCPs to the simple intersecting of propositional contents of the normal sort.

9. ALMOST DYNAMICS + EPISTEMIC MODALS = REAL DYNAMICS

One of the recurring themes we have stressed is the idea that there is reason to think that epistemic modals involve some sort of non-truth-conditional comment on their prejacents. Of course, as we have also stressed, making good on this idea is no easy task—in no small part because epistemic modals seem to mix and combine remarkably well with other, seemingly truth-conditional,

[23] The general result is due to van Benthem (1986), but see also Groenendijk and Stokhof (1990) and van Benthem (1996). Sometimes eliminative functions are called INTROSPECTIVE and distributive functions are called CONTINUOUS.

constructions. And so a version of the Frege–Geach problem looms. But not in a dynamic treatment. As a bonus, we will turn our previous update semantics into a genuinely dynamic semantics.

The basic intuition we begin with is that epistemic *might* serves to comment that its prejacent is compatible with the contextually relevant body of information. That is, it serves to comment that there is a world in the relevant context in which the prejacent is true. But, the idea is, this comment does not contribute to the propositional content of modal expressions like *might* ϕ—such expressions do not really traffic in propositions of the normal sort. There is a natural way to model this idea in the world of CCPs, making it both more precise and less exotic.

When we think of programs, we naturally think of programs like **set the value of variable x to 1** that have some non-trivial impact. But there are also programs whose whole point is to leave things exactly as they find them, *testing* whether certain conditions are satisfied. For instance, in the complex program **if** ϕ **then** α **else** β we want to check and see if the condition described by ϕ obtains or not and we do that by composing the test $?\phi$ with the non-test α and the test $?\neg\phi$ with the non-test β. If we are thinking of the denotation of a program as its set of input–output pairs, then tests are just those programs that are defined only on the diagonal: they always return their input states (if anything).

That is the simplest way of adding epistemic modals to our fragment: think of them as tests on the information state.[24] First, let's extend our intermediate language to L, defined as the smallest set including our set of atomic sentences that is closed under negation, conjunction, and the one-place epistemic modal operator *might*. We then add a single clause to (22) to cover the new bits of our (slightly) more expressive language:

(29) UPDATE SEMANTICS FOR L

(a), (b), and (c) as in (22),

(d) $s[\![might\phi]\!]^{\text{ccp}} = \{w \in s : s[\![\phi]\!]^{\text{ccp}} \neq \emptyset\}$.

This says that $[\![might\phi]\!]$ will take an information state s and either return all of it, or none of it, depending on whether or not the condition is satisfied. The condition is that the information that ϕ

[24] This is, plus or minus a bit, the first update system introduced by Veltman (1996). See also van der Does *et al.* (1997), Beaver (2001: ch. 5); and Gillies (2001).

carries be compatible with s. In other words, we could equivalently put the test behavior of *might* this way:

(30) $s[\![might\phi]\!] = \begin{cases} s & \text{if} s[\![\phi]\!] \neq \emptyset \\ \emptyset & \text{otherwise} \end{cases}$

If we let *must* abbreviate the $\neg$ *might* $\neg$ in our intermediate language, then the following CCP follows immediately from (29):

(31) (e) $s[\![must\phi]\!]^{\text{ccp}} = \{w \in s : s[\![\phi]\!]^{\text{ccp}} = s\}$.

Thus we have that *might*-statements act as tests (checking to see if the information carried by their prejacents is compatible with the contextually relevant body of information), and *must*-statements act as dual tests (checking to see if the information carried by their prejacents is already present in the contextually relevant body of information).

In fact, we can say something a little more definitive. The modals here do behave as quantifiers over information states since the following holds:

(32) If ϕ is non-modal, then:
 a. $s \models might\phi$ iff $s \cap [\![\phi]\!]^{\text{classic}} \neq \emptyset$,
 b. $s \models must\phi$ iff $s \subseteq [\![\phi]\!]^{\text{classic}}$.

We might well wonder in what sense we have made good on the promise of making the comment-intuition precise if the CCPs we have here could, after all, be reduced to the kind of complicated statics like we saw above. For then we have would not have managed to get propositions out of the semantics for the modals after all. This semantics, however, is non-trivially dynamic. It is still, of course, eliminative since the new clause for *might* will always either return its input state or the empty set—either way $s[\![might\phi]\!] \subseteq s$. For present purposes we would not want to do away with that property, since we are interested in monotonic information exchange in which the set of possibilities in a state shrinks as the conversation moves forward. But $[\![\cdot]\!]^{\text{ccp}}$ does not distribute, and this is, as we would expect, because of the test behavior of the modals.

Here is a simple counterexample to distributivity. Let $s = \{w_1, w_2\}$ where ϕ is true at w_1 and false at w_2. Since $s[\![\phi]\!] \neq \emptyset$, the test posed by *might* ϕ is one passed by s:

(33) $s[\![might\phi]\!] = s$.

But we get a different result if we take the worlds that make up s, one at a time. Of course, since ϕ is true at w_1, $\{w_1\}$ will pass the test posed by *might* ϕ. But w_2 will not. Since ϕ is false at w_2, $\{w_2\}[\![\phi]\!] = \emptyset$ and so $\{w_2\}[\![might\phi]\!] = \emptyset$. Thus we have:

(34) $\bigcup_{w \in s}\{w\}[\![might\phi]\!] = \{w_1\}$.

And these are different results.

One immediate consequence of this is that the CCPs associated with *might*-statements do not allow the kind of reduction we saw earlier. It is not generally true that:

(35) $s[\![might\phi]\!] = s \cap W[\![might\phi]\!]$.

And that means that $W[\![might\phi]\!]$ does not amount to the (static) propositional content of *might* ϕ. That is because *might*-statements, in this framework, make a kind of *global* comment about what is compatible with the current state. That is, they seem to say more about the information present than they do about the world. Which means that we cannot really factor out the current state from the interpretation in the way that we could in the static set-up. This way of making good on the intuition that epistemic modals involve a kind of comment dimension to them does not raise any Frege–Geach worries precisely because the semantic currency for the entire language—not just the modal stuff—is CCPs.[25] It just so happens that if we ignore the modals, those CCPs do not do anything that could not be done with propositions of the normal sort. But, as we have seen, things are different with the modals.

We also want to point out that although it can make perfect sense to assign *truth-conditions* to modal expressions—they, like the other sentences in our intermediate language, are true in a state iff that state is a fixed-point of the CCP—those truth-conditions are not about whether a proposition expressed by the sentence is true. So there is room to allow that epistemic modals have and contribute to truth-conditions, without requiring them to traffic in and express propositional contents. This is yet another way of exploring the idea that epistemic modals involve a kind of comment about the information carried by their prejacents.

[25] Of course, to really cash in on this claim, we would have to present dynamic semantic treatments of the whole panoply of embedding constructions that we used in section 4 to show that epistemic modals can embed. This goes way beyond what we can do in this paper, but the point is that there is no principled reason why this couldn't be done, whereas the embedding problem was severe for the two-dimensional approaches we considered there.

10. DYNAMIC EFFECTS IN NATURAL LANGUAGE

We seem to have checked our natural language interests at the door when we entered the world of CCPs. We want to now reclaim those interests, illustrating just a few ways in which the dynamic perspective is fruitful for thinking about epistemic modals.[26]

We are throwing a party, and exactly two guests—Alex and Billy—have yet to arrive. They will arrive one at a time. Consider the following minimal pair, where the dots indicate a pause to see who is at the door:[27]

(36) a. Billy might be at the door. ... It isn't Billy at the door.
b. ?? It isn't Billy at the door. ... Billy might be at the door.

Remember that we are limiting our attention to the monotonic shrinking of our uncertainty. We can interpret your utterance of (36a) perfectly smoothly. But things are different with (36b). Once we learn that Billy isn't at the door, it is very hard to interpret your claim that he might be. Assuming that a sequence of sentences is a conjunction of the sentences, and assuming the simple possible worlds treatment of modality, this asymmetry is rather unexpected. Letting ϕ be the atomic sentence *Billy is at the door* and B the epistemic conversational background:

(37) a. $[\![might(B)(\phi) \wedge \neg\phi]\!](w) = 1$ iff $w \in ([\![might(B)(\phi)]\!] \cap [\![\neg\phi]\!])$.
b. $[\![\neg\phi \wedge might(B)(\phi)]\!](w) = 1$ iff $w \in ([\![\neg\phi]\!] \cap [\![might(B)(\phi)]\!])$.

Given this analysis, there is no predicted asymmetry simply because set intersection is commutative. What we want, of course, is for the

[26] We won't go into it here, but the simple dynamic system here turns out to be pretty useful for thinking about some problems in formal epistemology as well. There is a well-known problem in belief dynamics—the Fuhrmann triviality result—that shows that conservative belief change is impossible for rational agents who have epistemic modal beliefs that are faithful to their non-modal beliefs. Diplomatically put: the dynamic perspective reveals an escape route that is hidden from view if we concentrate on revision models that have static entailment relations. Less diplomatically put: formal epistemology has a lot to learn from formal semantics. See Gillies (2006) for the details.

[27] This type of example is originally due to Veltman.

value of the conversational background B in (37b) to take into account the information introduced by the first conjunct—by the time we interpret *might* ϕ we have already learned that $\neg\phi$, and so B should not have any ϕ-worlds in it. Note that a consequence of this is that conjunction is not boolean intersection: $[\![\phi \wedge might(B)(\psi)]\!]^c$ is not, in general, $[\![\phi]\!]^c \cap [\![might(B)(\psi)]\!]^c$—$c$ may have to be ever so slightly shifted for interpreting B and so for assigning the right denotation to the second conjunct.

What this patch does in multiple steps is, in effect, exactly what the simple dynamic system above does in one step. Conjunction is interpreted not as intersection but as functional composition. So updating a state s with *might* ϕ and then with $\neg\phi$ will in general be very different from going the other way around. The former will, in many cases, be a fine way to proceed, but the latter will always result in a broken context, reducing the information state to absurdity.

A definition:

(38) a. A sentence is CONSISTENT iff for some state s, updating s with the sentence does not result in absurdity.
b. ϕ is consistent iff for some s: $s[\![\phi]\!] \neq \emptyset$.

Otherwise, the sentence is inconsistent. The prediction, then, is that (36a) is consistent but (36a) is not.

But the dynamic perspective also allows us to make distinctions between (36a) and more run-of-the-mill conjunctions like:

(39) a. Billy is at the door and Alex is in traffic.
b. Alex might be at the door and Billy might be at the door.

These are also consistent. But they are different from (36a). There it was crucial that we learned some new information midway through, but there is no similar requirement here. The information these sentences carry can hang together all at once.

(40) a. A sentence is COHESIVE iff there is a non-empty state that is a fixed-point of an update with it.
b. ϕ is cohesive iff for some $s \neq \emptyset$: $s[\![\phi]\!] = s$.

Clearly, cohesiveness implies consistency, but not the other way around.

Now we can mark the difference between (36a) and (39) easily: the latter are cohesive (and thus consistent) while the former is consistent but not cohesive.[28] The different information is crucial for keeping things running smoothly in that one. In the static framework, inconsistency and incohesiveness get lumped together. That is because "consistency" gets cashed out as "possibly true". But what we have here is a sort of case where a sentence like (36a) is not "possibly true"—there is no non-absurd fixed-point of an update with it—but that does not mean adding the information it carries always results in a broken context. One thing the dynamic perspective allows us is the expressive tools to mark these kinds of differences.

Since *might*-statements are expressions of ignorance—in view of the relevant set of facts, the prejacent cannot be ruled out—if the relevant set of facts grows it should be no surprise that *might*-statements that were once called for might not be called for later. That is:

(41) a. A sentence is PERSISTENT iff: if it is true with respect to a state s and s' contains as much information as s, then it is true with respect to s'.

b. ϕ is persistent iff $s \models \phi$ and $s' \subseteq s$ imply $s' \models \phi$.

The prediction, of course, is that sentences like *might* ϕ are not persistent. For suppose s has just two worlds in it, w_1 a ϕ-world and w_2 a $\neg\phi$-world. Although *might* ϕ is true at s, it is not true at $\{w_2\}$ even though $\{w_2\} \subset s$. Like we said, that is not very surprising given that *might* test for compatibility between the information carried by its prejacent and the contextually relevant body of information.[29]

Earlier we made a point of saying how epistemic modals are context sensitive and how that context-sensitivity ties in with *if*-clauses. We were highlighting just how tight the relationship is between context, modals, and other constructions. Of course, that *if*-clauses seem to function as restrictors for the conversational

[28] What we are calling "cohesiveness" is sometimes called COHERENCE. We prefer our term since there is nothing *incoherent* about (36a). It's just that what it says in the first conjunct doesn't stick to what it says in the second.

[29] The claim that epistemic modals are not persistent is not what's at stake in the debates between the "semantic relativists" mentioned in n. 1 and cooler heads. There the issue is over whether epistemic modals have context-dependent truth-conditions or whether they instead have some other more relativized kind of semantic value. Here the issue is over how stable the context-dependent truth-conditions end up being.

background is also a lot of trouble for some semantic theories. We want to now look briefly at this same phenomenon from the dynamic perspective.

Suppose we have lost our marbles. We have found all of them but two—the red one and the blue one—and know that exactly one of them is in the box. Thus:

(42) a. The marble in the box might be red, and might be blue.
b. If it's not red, it must be blue.
c. If it's not blue, it must be red.

In order to get these three sentences to all be true at once, there has to be some interaction between the *if*-clauses and the set of worlds that the modals act as (quantificational) tests on. Otherwise we get inconsistency. One way of doing this is to treat the *if*s as restrictors. But this simple dynamic semantics is another way. Take $\phi \rightarrow \psi$ to abbreviate $\neg(\phi \wedge \neg\psi)$, and treat the modals as having narrow scope in the conditionals, and you can easily show that all of these sentences are true in a state containing just two worlds: one a red-is-in-the-box world, and the other a blue-is-in-the-box world.[30] Having just assigned some homework, we think this is a good place to stop and sum up.

CONCLUSION

We began by noting that epistemic modals are interesting in part because their semantics is bound up both with our information about the world and with how that information changes as we share what we know. Our aim here has been to survey some of that territory. We have seen that epistemic readings of modal expressions are instantiations of a core meaning that is contextually filled in. They serve as evidential comments on the prejacent proposition, whose being put forward is often the *main point* of the utterance. They typically signal the presence of an indirect inference. Of course, there are a number of options open for exploring some of these issues, complicating the standard possible worlds approach in various ways. In the case of thinking of epistemic

[30] See Gillies (2007) for more on this and other puzzles about *if*s and modals.

modals as contributing more to *comments* than *contents*, we can complicate the semantic apparatus by including a distinct semantic dimension where comments live, we can complicate the pragmatics by saying that in uttering a modal a speaker manages to perform multiple speech acts, or we can redistribute some of the interpretive workload between the compositional semantics and pragmatics by making the semantics traffic in CCPs instead of contents. We have reservations about whether the first path here is really an option since embedding facts seem to doom it. The other two paths may well be related—the dynamic perspective is certainly the one that has been subjected to more formalization—but that sounds more like an open question than like material for a paper with our title.

REFERENCES

Beaver, David (2001) *Presupposition and Assertion in Dynamic Semantics*. Stanford, Calif.: CSLI.

van Benthem, Johan (1986) *Essays in Logical Semantics*. Studies in Linguistics and Philosophy (SLAP), 29. Dordrecht: Reidel.

—— (1996) *Exploring Logical Dynamics*. Stanford, Calif.: Center for the Study of Language and Information (CSLI).

Blain, Eleanor M. and Déchaine, Rose-Marie (2007) 'Evidential Types: Evidence from Cree Dialects', *International Journal of American Linguistics*, 73(3): 257–91. doi:10.1086/521728.

Copeland, B. Jack (2002) 'The Genesis of Possible Worlds Semantics', *Journal of Philosophical Logic*, 31(2): 99–137. doi:10.1023/A:1015273407895.

van der Does, Jaap, Groeneveld, Willem, and Veltman, Frank (1997) 'An Update on *Might*', *Journal of Logic, Language and Information*, 6(4): 361–80. doi:10.1023/A:1008219821036.

Egan, Andy (2005) 'Epistemic Modals, Relativism, and Assertion', in Gajewski *et al.* (2005).

—— Hawthorne, John, and Weatherson, Brian (2005) 'Epistemic Modals in Context', in Gerhard Preyer and Georg Peter (eds.), *Contextualism in Philosophy: Knowledge, Meaning, and Truth*, pp. 131–70. Oxford: Oxford University Press.

von Fintel, Kai (2005) 'Modality and Language', in Donald M. Borchert (2nd edn.) *Encyclopedia of Philosophy*, Macmillan. URL http://mit.edu/fintel/modality.pdf

—— and Gillies, Anthony S. (2007a) 'CIA Leaks', MS, MIT and University of Michigan, to appear in the *Philosophical Review*.

—— and —— (2007b). '*Might made Right*', MS MIT and University of Michigan, forthcoming in an OUP volume on epistemic models, edited by Brian Weatherson and Andy Egan.

—— and Iatridou, Sabine (2003) 'Epistemic Containment', *Linguistic Inquiry*, 34(2): 173–98. doi:10.1162/002438903321663370.

—— and —— (2006) 'How to Say "Ought" in Foreign: The Composition of Weak Necessity Modals', MS, MIT, to appear in Jacqueline Guéron and Jacqueline Lecarne (eds.), *Time and Modality* (Dordrecht).

Frege, Gottlob (1879) *Begriffsschrift, eine der arithmetischen nachgebildete Formelsprache des reinen Denkens*. Halle: L. Nebert. Tr. by Stefan Bauer-Mengelberg, from Jean van Heijenoort (ed.), *From Frege to Gödel: A Source Book in Mathematical Logic, 1879–1931*, Cambridge, Mass.: Harvard University Press. 1967.

Gajewski, Jon, Hacquard, Valentine, Nickel, Bernard, and Yalcin, Seth (eds.) (2005) *New Work on Modality*. MIT Working Papers in Linguistics, 52. Department of Linguistics and Philosophy, MIT.

Gillies, Anthony S. (2001) 'A New Solution to Moore's Paradox', *Philosophical Studies*, 105(3): 237–50. doi:10.1023/A:1010361708803.

—— (2006) 'What Might be the Case After a Change in View', *Journal of Philosophical Logic*, 35(2): 117–45. doi:10.1007/s10992-005-9006-7.

—— (2007) 'Iffiness', MS, University of Michigan.

Groenendijk, Jeroen and Stokhof, Martin (1990) 'Two Theories of Dynamic Semantics', in Jan van Eijck (ed.) *Logics in AI*, pp. 55–64. Berlin: Springer.

—— and —— (1991) 'Dynamic Predicate Logic', *Linguistics and Philosophy*, 14(1): 39–100. doi:10.1007/BF00628304.

Harel, David, Kozen, Dexter, and Tiuryn, Jerzy (2000) *Dynamic Logic*. Cambridge, Mass.: MIT Press.

Heim, Irene (1982) '*The Semantics of Definite and Indefinite Noun Phrases*', Ph.D. thesis, University of Massachusetts at Amherst. URL http://semanticsarchive.net/Archive/Tk0ZmYyY/dissertation.pdf

Hintikka, Jaakko (1962) *Knowledge and Belief*. Ithaca, NY: Cornell University Press.

Kamp, Hans (1981) 'A Theory of Truth and Semantic Interpretation', in Jeroen Groenendijk, Theo Janssen, and Martin Stokhof (eds.), *Formal Methods in the Study of Language*, pp. 277–322. Amsterdam: Mathematical Centre.

Kant, Immanuel (1781) *Critik der reinen Vernunft*. Riga: Johann Friedrich Hartknoch.

Karttunen, Lauri (1972) 'Possible and Must', in J. Kimball (ed.), *Syntax and Semantics*, i. 1–20. New York: Academic Press.

Karttunen, Lauri (1974) 'Presupposition and Linguistic Context', *Theoretical Linguistics*, 1: 181–93.

Kratzer, Angelika (1977) 'What *Must* and *Can* Must and Can Mean', *Linguistics and Philosophy*, 1(3): 337–55. doi:10.1007/BF00353453.

—— (1978) *Semantik der Rede: Kontexttheorie—Modalwörter—Konditionalsätze*. Königstein/Taunus: Scriptor.

—— (1981) 'The Notional Category of Modality', in H. J. Eikmeyer and H. Rieser (eds.), *Words, Worlds, and Contexts: New Approaches in Word Semantics*, pp. 38–74. Berlin: de Gruyter.

—— (1991) 'Modality', in Arnim von Stechow and Dieter Wunderlich (eds.), *Semantics: An International Handbook of Contemporary Research*, pp. 639–50. Berlin: de Gruyter.

Kripke, Saul (1963) 'Semantical Analysis of Modal Logic I: Normal Modal Propositional Calculi', *Zeitschrift für mathematische Logik und Grundlagen der Mathematik*, 9: 67–96.

Lewis, David (1979) 'Scorekeeping in a Language Game', *Journal of Philosophical Logic*, 8(1): 339–59. doi:10.1007/BF00258436.

MacFarlane, John (2003) 'Epistemic Modalities and Relative Truth'.

—— (2006) 'Epistemic Modals are Assessment-Sensitive', MS, University of California, Berkeley, forthcoming in an OUP volume on epistemic modals, edited by Brian Weatherson and Andy Egan.

Matthewson, Lisa, Rullmann, Hotze, and Davis, Henry (2006) 'Evidentials are Epistemic Modals in St'a?t'imcets', MS, University of British Columbia.

Potts, Christopher (2005) *The Logic of Conventional Implicatures*. Oxford: Oxford University Press.

Simons, Mandy (2006) 'Observations on Embedding Verbs, Evidentiality, and Presupposition', *Lingua*. doi:10.1016/j.lingua.2006.05.006.

Stalnaker, Robert (1978) 'Assertion', in Peter Cole (ed.), *Syntax and Semantics*, 9: 315–22. New York: Academic Press.

Stephenson, Tamina (2005) 'Assessor Sensitivity: Epistemic Modals and Predicates of Personal Taste', in Gajewski *et al.* (2005).

Swanson, Eric (2005) 'Something *Might* Might Mean', MS, MIT.

Veltman, Frank (1985) '*Logics for Conditionals*', Ph.D. thesis, University of Amsterdam.

—— (1996) 'Defaults in Update Semantics', *Journal of Philosophical Logic*, 25(3): 221–61. doi:10.1007/BF00248150.

Willett, Thomas (1988) 'A Cross-Linguistic Survey of the Grammaticalization of Evidentiality', *Studies in Language*, 12(1): 51–97.

Yalcin, Seth (2005) 'Epistemic Modals', in Gajewski *et al.* (2005).

3. Epistemic Conservatism: Theft or Honest Toil?

Richard Fumerton

Perhaps epistemic externalism's strongest sales pitch has always been that it alone can avoid radical skepticism. In recent years some epistemic internalists have been striking back with variations of a view sometimes known as epistemic conservatism. In its crudest form, epistemic conservatism takes the fact that a person believes a given proposition to be at least a prima facie epistemic reason in support of the proposition believed. In this paper I will distinguish a number of different versions of epistemic conservatism and examine the question of whether their desire to avoid skepticism is leading some internalists to favor theft over honest toil.

Ever since Quine (1969) urged us to naturalize epistemology, we have been told that traditional foundationalism has had its chance and has abjectly failed to show how we can legitimately gain epistemic access to the world of common sense. Certainly, once we restrict ourselves to the meager foundations of knowledge and justified belief recognized by the radical empiricist, the road back to the commitments of common sense is long, winding, and hard. Quine's observations predated careful statements of internalist/externalist controversies. Through the work of Alvin Goldman (1967, 1979, 1986, 1988) and others, externalists sought to analyze epistemic concepts in a way that would allow one to make sense of Quine's otherwise puzzling suggestion that we should investigate the sources of knowledge and justified belief employing the empirical methods of the natural sciences. In light of the internalist/externalist debate that ensued, it is natural to interpret the foundationalists Quine attacked as paradigmatic internalists. And it is striking that such externalists as Goldman (1999), Plantinga (2000), Van Cleve (2003), and Bergmann (2006), renew the attack on hard-core internalism as a view that will inevitably lead to a radical skepticism. Faced with a choice between skepticism and externalism, most will choose externalism.

To set the stage for the epistemic conservative's counterattack, we should briefly sketch the kind of internalism that its critics see as leading to skepticism. As I've argued elsewhere (1996), there are now a number of importantly different views associated with internalism. The view I call internal state internalism is perhaps the one most naturally suggested by the label. According to the internal state internalist, the epistemic justificatory status of a belief at t is constituted by or fully supervenes on the internal states of the believer at t. On this view if two believers are in identical internal states at t and there is justification for one to believe P at t then there is that same justification for the other to believe P at t.[1] A fully developed internal state internalism must make clear precisely what is meant by "internal state," a task not that easy to complete.[2] Depending on how precisely one characterizes internal states, and depending on one's analysis of mental states, it might be important to distinguish internal state internalism from what Feldman and Conee call "mentalism." [3] The mentalist agrees that two believers in identical *mental* states share the same justification for their respective beliefs, but their view leaves open the question of whether a mental state is a purely internal state. Given increasingly popular versions of semantic or methodological externalism, many philosophers have become convinced (mistakenly, I believe) that the identity conditions for many or all intentional states involve facts external to the person in such states. As the identity conditions for mental states expand to include external factors, "mentalist internalism" can begin to look like externalism in disguise.[4]

[1] It is important in this context to distinguish there being justification for S to believe P and S's belief that P being justified. The latter plausibly requires that S base his belief that P on the relevant justification there is for S to believe P. And if basing involves causation, and causation involves regularity, there is a sense in which having a justified belief might involve external factors even if the existence of the relevant justification does not. It should also go without saying that no internalist who recognizes a non-redundant truth-condition for knowledge should be an internal state internalist about knowledge.

[2] See Fumerton (1996). [3] Conee and Feldman (2004: 56).

[4] See Williamson (2000). Williamson thinks of knowledge as a mental state, and also that something is evidence if and only if it is knowledge. But because he thinks that the identity conditions for epistemic "mental states" involve external factors, he seems to me clearly to fall on the externalist side of the divide.

The internal state internalism and mentalism characterized above relativize the justification S has for believing P at a given time to the internal/mental states of S *at that time*. One can certainly distinguish that view from one that allows that the internal state/mental history of S is relevant to the epistemic status of S's belief at a given time. But few internalists would make such a move, in part because of their desire to connect their internalism with access requirements for justification and their concern that a past to which one has no access cannot play an epistemic role.

Indeed, epistemic internalism now is just as commonly associated with a number of theses about the connection between the justificatory status of a belief and the believer's access to that status. The strongest form of access internalism insists that if there is justification for S to believe P, then S also has noninferential justification for believing that there is that justification. A weaker requirement insists merely that S has justification for believing P only if S *could* get noninferential justification for believing that he has that justification (where the modal operator is typically understood in such a way that exercising the capacity would involve little more than concentrating hard on the relevant question). One can develop still more versions of access internalism by dropping the requirement that the access in question be noninferential or by weakening the interpretation of the modal operator.

There may, of course, be a close connection between internal state internalism and mentalism (on the one hand) and certain versions of access internalism given the once common view that the only contingent features of the world that one can noninferentially discover are facts about one's own psychological states. Externalism about mental states might, however, make more problematic the connection.[5] Whatever the connection is between internal state internalism and access internalism, it is important to distinguish both views from another very strong requirement on *inferential* justification. As I use the term, the inferential internalist is committed to the view that necessarily, if there is justification for S to believe P on the basis of E, there is justification for S to believe that E makes probable P (where entailment is the upper limit of making probable). Many

[5] Depending on the resolution of an ongoing debate concerning whether or not one can reconcile semantic externalism with introspective access to one's mental life. See Ludlow and Martin (1998) for one collection of papers devoted to the controversy.

internal state internalists explicitly repudiate inferential internalism, fearing that it leads to a vicious regress. The regress does loom unless one can get oneself noninferential justification for believing at least some propositions asserting evidential connections. But an internal state internalism that allows one to justifiably believe P on the basis of E when one neither sees nor understands the connection between E and P seems to me to defeat all of the intuitions underlying a commitment to internalism.

INTERNALISM AND SKEPTICISM

Most versions of internalism make it exceedingly difficult to avoid skepticism. Recognizing this, some internalists go out of their way to emphasize that their account of justification is intended to apply only to a kind of *ideal*, or philosophically *satisfying* justification. The more one is determined to secure a connection between having justification and being in a position to gain assurance of truth, the less surprising it might be that some version of skepticism is true. Internalists often accuse externalists of simply attempting to change the very subject-matter of traditional epistemology. A Descartes seeking secure foundations, or a Hume seeking vainly to satisfy the demands of reason, would be utterly bewildered, for example, by the reliabilist's suggestion that we have justification simply in virtue of having beliefs that are reliably produced (whether or not we have any reason to suppose that such beliefs have the relevant causal pedigree). The die-hard internalist forced to choose between an internalist analysis of intellectually satisfying epistemic justification and skepticism will always choose the internalism, perhaps suspecting with Hume (1888: 187) that with respect to the question of whether or not man should embrace commonsense beliefs "Nature has not left this to his choice, and doubtless esteem'd it an affair of too great importance to be trusted to our uncertain reasonings and speculations." But on this matter there is no doubt that the externalist has the rhetorical upper hand. I suspect that the vast majority of epistemologists share Chisholm's commitment to some form of epistemic particularism—they decide in advance that pre-philosophical views about what we reasonably believe are correct, and they are committed to adjusting their philosophical views until common sense is vindicated. It is understandable, then, that internalists are very concerned with responding to the externalist's charge that internalism (in most of its guises) leads to skepticism.

But what precisely is the problem? Why is internalism supposed to face such dismal prospects with respect to the refutation of skepticism? The answer isn't really all that hard to find. Consider internal state internalism, or versions of access internalism that require noninferential access to the epistemic status of one's beliefs coupled with a commitment to the view that one can have such access only to internal states. As Goldman (1999) points out, the problem is simply the paucity of internal states available as potential justifiers. Common sense allows that I have good reason to believe, indeed know, that the Battle of Hastings took place in 1066. What are the current internal states that serve as justifiers for that belief? Well, I do currently seem to remember hearing about it in a junior high history class taught by some really tall guy. Or perhaps, more accurately, I seem to remember having experiences as if I heard about it from some really tall guy teaching a history class. Perhaps the apparent memory gives me access to the prior experiences which in turn gives me access to the relevant facts about what actually happened in that classroom many long years ago. But that is, of course, just the start of the epistemic journey to the Battle of Hastings. On classical foundationalist views I've got to have reason to believe that the tall guy teaching that class was a reliable authority on British history and I've got to locate *that* reason in current internal states. I'd probably need something like the premises of an inductive argument or justified belief about the relevant hypothesis of reliability as the best explanation of the relevant data. If you gave me enough time I might be able to start telling some sort of story about what I seem to remember discovering with respect to correlations between junior high history teachers and historical facts, but the fact of the matter is that right now I don't recall ever having previously considered the question.

Can internalists solve the problem by appealing to the existence of a wealth of "stored" knowledge or justified belief that can serve as background evidence for commonplace beliefs? I don't really see how this even addresses the problem for the internalist committed to finding the sources of justification among the *current* internal states of the believers. The alleged "stored" knowledge or justified belief, either has or it doesn't have justification consisting of current internal states. If it does then we are back to searching for the relevant internal states. If it doesn't then we have just taken one large step towards abandoning internalism. If the conclusions of common sense rely on "evidence" in the form of propositions believed when we no longer have access to whatever justification we may have once had for such beliefs, we surely have some nerve complaining about the disconnect between satisfying externalist conditions on justification and gaining intellectually satisfying assurance.

Perhaps we were overly ambitious in beginning with a somewhat problematic example of a belief whose positive epistemic status is endorsed by common sense. After all, I used to go around telling people that Dedefre was an Egyptian pharaoh who built one of the three great pyramids. I believe I even used it as an example in papers I have published. Apparently it was a product of my decaying memory.[6] A commitment to avoiding skepticism surely doesn't involve ensuring that *I* get to know or even justifiably believe that the Battle of Hastings took place in 1066. The problem, however, is that even the most mundane of beliefs about physical objects in our immediate environment plausibly rely on a host of a background knowledge upon which we critically rely. Once we restrict the available justifiers for my belief that there is something red and square in front of me to my current internal states, it looks as if we are stuck with assorted sensations and, possibly, apparent memories of prior sensations. But surely to reconstruct an intellectually satisfying argument for the view that these psychological states are reliable indicators of the presence of the relevant object, I would need to rely on a host of background information about how objects of various sorts typically look under standard conditions of perception. And I'd need reason to believe (reason constituted by current internal states) that conditions of perception are, indeed, standard. Even as I try to begin a reconstruction of the relevant evidence I might possess, I constantly lose much of the precious "internal" evidence to the past.

[6] There was a Dedefre and he did build a pyramid—it just wasn't one of the three great pyramids at Gizeh.

EPISTEMIC CONSERVATISM

It is no wonder that in the face of such formidable obstacles to gaining intellectual assurance from an internalist perspective, some seek to cut a few corners. And there is no easier way to cut corners than to look to belief and related intentional states as potential justifiers.[7] As I indicated above, the crudest form of epistemic conservatism takes the mere fact that S believes P at t to be a prima-facie justification S has for believing P at t. But it is important to recognize that there are a host of related views that all qualify as versions of epistemic conservatism. Huemer (2001, 2006) and Conee (2004) both explicitly appeal to what one might call "seeming" epistemic conservatism, but many others flirt with views that bear at least a family resemblance to these. Huemer (forthcoming) characterizes his phenomenal conservatism this way:

> If it seems to S that p, then, in the absence of defeaters, S thereby has at least some degree of justification for believing that p.

According to Conee's (2004: 15) "seeming evidentialism":

> The general idea is that someone's evidence about a proposition includes all that seems to the person to bear on the truth of the proposition.

Applying the idea to evidence for believing epistemic propositions, he says that "whichever epistemic beliefs about cases of knowledge or general principles initially seem correct are thereby supported as data for theorizing" (Conee 2004: 19)

I think that both Huemer and Conee want seeming to be true to be something other than mere belief, though I'm not sure precisely what it is. At least for Conee it looks as if it might have something to do with a belief's being *spontaneous*. He says of one class of propositions that seem to be true the following:

[7] Although one shouldn't infer that the epistemic conservative faces nothing but smooth sailing if the view is true. As Russell and others have pointed out, common sense (how things seem) can turn on itself. It can seem to me that certain principles of reasoning are true and those very principles might defeat whatever justification I might otherwise have had for thinking that P is true (when it seems to me that it is). Or as Michael Tooley pointed out to me, it might seem to me that contraries of what I believe seem to be true to others, where it also seems to me that those others are just as reasonable as I am. That in turn can be grist for the skeptic's mill even within the framework of epistemic conservatism.

What seem to be true are propositions. They seem to be true in virtue of the fact that we are spontaneously inclined to regard something of which we are aware as indicative of their truth. (Conee 2004: 15)

For Huemer seeming to be true is surely something in the neighborhood of belief. The careful epistemic conservative, however, almost always allows that the justification provided by "seeming to be true" is defeasible, and for that very reason we can't straightforwardly identify seeming to be true with any species of belief. When we possess countervailing evidence, a proposition can still seem to be us to be true while we believe (all things considered) that it is false. Consider, for example, cases of illusion. After reading about it (or perhaps checking it out) we are no longer deceived by the Muller-Lyer illusion, even though, as Bealer (1999) points out, there is a perfectly clear sense in which the lines still seem to be of unequal length. I saw a movie in which a cowboy bet that he could hold his hand steadily against the side of a thick glass jar holding a rattlesnake as the coiled snake struck in vain at his hand. He lost the bet. In some sense he surely didn't *believe* the snake could hurt him, but he fell victim to a more "primitive" intentional expectation of harm. It's also useful to think about the emotional reactions we have upon seeing terrifying or sad movies. The audience can be weeping buckets at the plight that befalls the star-crossed lovers on the screen. Does the audience fail to realize that it sees only actors pretending to be suffering? Of course not. But the people reacting are in a state very much like belief—it still (at the time of their emotional reactions) seems to them as if the events portrayed are real.

While in its crudest form, epistemic conservatism might seem a somewhat odd and, even, desperate new move in epistemology, there is a sense in which a more careful look at the history of the field suggests that sympathy with the view was always quite prevalent. In his many famous discussions of the problem of the criterion, Chisholm distinguishes particularism from methodism as a way of searching for epistemic principles. The particularist decides in advance that most of the beliefs we take to be justified are, indeed, justified. And, as I indicated above, a great many philosophers, internalists and externalists alike, either explicitly or implicitly follow Chisholm's lead. But unless particularism is viewed as some sort of blind existential choice, it surely must be underwritten by something like a commitment to epistemic conservatism—the view that one is epistemically licensed to trust, at least initially, the deliverances of common sense, at the very least, the deliverances of common sense with respect to what we know and are justified in believing.

Of course, as the above remarks imply, the particularists might restrict their reliance on how things seem to a subclass of propositions. Conee himself emphasizes his conservatism in the context of a search for epistemic principles. But once one insists that one has an epistemic license to trust how things seem with respect to one kind of proposition, it is surely incumbent upon such a philosopher to explain why such trust wouldn't always be appropriate. Indeed, a great many philosophers who would, I suspect, distance themselves from epistemic conservatism, do talk a great deal about the importance of relying on intuition. Or if they don't talk about its importance, they are not shy about appealing constantly to intuitions in the course of presenting arguments. We intuit that a Gettier situation deprives the person with a justified true belief of knowledge. We intuit that it would be wrong to kill an innocent man to stop a vicious crime wave and, for that reason, reject utilitarianism. We intuit necessary truths of logic, mathematics, and geometry. These appeals to intuition are often frustratingly unaccompanied by any account of what intuition is supposed to be. At least sometimes, however, one suspects that the appeal to intuition is just appeal to how things seem, and if intuition does degenerate into such a fallible intentional state, the intuitionism in question can look again very much like a version of epistemic conservatism.

As one examines closely the critical epistemic role various mental states play for philosophers, the more often one can find the seeds of an implicit epistemic conservatism. Consider the classic empiricists. Although most of them did not explicitly take sensation to be anything like belief, it has become increasingly more common for philosophers to argue that sensation is itself an intentional state, a state that *represents* the world as being a certain way.[8] Construed as intentional states that make a claim on reality, then, even the view

[8] One might suppose that all of the classical representational realists took sensation to represent. But most did not, at least in the sense I mean here. I think for most representational realists, sensations only represent to the person who has those sensations in virtue of legitimate inferences that the person could make to the

that takes my current sensations to be justification for believing commonplace truths about the breadbox-sized objects around me is closely related to epistemic conservatism.[9]

The coherence theory of justification is usually thought of as one of the classic rivals to foundationalism. But as Plantinga (1993: 79–80) has pointed out, it is not all that implausible to suppose that the coherence theorist is a closet foundationalist. Plantinga's suggestion is that a coherentist really holds that a belief's being *foundationally* justified is just a matter of its being a member of a coherent set of beliefs. But one might take Plantinga's suggestion a step further and wonder whether a more plausible coherence theory still might not be construed as endorsing a crude version of epistemic conservatism. Why would anyone take coherence among one's beliefs as something that yields *all-things-considered* justification unless one takes the mere fact that one has a belief to confer at least *some* slight justification in support of the proposition believed?

FOUNDATIONALIST, NONFOUNDATIONALIST, AND SPURIOUS VERSIONS OF CONSERVATISM

The internalist can recognize an evidential role for "seeming to be true" in one of two importantly different ways. The foundationalist conservative takes the mere fact that it seems to one as if P to constitute a kind of noninferential (albeit defeasible) justification for one to believe P. The inferential conservative takes the truth that it seems to one as if P as a potential premise that can be known noninferentially, a premise from which one can infer (in the absence of defeating evidence) that P. The inferential internalist, for example, might claim that one can get justified belief that P through introspective knowledge that it seems to one as if P, coupled with a priori knowledge that seeming to one as if P makes likely P. It is easy to confuse the two views, particularly if one takes the claim that appearances confer prima-facie justification

existence of the cause of those sensations. The sensations did not intrinsically represent.

[9] Though most versions of classical empiricism would still end up being versions of the spurious conservatism discussed below.

to be knowable a priori and one couples that claim with the allowance that one can introspectively discover how things appear to one. The very intentional state that constitutes justification for the foundationalist conservative is also a state that *can* be described by a proposition from which one also can legitimately *infer* the truth of the proposition that seems to be true. But this is obviously compatible with the foundationalist conservative's position that there *need* be no such inference in order for the "seeming" to yield justification.

The epistemic conservative must be carefully distinguished from a spurious epistemic conservative—the philosopher who recognizes the importance of how things seem but only as the subject matter of premises to be used in an *inductive* argument in support of various conclusions. Those of us lucky enough to be right most of the time when things seem to us a certain way may be in a position to formulate a "track record" argument for trusting such seemings (assuming that we have *independent* solutions to the epistemological problems of perception, induction, and memory). I remember it seeming to me that Wittgenstein's argument against the possibility of a private language was bad and I was right. I remember it seeming to me as if the Slingshot argument against the correspondence theory of truth was bad and I was right. I remember it seeming to me as if Quine's argument against the analytic/synthetic distinction was bad and I was right, and so on. Lucky me. I might be able to build an inductive argument for trusting how things seem to *me*. I suspect that most of us do, in fact, trust our "intuitions" based on a vague sense that they have been more or less reliable guides to the truth in the past. Some may even have supplemented that vague track-record justification with a more sophisticated argument relying on the likelihood of evolution selecting for beings whose "instinctual" judgments are more or less correct.

I'm not interested here in the question of whether track-record or evolutionary arguments are or are not plausible ways of incorporating information about "seemings" into our justification for commonsense beliefs. Both are, of course, problematic. An internalist who uses the track-record argument had better have some *independent* way of ascertaining the truths allegedly correlated with the intuitions. The evolutionary theorist had better have some response to the kind of arguments presented by Plantinga (1993:

chs. 11 and 12). The important point to emphasize here is that the mere fact that one employs arguments for various conclusions that incorporate premises describing how things seem to us does not make one an epistemic conservative in any of the senses described above. The epistemic conservatists we are interested in here either take the relevant appearances to constitute a noninferential justification or to constitute the subject-matter of propositions which *by themselves* constitute prima-facie evidence in support of the conclusion that things are as they appear.

A similar point might apply to Descartes and the role played in his epistemology by clear and distinct ideas. I've never really understood what he was talking about when he described himself as having a clear and distinct idea, but I suppose it might bear at least a superficial resemblance to some version of epistemic conservatism. After all, clearly and distinctly perceiving something is presumably an intentional state of *some* sort. But on the most natural reading of Descartes's argument purporting to establish the epistemic relevance of clarity and distinctness, these properties of belief enter the picture only after an *independent* argument for the conclusion (I exist) that is said to be clear and distinct. If the relevance of clarity and distinctness is parasitic upon discovering a correlation between it and truth, Descartes was no epistemic conservative. Descartes also urged us, of course, by Meditation VI to trust our instincts. But again it is surely clear that the legitimacy of such trust was, for Descartes, parasitic upon his successful defense of the existence of a non-deceiving God. Our instincts by themselves were viewed by Descartes as epistemically worthless. Even Reid, who many epistemic conservatives eagerly embrace as one of their own, *sometimes* sounds much more like Descartes when it comes to answering the question of *why* we should put trust in the ways we form beliefs. He sometimes seems to concede straight out that his faith in how things seem is no more justified than his belief in a providential God.[10]

There is another view that may only masquerade as a version of epistemic conservatism, this time in a more subtle way. Some philosophers will argue that certain beliefs carry with them

[10] For a plausible characterization of Reid as a "providentialist," see Sandberg (2004).

justification for what is believed in virtue of factors that are partially constitutive of the belief. So, for example, one might suppose that one can have a *de re* belief about some object only in virtue of one's being directly or immediately aware of the object (and perhaps its properties), an object that literally becomes, in virtue of that awareness, a constituent of the belief state. One might then go on to argue that the very awareness that makes possible the belief also constitutes a kind of justification for the belief.[11] Such a view may end up sounding like a version of epistemic conservatism—having the right sort of belief will *carry with it* a certain justification for the belief. But arguably it is the direct awareness or direct acquaintance that makes possible the belief that is the real source of justification. The view might just be a roundabout way of endorsing the classical version of foundationalism that seeks to identify foundations with propositions believed when one is directly acquainted with the truth-makers for those propositions.

In a similar way, it may be possible for externalists about the content of belief to argue that the conditions that make possible a certain belief ensure that the belief is at least likely to be true. On an absurdly crude and implausible version of content externalism, for example, one might hold that one can have a belief about Julius Caesar only in virtue of being in some internal state whose cause can be traced all the way back to Caesar himself. If such a view were true, one might hold that my belief that Caesar existed guarantees its truth. Furthermore, if I could know that I have the belief and know the relevant truth about the factors that determine its content, I would, presumably be in a position to infer from my belief its truth. But again, it wouldn't be the belief by itself that provides the relevant justification. It would be the belief coupled with the problematic theory of intentional states that allows me to draw the relevant conclusion. That it would be absurd to suppose that we can discover the truth of beliefs this way is a reason to think long and hard before embracing crude forms of content externalism.[12]

[11] See, for examples, McGrew (1999) and Brewer (1999). Brewer would probably be exceedingly uneasy about the suggestion that it is direct awareness or direct acquaintance as the classical empiricist understood it that makes possible the relevant de re beliefs.

[12] This cryptic remark does not do justice to the complexity of the issues lurking in the background. See Fumerton (2003) for further exploration of the tensions

EVALUATION

1. *Foundationalist Conservatism*

So what can be said for or against various versions of epistemic conservatism? Let's begin by looking at the foundationalist versions of the view. Why should we think that the mere fact that it seems to me as if P makes P prima facie probable for me? Of course, if epistemic conservatism *is* true your reasons for thinking that it is true might include the fact that you think that it's true. By the same token, if epistemic conservatism is true then I probably have a prima-facie reason for thinking that it isn't true, because it doesn't seem to me that it is. We're not getting anywhere this way. We need some independent reason for thinking that the antecedent of the conditional is true.

Nor are we likely to make much progress attempting to employ straightforward argument by counterexample. To be sure, the epistemic conservative's opponent might get some mileage out of asking us to imagine a person who whimsically finds some bizarre proposition attractive. I start thinking about whether or not life as we know it will end tomorrow and find myself strangely inclined to believe it. *Surely*, I haven't even the slightest reason to accept such a bizarre proposition, one suggests in one's most sarcastic tone of voice. But in the final analysis the argument is clearly question-begging. The consistent epistemic conservative will allow that even in such an odd case there is *some* (with a strong emphasis on "some") reason for me to accept the proposition, a reason that is almost immediately swamped by available counterevidence. To evaluate the view we'll need to find more abstract considerations that tell for or against it.

In his excellent article on epistemic conservatism, Foley (1983) employs a more subtle thought experiment (a variation of which is also presented by Feldman, 2003). He asks us to imagine someone who is trying to figure out what to believe about some matter—let's say it is a juror trying to reach a conclusion about the guilt or innocence of a defendant. After carefully considering all of the evidence presented at the trial, our juror concludes that the evidence

between plausible epistemological premises and externalism about the content of representational mental states.

weighs equally on either side of the issue. Surely the epistemically rational thing to do at this point is to withhold belief. But let's suppose that instead the juror perversely finds himself suddenly inclined to think that the defendant is guilty. Do we really want to conclude that through an odd act of cognitive whimsy the juror *now* has a total body of evidence that tips in favor of a guilty conclusion?

The objection is related to another somewhat vague concern. We might suppose that an epistemic theory has value only in so far as it gives one guidance with respect to what to believe. Epistemological questions typically arise in the context of a concern over whether one should or shouldn't believe some proposition. Now consider the person who is genuinely puzzled as to whether or not he should believe that a God exists. Isn't there something very odd about the following advice. Believe that God exists if you find yourself believing (or inclined to believe, or in a state very much like belief) that God exists. Disbelieve that God exists if you find yourself disbelieving (or inclined to disbelieve or in a state very much like disbelief) that God exists. I presumably already know what I do or don't believe. What I need is something that tells me what I (epistemically) ought to believe.

In the final analysis, I'm not sure that the above objections will have much force against the committed epistemic conservative. I noted earlier that the pure internalist will relativize justification to a time. In Foley's thought experiment we have a person who at t had a body of evidence that justified withholding belief with respect to whether or not the defendant is guilty. At $t + 1$, something new was added. In addition to the other evidence, it now suddenly seemed to our juror that the person was guilty. Of course, *I* don't think that the new intentional state (by itself) has any epistemic significance, but that is surely just because I don't think that epistemic conservatism is plausible.

Nor is it clear to me that the epistemic conservative isn't giving advice. Once we distinguish what one believes all things considered from "seeming to be true," it's not clear that the "magnetism" of that appearance can't give one guidance. When lining up a putt golfers are often told to "trust their instincts." One can plumb the line, or try to learn from another golfer's putt. There are other ways to reach a conclusion about which way the ball will roll. The advice to trust your instincts, if followed, will often lead to a different conclusion than otherwise would have been reached. To put it overly crudely, the epistemic conservative is just urging us to "trust our cognitive instincts" in the absence of countervailing evidence.

So it seems to me that the epistemic conservative shouldn't be construed as failing to offer a theory that gives genuine advice. But even if the charge were correct, it is not clear that it should be viewed as fatal, particularly in the context of a view about noninferential justification. While there are certainly contexts in which one might be genuinely puzzled about what to believe and, consequently, be interested in some sort of advice, there are other contexts in which the presupposition that a believer is "choosing" what to believe seems implausible. And perhaps the most obvious context in which the notion of choosing to believe seems incongruous is that of the noninferentially justified belief. To be sure, as an epistemologist I'm interested in coming to some rational conclusion about just precisely what justifies me in believing that I'm in pain when I am. But it's not as if my interest in this theoretical question arises in the context of a decision about whether or not I should be believing that I am in the searing pain that arises from accidentally placing my hand on the red-hot burner! The belief is a spontaneous reaction to its immediate cause (the pain), and I'm not interested in getting advice in this context about what I should be believing. That I believe that I'm in severe pain and that I am justified in believing that I'm in severe pain, both seem utterly obvious. The philosophical task is to discover why the belief that I'm in pain is interestingly different from other beliefs by virtue of needing no further justification in the form of other different beliefs. The epistemic conservative's suggestion is that my belief that I am in pain is justified in virtue of the fact that it seems to be so patently obvious that I'm in pain.

At this point, there may be no alternative than to retreat to yet more abstract considerations, and for that reason more controversial considerations, concerning the nature of noninferential justification. I've argued in a number of places that the key to developing a plausible account of noninferential justification is to get the truth-maker for the belief into the story about what constitutes noninferential justification. My own view is that the belief that I'm in pain when I am is epistemically special precisely because the truth-maker for the belief is immediately present to consciousness. The pain itself is a constituent of a conscious state that accompanies my belief that I'm in pain (as is the transparent correspondence between the belief state and the pain). The foundationalist epistemic conservative suggests an account of noninferential justification according to which it is the occurrence of an intentional state (it's seeming to me as if I'm in pain) that constitutes the noninferential justification. To me the occurrence of that intentional state is no more plausible as an indication that no further justification is needed than is the occurrence of any other intentional state. It seems to me that I might just as well argue that my hoping that I'll be very wealthy is a prima-facie (noninferential) justification for believing that I'll be very wealthy, as that it's seeming to me that I'll be very wealthy some day is a prima-facie (noninferential) justification for believing that I'll be very wealthy some day. Why should either intentional state (a state that can so obviously occur without its satisfaction conditions) constitute any source of justification at all for believing that those satisfaction conditions obtain?

Just as it seems to me that any plausible account of my noninferential justification for believing that I am in pain must bring the pain itself into the story of what justifies my belief, so also it seems to me that other candidates for the epistemic conservatist's noninferential justification leave out of the picture critical experiential states. So suppose that an epistemic conservative claims that when an object appears red I'm typically noninferentially justified in believing that there is something red before me. But, the epistemic conservative claims, it is not the sensory state that justifies my belief, but the "taking the object to be red," a state that is causally prompted by the sensory state, that does the epistemic work. But surely that's an odd view. Is there really no epistemic connection between the red appearance and the justification I have for believing that the object is red? Would the fact that the object looks blue be irrelevant to the justification I have for believing that there is a red object in front of me if I am so constituted that when things look blue I take them to be red? Of course one might deny that there is this raw sensory state the occurrence of which I am presupposing. One might claim, in Chisholm's terminology, that there is only the epistemic use of "appears" or "looks." Talk about how things look or appear just is talk about the very intentional state to which the epistemic conservative appeals. But although it's a long story, that view just seems to me to be wrong. It seems to me that even if we rarely focus on the phenomenological character of how things look, we certainly can do just that, and when we do, we find a state with an intrinsic character not exhausted by our judgments about the external world. Furthermore, although this is even a longer story, it seems to me that our very understanding of what makes an object red involves critical reference to the way in which such objects cause certain sensory states, and that this is critical to understanding precisely why how things look is epistemically relevant to how things are.

There is a more abstract concern still that should worry the epistemic conservative trying to identify the foundations of justification with what "seems to be true." Foundationalists (internalists and externalists alike) are typically interested in preventing not just one but two potentially vicious regresses. The more familiar is the epistemic regress. If all justification were inferential and one can justifiably infer P from E only if one is justified in believing E, it looks as if we would need to complete an infinitely long chain of reasoning to be justified in believing anything. But of equal concern to the classic foundationalist is a potential conceptual regress. In analyzing the concept of inferential justification we need to appeal to the epistemic status of the premises from which the inferential justification flows. I believe that it is part of what it *means* to say of S that he justifiably believes P on the basis of E that he is justified in believing E (and, I would argue, that he is justified in believing that E makes probable P). To deal with the threatening conceptual regress, the classical foundationalists (and their new externalist cousins) develop a *recursive* analysis of justification. Their recursive analyses require a base clause—a base clause that does not employ a concept of justification. The acquaintance theorist identifies the base clause with a proposition describing one's being directly acquainted with a belief and its correspondence to a truth-maker. The hard-core reliabilist identifies the base clause with a proposition describing a belief's being the result of a belief-independent unconditionally reliable process. The base clause is supposed to identify a *sufficient* (though not necessary) condition for a belief's being justified, and to do so in a way that does not invoke the concept of justification or one of its synonyms.

Why should this pose a problem for the foundationalist version of epistemic conservatism? The epistemic conservativist's "foundations" are *defeasible*. As we saw earlier, without the assumption of defeasibility, the view is hopelessly implausible. But one must wonder how defeasible foundations successfully end the threatening *conceptual* regress that our recursive analysis is supposed to foil. The following is unacceptable as a base clause: S is justifed in believing P when it seems to S as if P and there is no other proposition that S is *justified* in believing that counts against P. One might reply that the base clause without its protecting subclause is fine provided that it is construed only as stating a sufficient condition for prima-facie justification, but it is not clear to me that one can even understand the concept of prima-facie justification without understanding the concept of justification. To be prima-facie justified in believing some proposition P is to be justified in believing P in the absence of other *epistemically relevant justifiers*. I realize full well that among the dwindling class of classical foundationalists, so-called modest foundationalism (a foundationalism that allows foundational justification at t to be defeasible at t) is now the norm. But as I have argued it is not clear to me that the modest foundationalist has the resources to end the conceptual regress that arises in trying to analyze the concept of justification.[13]

2. *Inferential Conservatism*

The inferential conservatives don't face the above problem. Their claim is only that we have unproblematic access to how things seem, an access that provides us with a premise from which we can infer in the absence of other relevant evidence that things are as they seem. Earlier I distinguished inferential internalism from inferential externalism. The inferential externalist needs nothing other than the relevant probabilistic connection between how things seem and how things are to allow the relevant conclusions to be legitimately drawn. The inferential internalist, by contrast, insists that we must have a reasonable belief that our premise about how things appear makes probable our conclusion how about how things are. I have argued in a number of places that a commitment to inferential internalism lies at the very heart of internalist intuitions. As I see it, an internalist is determined to link possessing justification for a belief to gaining

[13] For a more detailed defense of this position see Fumerton (1988). I make the argument in connection with Goldman's (1979) attempt to "protect" his base clause, but the point can be generalized.

assurance of truth. If I can't see the connection between my premises and my conclusion, I don't see how the mere existence of the connection does me any good in gaining such assurance. I have also argued elsewhere (1996) that the prospects of avoiding skepticism within the framework of inferential internalism are not bright. To end a threatening regress, there must be some propositions of the form E makes probable P that one can know noninferentially. And such noninferential knowledge will presuppose the existence of something like a Keynesian view of epistemic probability—the view that there are a priori necessary truths concerning probabilistic connections between propositions.[14]

If inferential *externalism* is true, then to get inferential justification through inference, all that need be true is that the relevant probabilistic connection holds between my premises and my conclusion. As I have argued elsewhere (2004), the inferential externalist is free to explore ways of understanding evidential connections in terms of frequency conceptions of probability. Crudely put, the idea is that we formulate the truth-conditions for non-deductive probability claims by assigning a pair of propositions to a class of pair kinds where the probability in question is understood in terms of the frequency with which propositions of the conclusion "kind" are true when propositions of the premise "kind" are true. Because there are many kinds to which any given premise and conclusion belong, there are many ways to assign propositions to relevant classes—this is the analogue of the generality problem for reliabilism. We also need to decide whether to go counterfactual in the analysis of the relevant frequency—it's almost always necessary to do so to avoid devastating counterexamples. To develop any such view in detail is a task for a full paper or a book, and because I'm not at inferential externalist I'm not really interested in the task. The above should give you a feel, however, for the way in which an inferential externalist might approach the analysis of probability relations the existence of which will make rational on their view the inferences people make.

Now for all I know there are non-accidental statistical correlations (probabilistic connections understood in terms of frequency) between how things seem to people and how things are. And as I

[14] See Fumerton (2004) for a more detailed defense of this view.

said, if inferential externalism is true, the existence of these correlations will underwrite the legitimacy of the inferential conservative's controversial inference. (If those connections exist and it is possible to discover them, they can also be described in the spurious conservative's defense of an epistemic role for how things seem to one.) But I'm interested here in epistemic conservatism as a view that might save the commited internalist from skepticism, and as I see it inferential externalism undercuts the intuitions underlying internalism. Spurious conservatism, as we saw earlier, isn't even in tension with internalist principles. If you can figure out how to get internal evidence justifying belief in correlations between how things seem and how things are, no internalist will complain about relying on appearance as a source of evidence.

For the inferential conservative's program to succeed, there must be some truths knowable a priori asserting a probabilistic connection between how things seem and how things are. In general, the inferential internalist needs knowledge of such truths to end both a conceptual regress and an epistemic regress of justification. If I have to know that E makes probable P before I can legitimately infer P from E, the question arises as to how such knowledge is possible. I might be able to infer the probability connection from yet some other proposition F, but that just raises the question of how I can justifiably believe that F makes probable that E makes probable P. The regress won't end until we find a plausible proposition of the form *e makes probable p* that can be known without inference. That's why the inferential internalist's only hope is that there be the Keynesian relation of making probable understood as a quasi-logical relation holding between propositions, a relation that obtains as a matter of (synthetic) necessity and that can be known a priori and noninferentially.

The dialectically attractive feature of Keynesian epistemic probability is that philosophers bent on avoiding skepticism can "find" the relevant probability relations whenever they get backed into a corner by the skeptic. Convinced by the skeptic that we can't get justified beliefs about the external world from available foundations relying only on enumerative inductive principles, we "discover" that facts about our sensory states make probable logically distinct propositions about mind-independent enduring objects. Facing the daunting problem of getting knowledge of past experience while imprisoned in the present, one "discovers" relevant epistemic truths sanctioning inference from what we seem to remember to what has happened. We could do this piecemeal, but the epistemic conservative has found a short-cut. Why does the epistemic particularist—the philosopher absolutely committed to avoiding skepticism—recognize the epistemic principles he does? How does he decide what conclusions he wants justified? The obvious answer is that he starts with the conclusions that seem to him to be true—that's his guide. So why not save everyone a lot of trouble and keep things simple? Why not postulate a nice simple epistemic principle that will sanction all of the inferences that the more specialized principles are designed to underwrite anyway? Why not simply claim to know a priori that its seeming to one that P makes probable P. That it is necessarily true that E makes probable P is perfectly consistent with its being false that E + X makes probable P, so we can recognize the defeasibility upon which the careful epistemic conservative insists.

Well why not? Why not make our epistemic life easy? The fact is that I can't give a non-question-begging answer. There is no doubt that the view is dialectically attractive. If I were a lawyer paid to defend common sense against skepticism I might appeal to it. The wonderful thing about embracing an epistemology that recognizes noninferentially justifiable epistemic principles is that one needn't (and had better not) fall into the trap of offering an argument for the principles. Such principles are, after all, supposed to be knowable a priori. But one still needs a more general account of a priori knowledge complete with an explanation of its source. And such an account must fit plausibly with one's general account of noninferential justification and knowledge. To defend the claim that one can know noninferentially an epistemic principle, the direct acquaintance theorists will need to argue that one can be directly aware of both the relata and the relation of making probable when one is directly aware of one proposition's making probable another. They will model knowledge of (epistemic) probability connections on knowledge of logical entailment. The foundationalist conservative might claim to intuit the truth of the principle where the relevant "intuition" is just one more species of a proposition's seeming to be true that yields justified belief in the proposition. The latter obviously presupposes the problematic foundationalist conservativism under discussion. But I'm not accusing the conservative of problematic circularity in this regard. If one accepts the view, one should surely accept its implications concerning how one can get oneself justification that the view is true. But *rhetorically* one can't presuppose the view when trying to convince someone of its truth.[15] The acquaintance theorists need to convince themselves that they are directly acquainted with the relevant quasi-logical relation between how thing seem and how things are. I've convinced myself (rightly or not) that I am directly acquainted with all sorts of truth-makers for all sorts of propositions, but when I look for the inferential conservative's probability connection I find only the not very surprising contingent fact that I usually end up believing P when I find myself inclined to believe P. I don't find any logical or quasi-logical connection between it seeming to me as if P and P. Foundationalists who embrace foundational knowledge of epistemic principles must always exercise philosophical self-discipline to ensure that their choice of principles is not guided solely by their overwhelming desire to avoid skepticism. I can't help but feel that to defeat skepticism wielding the weapon of epistemic conservatism shows all the signs of theft over honest toil.[16]

REFERENCES

Bealer, George (1999) 'A Theory of the A Priori', *Philosophical Perspectives*, 13: 57–89.

Bergmann, Michael (2006) *Justification Without Awareness* (Oxford).

Brewer, Bill (1999) *Perception and Reason* (Oxford).

Conee, Earl (2004) 'First Things First', in *Evidentialism* (New York).

—— and Richard Feldman (2004) *Evidentialism* (New York).

Feldman, Richard (2003) *Epistemology* (Upper Saddle River, NJ).

Foley, Richard (1983) 'Epistemic Conservatism', *Philosophical Studies*, 43: 165–82.

Fumerton, Richard (1988) 'Foundationalism, Conceptual Regress, and Reliabilism', *Analysis*, 48: 178–84.

—— (1996) *Metaepistemology and Skepticism* (Lanham, Md.).

[15] See Peter Markie (forthcoming) for a plausible defense of the distinction between unproblematically getting justification for believing a principle employing the principle, and unproblematically arguing for a principle, presupposing the principle.

[16] I thank my colleague, Diane Jeske, for comments on a draft of this paper.

____(2003) 'Introspection and Internalism', in Susana Nuccetelli (ed.), *New Essays on Semantic Externalism, and Self-Knowledge* (Boston), 257–76.
____(2004) 'Epistemic Probability', *Philosophical Issues*, 14: 149–64.
Goldman, Alvin (1967) 'A Causal Theory of Knowing', *Journal of Philosophy*, 64: 355–72.
____(1979) 'What is Justified Belief?', in George Pappas (ed.), *Justification and Knowledge* (Dordrecht), 1–23.
____(1986) *Epistemology and Cognition* (Cambridge).
____(1988) 'Strong and Weak Justification', in James Toberlin (ed.), *Philosophical Perspectives 2: Epistemology* (Atascadero, Calif.), 51–69.
____(1999) 'Internalism Exposed', *Journal of Philosophy*, 96: 271–93.
Huemer, Michael (2001) *Skepticism and the Veil of Perception* (Lanham, Md.).
____(2006) 'Phenomenal Conservatism and the Internal of Intuition', *American Philosophical Quarterly*, 43: 147–58.
____(forthcoming) 'Compassionate Phenomenal Conservatism', *Philosophy and Phenomenological Research.*
Hume, David (1888) *A Treatise of Human Nature*, ed. L. A. Selby-Bigge (London).
Ludlow, Peter, and Norah Martin (eds.) (1998) *Externalism and Self-Knowledge* (Stanford, Calif.).
McGrew, Timothy (1999) 'A Defense of Classical Foundationalism', in Louis Pojman (ed.), *The Theory of Knowledge*, 2nd edn. (New York), 224–35.
Markie, Peter (forthcoming) 'Easy Knowledge', *Philosophy and Phenomenological Research.*
Plantinga, Alvin (1993) *Warrant and Proper Function* (Oxford).
____(2000) *Warranted Christian Belief* (New York).
Quine, W. V. O. (1969) 'Epistemology Naturalized', in *Ontological Relativity and Other Essays* (New York).
Sandberg, Thomas (2004) 'Thomas Reid's Providentialist Epistemology', Ph.D. thesis, University of Iowa.
Van Cleve, James (2003) 'Is Knowledge Easy—or Impossible: Externalism as the Only Alternative to Skepticism', in Steven Luper (ed.), *The Skeptics* (Aldershot), 45–60.
Williamson, Timothy (2000) *Knowledge and its Limits* (Oxford).

4. The Evolution of Irrationality: Insights from Non-Human Primates

Laurie R. Santos

Making decisions is like speaking prose—
people do it all the time, knowingly or unknowingly.
(Kahneman and Tversky, 1984)

1. INTRODUCTION

From the moment we wake up in the morning, we are confronted by a staggering array of choices. (Should I hit the shower or the snooze button, the highway or the byway?) Though sometimes our preferences are well-known to us, often we must make decisions with limited information about how different outcomes will affect our overall happiness and utility. (Having never tried Korean *sannakji*[1] for example, I am unsure whether I would find the experience glorious or repulsive.) Moreover, we can rarely be certain of what the outcome of our choice will be. (Generally, taking the highway increases my overall well-being, but if I have an accident, the utility is decidedly otherwise.)

As decision-makers go, however, human adults are fairly lucky: we have large brains, language, psychic advisers, and Blackberries to help us navigate our myriad choices. Non-human animals face a corresponding array of complex options with a rather more limited

The author would like to thank Mark Maxwell and the editors for helpful comments on an earlier version of this paper. Address correspondence to Laurie R. Santos, Yale University, Department of Psychology, Box 208205, New Haven, CT 06510 or via email at laurie.santos@yale.edu.

[1] *Sannakji*, I'm told, is a Korean delicacy. To prepare it, the chef slices the tentacles off of a small live octopus, which arrive at the table still moving around using their suction cups. Though the squirming is considered a highlight of the experience, it does pose a health hazard; every once in a while a diner chokes as the suction cups stick to his mouth and throat.

set of resources. Like us, non-human animals have constrained time and energy, and must decide between different time- and energy-use alternatives. A female capuchin monkey waking up in the canopy, for example, must decide whether to get up or stay asleep, forage in well-trod paths or try new areas, lunch on boring leaves or search out rarer but more delicious insects, and so on. Such daily decisions may have far-reaching consequences, both in terms of immediate individual utility—how full, tired, comfortable, and happy she is that day—and for her survival and reproductive success.

How do humans and other animals actually navigate the decisions that we face each day? In this chapter, I will challenge what has typically been considered the standard descriptive account of the mechanisms underlying human and animal decision-making, the notion of *rational utility-maximization*—the idea that organisms make decisions rationally, choosing alternatives that maximize their expected payoffs. After presenting a brief overview of this standard theory (section 2) I will review the results of classic studies on decision-making in humans which suggest that even experienced decision-makers violate rationality in a number of systematic and important ways (section 3). (Readers familiar with this literature may wish to skim these portions of the paper.) I will then present new evidence from my lab on decision-making in non-human primates indicating that humans are not alone in their irrational decision-making tendencies (section 4). I will then use this evidence to support an alternative claim—that humans and other animals make decisions using evolutionarily shared (possibly innately specified) cognitive shortcuts, ones that do not adhere strictly to the rules of rationality. I will then very briefly discuss some implications of this notion for cognitive evolution generally and for the idea of rationality in humans and animals (section 5).

2. THE CLASSICAL APPROACH TO RATIONAL CHOICE: EXPECTED UTILITY MAXIMIZATION

The classical view of human decision-making—which I'll refer to throughout this article as rational expected-utility-maximization—starts with a simple assumption about decision-making organisms:

they are rational. Rationality in this case means that organisms will behave in ways that they believe will maximize their own utility. For this notion to make sense, we must presuppose a few things about rational agents. First, self-interested rational agents must have more and less preferred consequences—*preferences*—which are *reasonable,* in the sense that they are consistent over time and transitive across different options (if an agent prefers A to B and B to C then he must also prefer A to C). Second, rational agents must be endowed with certain *reasoning capacities*. They must, at least at some level, be able to make connections between the actions they take and the consequences of those actions, and when actions do not consistently lead to the same consequences, rational organisms must employ the basic tenets of probability to determine the likelihood that a particular action will yield a given consequence. In this way, organisms must factor likelihood information into their calculation of which behaviors can be expected to bring them the best returns. Thus rational agents are assumed to compute *expected utilities*—the value of the consequences of each action adjusted by the likelihood that this consequence will actually occur—for each possible action and then choose the action that, on average, leads to the maximum expected utility. Finally, rational organisms must *consistently behave rationally*—that is, they must always act in ways that are consistent with their own self-interest and preferences, and must always choose options that maximize their own average expected utility, no matter what their current wealth level or situation.

Although the basic idea of rational expected-utility-maximization was first described hundreds of years ago, its popularity reached a pinnacle in the mid-twentieth century when two very separate fields, behavioral ecology and economics, attempted to formulate normative models of optimal behavior. Behavioral ecologists in the 1950s were centrally concerned with the adaptive nature of animal behavior, the extent to which an individual animal's behavior was optimized by natural selection for maximizing that individual's survival and reproductive success. With this in mind, behavioral ecologists became interested in the behavioral trade-offs that animals make on a daily basis, particularly within the domain of foraging (for elegant reviews of this literature, see Glimcher, 2003; Krebs and Davies, 1993). This interest led to the development of *optimal foraging theory*, a normative model of optimal choice behavior and a set of mathematical predictions governing how the ideal rationally self-interested individual animal should forage given different environmental payoffs. Optimal foraging theory was thus concerned both with determining how organisms maximize expected daily payoffs, like overall daily energy attainment, and with how they maximize the ultimate evolutionary currency, survival, and reproductive success.

At around the same time that behavioral ecologists were formulating normative models of animal decision-making, economists were developing normative models for human decision-making. Conceptualizing economic situations as multi-player games, these models allowed individual decision-making to be described in terms of choices among different "gambles," each with its own associated payoff and probability of occurring. Under this framework, optimal human decision-making could be understood as a process of computing and comparing different average expected payoffs with the goal of maximizing utility. Such models were taken to apply to the behavior both of individuals (persons) and groups (corporations or markets).

Though rational expected-utility-maximization models were originally formulated as *normative* models, both economists and behavioral ecologists have often adopted the same models as a *descriptive* framework. The idea that rational expected-utility-maximization models accurately describe the behavior of individual animals and investors has held intuitive appeal for economists and biologists for a number of reasons. First, these models fit well with the widespread belief that, in general, people and animals behave in ways that cause their desires to be satisfied. Second, rational expected-utility-maximization models are attractive to economists and biologists because they have a formal appeal; such models are easy to quantify mathematically, and therefore allow for the types of predictive modeling to which economists and mathematical biologists are accustomed. Third, rational expected-utility-maximization models provide a natural explanation for the observation that, in general, large groups of decision-makers—markets in the case of economics and species in the case of ecology—do seem relatively optimized to solve particular problems and achieve specific goals. Finally, rational utility-maximization models mesh well with the first-principle assumptions of each of these two fields. Behavioral ecologists work under the assumption that the behavior of modern organisms has been shaped over time by the process of natural selection: behavioral strategies observed today are the result of generations of competition for scarce resources. Because optimal decision-making behavior should increase an organism's chance of survival in harsh competitive times, optimal behaviors are more likely to persist across generations of evolutionary selection. In the same way, economists assume that market competition should serve as a strong selection force against suboptimal decision-making strategies. In this way, generations of market forces should select for normatively optimal decision-making behavior. As such, observed market strategies should on average yield relatively optimal payoffs, just as observed animal behavior should yield relatively optimal energy returns that can be translated into relatively optimal reproductive fitness returns.

3. THE MODERN SYNTHESIS: CHOICES, VALUES, AND FRAMES

The normative appeal of rational expected-utility-maximization models led many to the view that such models provide adequate descriptive accounts of behavior, both that of individual human investors and other non-human species. But an enormous (and still growing) body of empirical work suggests that human agents diverge from what rational expected-utility-maximization models would predict, both in the laboratory and in the real world.

Rational expected-utility-maximization models were first questioned by the behavioral economists Daniel Kahneman and Amos Tversky. One of Kahneman and Tversky's earliest and most important observations was that human decision-makers seem to violate a primary assumption of rational expected-utility-maximization models—they don't *always* choose the option with the highest expected utility. In addition, human decision-makers (including experienced ones like economists and investors) generally do not describe the outcomes of their choices in terms of overall utility. In ordinary conversation, people tend to refer to the outcome of their choices as a gain or loss relative to some starting point (e.g.

"I lost $20 because of that parking ticket!") rather than in terms of their overall utility or wealth level (e.g. "My entire net worth is now only $227,364 because of that parking ticket!") Kahneman and Tversky wondered if this relativist rather than absolutist perspective actually affected people's choices. Would people behave differently when faced with outcomes that felt like relative gains than they would for ones that felt like relative losses? They presented participants with the one of the two following scenarios (see Kahneman and Tversky, 1979). The actual percentage of participants that chose each scenario is given in brackets after each scenario.

Scenario 1. You have been given $1000. You are now asked to choose between: (A) a 50% chance of receiving another $1000, and 50% chance of receiving nothing [16%], or (B) receiving $500 with certainty [84%].

Scenario 2. You have been given $2000. You are now asked to choose between: (C) a 50% chance of losing $1000, and a 50% chance of losing nothing [69%], or (D) losing $500 with certainty [31%].

From the perspective of overall utility maximization, each scenario has exactly the same two choices: options A and C each give a 50% chance of a final result of $1000 and a 50% chance of a final result of $2000, and options B and D each guarantee $1500. Rational expected-utility-maximization models would thus predict that human subjects should show the same preference in each of the two scenarios. In contrast to this prediction, participants show quite different preferences across the two scenarios. In the first situation, where both options are framed as gains, participants reliably preferred the safe option B over the risky option A; in the second situation, where options are framed in terms of losses, participants reliably preferred the risky option C over the safe option D.

Kahneman and Tversky used evidence from this and numerous similar cases to argue that human decision-makers do not evaluate choices in terms of overall utility, as the classic rational descriptive account predicts. Instead, they seem to consider different options in regards to a particular (usually arbitrary) *reference point* (e.g. one's current position in a particular experimental gamble, etc.). Kahneman and Tversky further observed that subjects seemed to treat changes from a reference point differently depending on whether those changes were positive (gains) or negative (losses): people tended to be risk averse when dealing with perceived gains—they chose sure, smaller gains over larger, riskier gains—but risk-seeking when dealing with perceived losses—they preferred a risky chance not to have any loss over a sure small loss. This phenomenon of changing risk-preferences—often termed the *reflection effect*—is observed even in decisions that don't involve monetary gains. Consider another problem presented by Tversky and Kahneman (1981), a scenario commonly referred to as the "Asian disease problem":

Imagine that the U.S. is preparing for the outbreak of an unusual Asian disease, which is expected to kill 600 people. Two alternative programs to combat the disease have been proposed. Assume that the exact scientific estimates of the consequences of the programs are as follows:

If Program A is adopted, 200 people will be saved [72%]
If Program B is adopted, there is a 1/3 probability that 600 people will be saved, and 2/3 probability that nobody will be saved [28%]
If Program C is adopted 400 people will die [22%]
If Program D is adopted there is a 1/3 probability that nobody will die, and 2/3 probability that 600 people will die [78%]

As in the previous set of scenarios, programs A and C are equivalent (200 people will live for sure, and 400 will die for sure), and programs B and D are equivalent (there is a 1/3 chance of 600 people will live and zero will die, and a 2/3 chance that no one will live and 600 die). Nevertheless, as in the case described above, participants presented with the first two options preferred the certain gain (A) to the risky gain (B), while those presented with the second two options preferred the risky loss (D) to the certain loss (C). Participants' choices thus seemed to be based solely on how the problem was written or *framed*: when the choice was described in terms of people dying (i.e. lives *lost*) people chose to avoid a sure loss; when the mathematically identical choice was described in terms of survival rates (i.e. lives gained, so to speak), participants switched their preference and sought out safe options. As Kahneman and Tversky (1981) observed in this and other problems (see Kahneman and Tversky, 2000, for a review), the utility that decision-makers feel they lose with losses tends to be greater than the utility they feel they obtain with identically sized gains. This feature leads to *loss aversion*—people tend to avoid losses more than they tend to seek out equally sized gains. (Human loss aversion can also be observed in the fact that most average-salaried academics would pass up the following gamble: a 50% chance to win $1001 and a 50% chance to lose $1000.)

The phenomenon of reference dependence and loss aversion led Kahneman and Tversky (1979, 1981) to develop a new descriptive account of human decision-making under uncertainty. This new account, *prospect theory*, begins by treating decisions as measuring value (described in relative terms like gains or losses) rather than overall utility. Under prospect theory, values are measured as losses or gains relative to a specified (yet often arbitrary) reference point. Because of loss aversion, there is a kink in the value curve at the reference point, such that a given absolute-sized loss (e.g. a $5 loss) will decrease value more than an identically sized gain (e.g. a $5 gain) will increase value. One of the major implications of prospect theory is that people naturally frame their decisions as gains or losses relative to a particular reference point. This feature of prospect theory leads to odd and often irrational *framing effects*, in which decision-makers' responses may vary with how the choice is presented, worded, or described. Because of loss aversion, framing effects may cause decision-makers to make decisions that lower their overall expected utility.

We can see these effects in a number of real-world economic situations. Take, for example, the tendency for people to overvalue objects that they own relative to objects that they don't yet own, a phenomenon that Thaler (1980) christened "*the endowment effect.*" In one classic study, Kahneman and colleagues (1990) gave one of two identically priced items—either a coffee mug or a box of pens—to each member of a participants group. They then examined subjects' willingness to trade the item they were given for the alternative item. Interestingly, the researchers observed very few examples of trading. Instead, coffee mug owners tended to demand a larger price to sell or trade their mug than non-owners were willing to pay to buy or trade for it. Kahneman and colleagues hypothesized that the act of becoming an owner of an object changes one's view of that object because it changes one's reference point—object owners will experience a loss when trading an object (and thus, value it more strongly) while object buyers will experience the new object as a gain (and thus, value it less strongly than they would if they were experiencing it as a loss). Because of loss aversion, people's willingness-to-sell an item is often less than their willingness-to-buy an identical item.

4. NEW EMPIRICAL WORK ON IRRATIONALITY: FRAMING EFFECTS IN ANIMALS

The ground-breaking work of Kahneman and Tversky led to a new view of human decision-making: we, humans, are not the normatively obedient decision-makers we had once assumed. Instead, humans behave in ways that violate a number of the major tenets of economic rationality. We have preferences that are inconsistent across time and presentation. We evaluate our payoffs in relative rather than absolute terms, and therefore occasionally fail to choose options with the highest absolute payoffs. Finally, and perhaps most problematic, our view of a decision can be changed arbitrarily by framing—simply wording a problem differently or changing how it's presented can affect both how we value our alternative outcomes and how we behave.

The finding that human decision-making violates these normative standards leads to a number of questions concerning where these decision-making biases come from. How is it that adult human decision-makers (like those tested in studies) came to be loss averse and reference dependent? Do these decision-making biases come about because of specific economic experiences or cultural training? Or are these biases instead a more basic feature of the way humans make decisions? Could they even be present as part of our evolutionary heritage?

My colleagues and I have taken a somewhat radical view of the origins of our own species' irrational decision-making biases (see Chen *et al.*, 2006; Santos and Lakshminarayanan, in press): we hypothesize that at least some aspects of our irrational decision-making are innately specified. More specifically, we have argued that phenomena like loss aversion and reference dependence are not solely the result of experience and cultural learning. Instead, we hypothesize that these decision-making biases result from more evolutionarily ancient tendencies, ones that are likely to be present in the decision-making of other non-human species as well.

To test our somewhat radical idea, my colleagues and I have begun to examine whether the irrational biases that govern human choice are demonstrated in the choice behavior of other animals as well (see Marsh and Kacelnik, 2002, for a similar approach). In particular, we examined whether a closely related non-human primate species, the capuchin monkey (*Cebus apella*) exhibits reference dependence and loss aversion when making decisions conceptually similar to those of the Kahneman and Tversky studies. We chose to begin our comparative investigation with a primate comparative model for a number of reasons. First, non-human primate (hereafter, "primate") models provide one of the best windows into the evolutionary origins of human cognition. Much of human cognition was likely to have been shaped for problems that our ancestors faced over their evolutionary history. The ancestors of closely related primates presumably faced selection pressures similar to those that plagued our human ancestors; as such, modern primates can often provide a useful model for determining the strategies that our ancestors may have used to solve ancestral problems. In addition, primate models can be particularly useful tools for examining the role of experience in shaping how a particular cognitive mechanism operates. Adult primates, unlike adult humans, have little experience in real-world economic markets, and thus they provide an excellent test case for what economic decision-making looks like in the absence of market training and experience. Third, because primates do not naturally use money, any decision-making mechanisms we observe in primates could not have evolved for economic exchange *per se*. Instead, if loss aversion and reference dependence were observed in primates, they would have to be mechanisms that evolved not for market use, but instead as general problem-solving and decision-making strategies.

The overarching goal of our work, then, was to examine how capuchin monkeys would perform on the gambles presented to human participants in classic behavioral economic studies (see reviews in Kahneman and Tversky, 2000). The first challenge of this approach was to develop a way to measure and quantify monkey preferences. Unlike human participants, our capuchin subjects were unable to fill out questionnaires, list what they prefer, or verbally report how much they'd be willing to spend to take part in a particular gamble. We therefore needed to develop a method for testing primate preferences that could approximate the tasks typically used to test human subjects in choice experiments. In addition, we also hoped to find a capuchin choice method that required as little training as possible. Spontaneous studies, which require very little reinforced training, represent a particularly useful way of assessing how an animal would make decisions in its natural environment. We therefore wanted to develop a task that required little training with the specific gambles in which we were interested in testing.

In the end, we decided that if we really wanted to test monkeys' preferences in a way that was directly comparable to that used by economists to test humans, then the easiest course of action was to teach our monkeys how to use a fungible currency like money and let them use this currency to establish preferences as humans did. Although teaching monkeys to use money might seem a daunting task, a number of labs had previously taught primates to trade token-like "money" in exchange for food (see Brosnan and de Waal, 2003, 2004; Liv *et al.*, 1999; Westergaard *et al.*, 1998, 2004). These labs had used token-trading methods as an easy way of getting monkeys to make choices, but no one to date had used monkey tokens to set up a real economy, one geared to illustrate monkeys' economic preference patterns and compare such patterns with those of human participants.

We began by presenting monkeys with novel tokens—small metal discs. Once monkeys became familiar with the tokens, we then began reinforcing them for an exchange, basically handing them food whenever they gave one of their tokens to a human experimenter. Monkeys quickly got the hang of the set-up, spontaneously taking tokens when they were available and waiting patiently with the tokens for a human willing to trade (see Figure 4.1 for a

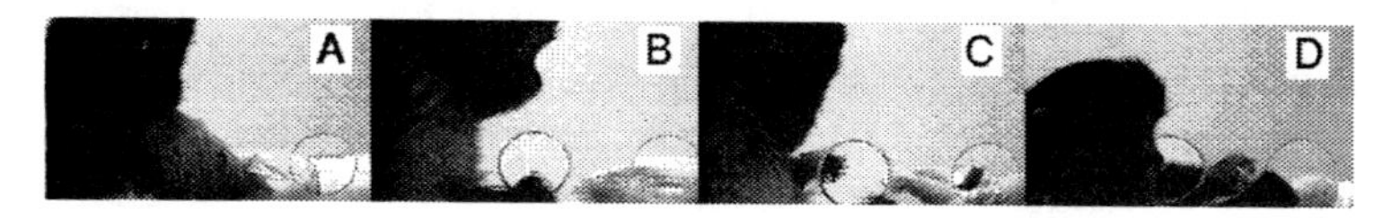

Figure 4.1. Depiction of the Trading Situation. The capuchin trader delivers a token to the salesman's hand (A). He then takes it away (B), and delivers a piece of food in return (C), which the monkey then takes and eats (D).

depiction of a single exchange). Within a few weeks of this simple training, our monkey economy was born. Each morning before testing, we handed monkeys a wallet of tokens and let them enter into a "market," in which two different experimental salesmen—two different research assistants dressed in dissimilar outfits—offered different kinds of food at different prices. Monkeys were then given a set amount of time in the market in which they could spend their wallet of tokens however they chose, buying goods from one or both of the salesmen. With this set-up, we could observe monkeys' preferences just as economists observe human preferences—by looking at what options the monkeys are interested in buying and the proportion of their budget they're willing to spend to obtain these different options.

Our first task was to demonstrate that our new monkey market worked in an economic sense, that is, that monkeys acting in our new market would reveal preferences that generally remained stable over time and responded rationally to price changes (Chen *et al.*, 2006). To assess this, we presented the monkeys with a market that involved a choice between two equally preferred goods, which for most monkeys involved a slice of Jello and a small apple chunk. Monkeys liked these two types of food about equally, so they tended to purchase them at equal rates—spending half of their budget on Jello and half on apples. We then presented monkey buyers with a situation in which the price of one of the two equally preferred goods fell by half—monkeys who previously paid one token for a small chunk of apple now got two chunks for the same price. If monkeys, like humans, adjust their preferences based on the price of the objects, then they should buy more of the cheaper good. Monkeys did just this, switching to buying more apples and avoiding goods that cost more. Like human economies, our newly introduced monkey market seemed to pay attention to price shifts, with their previously established preferences remaining stable across changes.

Having established that monkeys performed rationally in the types of situations where human agents performed rationally, we then turned to our real question of interest: whether monkeys would demonstrate the *irrationalities* that humans classically demonstrate—reference dependence and loss aversion. Put more specifically, could we get monkey buyers to change their preferences based simply on how a salesman framed his offer? To explore these questions, we presented monkeys with a market in which the two experimenters each offered different numbers of apples. Importantly, however, the experimenters in this market didn't always hand over the number of food pieces they originally displayed—some experimenters gave more pieces of food than they originally offered, whereas others gave less. Our hypothesis was that monkeys might decide between the two offers not just based on how much food they get, but how much food they get relative to what they were originally offered. In other words, we predicted that monkeys might use the original offer as a reference point, and frame their final outcome not in terms of its overall value, but instead, as a loss or gain relative to that initial reference point, with less food being considered a relative loss and more food being considered a relative gain.

In the first study (Chen *et al.*, 2006), monkeys had a choice between two experimenters. The first experimenter offered two pieces of food but, half the time, only handed over one of the promised pieces of food. As such, this experimenter represented a risky chance of losing one piece of food. The second experimenter always offered one piece of food but, half the time, added a second unexpected piece of food. In contrast to the first experimenter, the second experimenter represented a risky chance of gaining one piece of food. As such, the only thing that differed across the two experimenters was how their actual offering was framed relative to what they had originally promised. Overall, both of the two experimenters delivered the same amount of food; on average, each experimenter gave 1.5 pieces of apple. But our monkey participants did not treat the two offers similarly—all of our monkey buyers significantly preferred the experimenter who appeared to give them gains, the salesman who promised only one piece and sometimes gave more. Like humans, our monkey buyers seemed to like receiving things that appeared to be gains more than they liked experiencing perceived losses, even though this didn't increase the overall amount of food they received on average.

But were our monkey buyers seeking out perceived gains or were they, like human actors, actively avoiding losses? To test this, we presented monkeys with a choice between an experimenter who always delivered what he initially offered and an experimenter who always delivered less than he initially offered. Monkeys chose between one experimenter who promised and delivered one chunk of apple and an experimenter who promised two chunks and always delivered only one. Again, monkeys avoided the experimenter giving losses, and this time they showed an even stronger preference than in the previous study. Monkeys thus seemed to avoid a 100 per cent chance of loss even more than they avoided a 50 per cent chance of loss.

In a later study (Lakshminarayanan *et al.*, in preparation), we went on to explore whether monkeys' risk-taking behavior is also susceptible to framing effects. To do so, we developed a monkey version of Kahneman and Tversky's Asian disease problem. We presented monkeys with a choice between two salesmen that varied in their riskyness: the first salesman was a safe trader—he always did the same thing on each trial. The second salesman, in contrast, was a risky trader—he varied what he did from trial to trial. We then altered how the risky and safe salesmen framed what they offered. In the first condition, both salesmen framed their offer as a gain. The safe trader promised one piece of apple and, on every trial, added a second piece to his actual offer. The risky trader on the other hand always began by offering one piece of apple, but then varied his final offer: on some trials he gave a large gain of two apples (for a resulting offer of three) while on other trials he gave no bonus. With this set-up both the safe and the risky trader resulted in an average absolute offer of two pieces of apple. Nevertheless, our monkey subjects did not treat them equally. Our monkey buyers preferred to trade with the safe experimenter over the risky experimenter. The second condition, in contrast, presented monkeys a choice between risky and safe options that were instead framed as losses. Monkeys were allowed to choose between a safe salesman and a risky salesman, each of whom began by offering three chunks of apple. Both salesmen then delivered a loss relative to this initial reference point: the safe salesman always delivered a small loss of one apple piece (resulting in an offer of two pieces), whereas the risky salesmen sometimes delivered no loss (resulting in an offer of three pieces) and sometimes delivered a big loss (resulting in an offer of only one apple piece). Like human subjects, monkeys changed their risk seeking when problems were framed as losses rather than gains. When the options were framed as losses, monkeys behaved more risk-seeking—they reliably preferred to trade with the risky salesman over the safe salesman. Even when evaluating when to take risks, monkeys seem to respond to how a particular problem is framed and whether options appear to be gains or losses relative to an arbitrary reference point.

In our most recent study (Lakshminarayanan, Chen, and Santos, in preparation), we examined whether our monkeys' loss aversion would also lead them to experience an endowment effect, an asymmetry between their willingness-to-buy and willingness-to-sell the same good. To test this, we identified another set of two different foods that the monkeys preferred about equally, in this case, cereal and pear pieces, and therefore purchased at equal rates. We then changed the trading task just a bit. Rather than provide the monkeys with a wallet of tokens, we instead gave them a wallet of one of these two goods. Half our monkeys, for example, became an owner of several wheat cereal pieces, which they could then trade for equally valued pear slices. Because these pear and cereal pieces are equally preferred, one might predict that monkeys should be willing to trade about half of their cereal pieces for pear slices. However, if monkeys, like humans, experience an endowment effect then they should be reluctant to trade the good that they own for an equally preferred good that they do not own. This is just what we observed. Like humans, monkeys who are made owners of one kind of food are reluctant to trade this food for another equally preferred option. Even across control conditions in which monkeys are compensated for any perceived transaction costs, our capuchin participants failed to trade the owned good for an equally preferred or slightly more valuable good. As in humans, it seems that when a monkey becomes an owner of an object, his views about the value of that object change. Monkey owners seem to avoid losing objects that they already own even if it means forgoing the gain of an equally valued alternative object. As with loss averse humans, monkeys' willingness-to-sell an item is less than their willingness-to-buy an identical item.

Taken together, the studies described above suggest that monkeys share a number of the irrational tendencies that humans demonstrate. First, they seem to evaluate their choices not in terms of their overall utility, but instead in terms of arbitrary reference points—how much food they currently have or how much food they are expecting. In addition, monkeys seem to pay more attention to losses than they do to gains, demonstrating an asymmetry in the amount of work they will expend to avoid losses as opposed to seeking out equally sized gains. Such loss aversion also plays out in the way monkeys deal with risk—they seem to choose risky situations more when they think they are gambling to lose than when they think they are gambling to gain. Finally, monkeys' loss aversion also leads to problems with trading that humans experience; like human traders, monkeys demonstrate an endowment effect when trading equally priced goods.

5. INNATE IRRATIONALITY? CHALLENGES FOR PSYCHOLOGISTS (AND PHILOSOPHERS)

I began this article with the claim that humans and other animals do not behave according to the tenets of the most widely accepted normative account of decision-making, the model of rational expected-utility-maximization. Having reviewed evidence that human and primate participants behave in ways that systematically violate the predictions of rational expected-utility-maximization models, I have argued that a better descriptive model of human and non-human decision-making involves evaluating payoffs in terms of their relative value rather than their absolute utility. This new model incorporates two cognitive biases—reference dependence and loss aversion—that produce framing effects in a number of situations. In addition, our new evidence seems to suggest that such effects are not the result of economic experience: capuchin monkeys (and possibly other animals, see Marsh and Kacelnik, 2002) seem to employ the same biased decision-making strategies as do human participants.

The findings reviewed above suggest that humans and animals share a set of decision-making strategies that deviate from classic normative utility maximization models. My colleagues and I have interpreted these collective findings not only as evidence that capuchins (and probably other animals) share the underlying decision-making heuristics that give rise to the irrationality of human choice, but also that these biases result from homologous cognitive mechanisms, ones that stem from a shared innate evolutionary history.

Let me close this chapter by very briefly highlighting three sorts of challenges that this comparative line of research raises for a psychological (and philosophical) understanding of the evolution of decision-making and rationality more generally. The first challenge concerns the claim that the biases we have observed in capuchin monkeys are part of an innately specified system and the question of how these purportedly innate biases came about over evolutionary time. Typically, when psychologists talk about an innately specified cognitive strategy, they at least implicitly assume that the strategy they're talking about is one that works pretty well. Take, for example, the nativist claim that human infants possess innate cognitive strategies for tracking objects as they move through time and space (see e.g. Spelke *et al.*, 1992). Although many have taken issue with the evidence for such an innate object knowledge system (e.g. Smith, 1999), no one would argue that such an innate system would constitute a bad evolutionary idea. In fact, possessing an innately specified set of cognitive strategies to accurately make sense of the physical world can only be thought of as an evolutionary blessing. Intuitively, at least, this *does not* seem to be the case for an innate system for making biased decisions (see also Santos and Lakshminarayan, in press). Rather than an evolutionary blessing, a set of cognitive strategies that systematically leads an individual away from normatively better choices would seem to be a pretty major evolutionary inconvenience, one that might systematically reduce an organism's chances of maximal reproductive success. How, then, could an innate system of biased decision-making strategies have come about over evolutionary time? To the extent that the strategies I've described cause both humans and non-humans to behave in ways that systematically deviate from what normative models dictate, how could they have been selected via natural selection? The question of whether and how these biased decision-making strategies are able to confer a selective advantage is a major challenge facing this research program, one with which philosophers interested in the evolution of rationality may have to contend.

The next set of challenges facing the comparative research program I've described—and one that also plagues work in human behavioral economics—arises from considering the contrast between poor individual performance on the tasks described above and the proficient aggregated performance demonstrated by groups of those same individuals in a variety of macroeconomic situations. Whereas individual human decision-makers regularly make decisions that violate the maxims of rationality and utility-maximization, markets—which are in some ways just aggregates of individual decision-makers—*do not* seem to behave in these ways. Indeed, neo-classical economists critical of experimental work in behavioral economics have long pointed out that markets, on average, seem to approximate what rational expected-utility-maximization models predict. A parallel question arises for aggregates of non-human decision-makers. Whereas the studies described above suggest that at least one non-human species (the capuchin monkey) demonstrates irrational decision-making behavior involving reference dependence and loss aversion, most species do impressive jobs of maximizing their expected energy and mating payoffs over time. How could seemingly irrational strategies like framing and reference dependence at the proximate or individual level translate into seemingly rational strategies of payoff-maximization at the ultimate or group level? The idea that strategies at the individual level do not necessarily translate into strategies at the aggregated level suggests that researchers must be careful when discussing the idea of rationality. In particular, those interested in the evolution of rationality might need to be more careful in specifying the proper unit of analysis for the investigation—either at the level of individual strategies or at the level of an aggregated group-level strategy.

A third challenge facing researchers interested in rationality concerns the question of what these new (possibly adapative) descriptive models of decision-making mean for normative models of behavior and choice. Gigerenzer and colleagues (e.g. Gigerenzer and Selton, 2001; Gigerenzer and Todd, 1999) have forcefully argued that "irrational" strategies may outperform rational expected-utility-maximization models when time and energy are of the essence. Because rational models require agents to spend unusually large amounts of time computing difficult-to-calculate expected payoffs, organisms may sometimes do better by simply "satisificing" with a rough yet quick solution to complex problems. Prospect theory, then, may provide not just a better descriptive account of organisms' actual reasoning, but it might also be a normatively better way to make decisions than classic models because relative judgments require less time and computation. In this way, an organism might be better off bearing the cost of irrationality's imprecision and making relative judgments than they would be bearing the cost of time and calculation energy required to make a rational estimate. If Gigerenzer and colleagues' view of biased thinking is correct, philosophers and psychologists may need to radically rethink the status of traditional rationality as a *normatively viable* decision-making model.

The first goal of this article was to provide yet another empirical challenge to the once (and—in some circles—*still*) dominant descriptive account of human and animal decision-making, the idea that organisms make decisions in ways that serve to maximize their expected utility. To do so, I describe new work demonstrating that humans are not the only species to violate the predictions of expected utility models. Capuchin monkeys, who lack cultural training and experience in economic markets, exhibit biases that are analogous to those of human subjects in classic behavioral economic studies. The second goal of this article was to briefly consider what these findings mean for the nature and development of human decision-making strategies. My lab's capuchin results suggest that the decision-making heuristics used by human adults may emerge in the absence of culture, pedagogy, and experience. As such, I have interpreted these findings as evidence that our human decision-making biases result from innate cognitive strategies, ones with a lengthy evolutionary history. My hope is this new evidence for irrational decision-making in closely related non-human primates will help to inform and constrain the way that philosophers come to think about the broader question of rationality and its evolution.

REFERENCES

Brosnan, S. F., and F. B. M. de Waal (2003) 'Monkeys Reject Unequal Pay', *Nature*, 425: 297–9.

—— and —— (2004) 'Socially Learned Preferences for Differentially Rewarded Tokens in the Brown Capuchin Monkey (Cebus apella)', *Journal of Comparative Psychology*, 118: 133–9.

Camerer, C. F., G. Loewenstein, and M. Rabin (eds.) (2003) *Advances in Behavioral Economics* (Princeton).

Chen, M. K., V. Lakshminarayanan, and L. R. Santos (2006) 'The Evolution of our Preferences: Evidence from Capuchin Monkey Trading Behavior', *Journal of Political Economy*, 114: 517–37.

Genesove, D., and C. Mayer (2001) 'Loss Aversion and Seller Behavior: Evidence from the Housing Market', *Quarterly Journal of Economics*, 116: 1233–60.

Gigerenzer, G., and D. G. Goldstein (1996) 'Reasoning the Fast and Frugal Way: Models of Bounded Rationality', *Psychological Review*, 103: 650–69.

—— and R. Selten (eds.) (2001) *Bounded Rationality: The Adaptive Toolbox* (Cambridge).

—— and P. M. Todd (1999) *Simple Heuristics that Make us Smart* (Oxford).

Glimcher, P. W. (2003) *Decisions, Uncertainty, and the Brain: The Science of Neuroeconomics* (Cambridge).

Hardie, B. G. S., E. J. Johnson, and P. S. Fader (1993) 'Modeling Loss Aversion and Reference Dependence Effects on Brand Choice', *Marketing Science*, 12: 378–94.

Hastie, R., and R. M. Dawes (2001) *Rational Choice in an Uncertain World* (Thousand Oaks, Calif.).

Kahneman, D., and A. Tversky (1979) 'Prospect Theory: An Analysis of Decision under Risk', *Econometrica*, 47: 263–92.

—— and —— (2000) *Choices, Values, and Frames* (Cambridge).

—— J. L. Knetsch, and R. H. Thaler (1990) 'Experimental Tests of the Endowment Effect and the Coase Theorem', *Journal of Political Economy*, 98: 1325–48.

—— —— and —— (1991) 'Anomalies: The Endowment Effect, Loss Aversion, and Status Quo Bias', *Journal of Economic Perspectives*, 5: 193–206.

—— P. Slovic, and A. Tversky (eds.) (1982) *Judgment under Uncertainty: Heuristics and Biases* (Cambridge).

Krebs, J. R., and N. B. Davies (1993) 'An Introduction to Behavioural Ecology', *Blackwell Scientific Publications*, 57.

Lakshminaryanan, V., L. R. Santos, and M. K. Chen (in preparation) 'The Evolution of Risky Choices: Framing Effects in Non-Human Economic Behavior', *Current Biology*.

Liv, C., G. C. Westergaard, and S. J. Suomi (1999) 'Exchange and Value in Cebus apella', *American Journal of Primatology*, 49: 74–5.

Marsh, B., and A. Kacelnik (2002) 'Framing Effects and Risky Decisions in Starlings', *Proceedings from the National Academy of Sciences*, 99: 3353–5.

Odean, T. (1998) 'Are Investors Reluctant to Realize their Losses?', *Journal of Finance*, 5: 1775–98.

Santos, L. R., and L. Lakshminarayan (in press) 'Innate Constraints on Judgment and Choice: Insights from Children and Non-Human

Primates, in P. Carruthers (ed.), *The Innate Mind Foundations and the Future* (Oxford).
Smith, L. B. (1999) 'Do Infants Possess Innate Knowledge Structures: The Con Side', *Developmental Science*, 2: 133–44.
Spelke, E., K. Breinlinger, J. Macomber, and K. Jacobson (1992) 'Origins of Knowledge', *Psychological Review*, 99: 605–32.
Thaler, R. H. (1980) 'Toward a Positive Theory of Consumer Choice', *Journal of Economic Behavior and Organization*, 1: 39–60.
Tversky, A., and D. Kahneman (1974) 'Judgment under Uncertainty: Heuristics and Biases', *Science*, 185: 1124–31.
____ and ____ (1981) 'The Framing of Decisions and the Psychology of Choice', *Science*, 211: 453–8.
____ and ____ (1986) 'Rational Choice and the Framing of Decisions', *Journal of Business*, 59: 251–78.
____ and ____ (1991) 'Loss Aversion in Riskless Choice: A Reference-Dependent Model', *Quarterly Journal of Economics*, 106: 1039–61.
Westergaard G. C., C. Liv, T. J. Chavanne, and S. J. Suomi (1998) 'Token Mediated Tool-Use by a Tufted Capuchin Monkey (Cebus apella)', *Animal Cognition*, 1: 101–6.
____ ____ A. M. Rocca, A. Cleveland, and S. J. Suomi (2004) 'Tufted Capuchins (*Cebus apella*) Attribute Value to Foods and Tools during Voluntary Exchanges with Humans', *Animal Cognition*, 7: 19–24.

5. Basic Justification and the Moorean Response to the Skeptic

Nicholas Silins

INTRODUCTION

Suppose that, having concluded that there's an external world, Moore forges on, and reasons along the following lines (BIV):

(HANDS) I have hands.

(LINK) If I have hands, then it's not the case that I'm a brain in a vat (BIV) who merely seems to have hands.

So,

(¬BIV) It's not the case that I'm a BIV who merely seems to have hands.

My focus will be on two questions about Moore's justification to believe the premises and the conclusion of the argument above. At stake is what makes it possible for our experiences to justify our beliefs, and what makes it possible for us to be justified in disbelieving skeptical hypotheses about our experiences.

The first question is,

(A) How is Moore justified in believing HANDS?

Here my aim is to clarify and to defend the view that Moore's experience gives him immediate or non-inferential justification to believe that he has hands (Pollock, 1974; Pryor, 2000, 2004, forthcoming *a*; Peacocke, 2004; Davies, 2004).[1] Doing so will be the

For their helpful comments and questions, thanks to Richard Boyd, Stewart Cohen, Louis DeRosset, Ross Ford, John Hawthorne, Elizabeth Harman, David Jehle, Geoffrey Lee, Ram Neta, James Pryor, Stephen Schiffer, Declan Smithies, Scott Sturgeon, Adam Wager, Brian Weatherson, Ralph Wedgwood, Timothy Williamson, and Roger White. Special thanks to Matt Kotzen. I'm also grateful to audiences at the Universities of Calgary, Geneva, Kansas, Montana, Vermont, and North Carolina at Chapel Hill; Auburn, Columbia, Cornell, and Oxford Universities; and at MIT, SMU, and the ANU.

[1] Also relevant are Burge (1993, 2003) or Huemer (2001).

task of sections 1 and 2. Following the terminology of Pryor (2004), we can call the view *Liberalism*.

The second question is,

(B) How is Moore justified in believing ¬BIV?

Here I will defend the unorthodox view that, although Moore's experience does give him immediate justification to believe that he has hands, Moore's experience does not give him justification to believe ¬BIV. Moore does have justification to believe ¬BIV, but that justification is such that he could have it even if he didn't have his particular experience. I will defend this view in section 3. I will also show how the view undermines the core argument against Liberalism about how experience justifies belief.

My main aim, then, is to hold on to the insight of the Liberal position while rejecting the Moorean response to the skeptic. In section 4 I will respond to the main objections to the overall package I endorse.

1. SOME DISPUTES ABOUT PERCEPTION AND JUSTIFICATION

In order to assess the main claims of this paper, we need a much sharper sense of what they are. I'll start with some general preliminaries, and then move on to formulations.

First, a proposition might have a good epistemic status for a thinker, even though she does not believe the proposition, or believes the proposition though not on a justifying basis. In such a scenario, I will say that the thinker has *propositional justification* to believe the proposition. When a thinker has based her belief on something that justifies the belief, I will say that the belief is *well-founded* (Feldman and Conee, 1985). My concern in the paper will typically be with what a thinker has propositional justification to believe, although at some points it will be crucial to consider well-founded belief. I'll remain neutral on how exactly to explain these notions, and about which if any is prior to the other. Second, my focus will primarily be on what a thinker has *perceptual justification* to believe. As I will use the expression, a thinker has perceptual justification to believe P just in case she has a possibly non-veridical experience with the content P, and her experience gives her justification to believe P.[2] According to the particular framework in which I working, Moore's perceptual evidence is that it visually seems to him that he has hands, rather than his seeing that he has hands (which he cannot do in a case of illusion or hallucination), or his seeing some objects as being his hands (which he cannot do in a case of hallucination).

Finally, I will focus throughout the paper on the case of justification provided by visual experiences, thereby leaving open the possibility for different treatments of sources of justification such as testimony or memory, and even leaving open the possibility for different treatments of different types of experiences such as auditory or tactile experiences.

1.1. *A Dispute About How Experiences Justify Belief in Their Contents*

In order to clarify the rival views about how Moore's experience justifies him in believing that he has hands, we need to introduce one more piece of terminology. Let's say that, when one has an experience which represents it to be the case that P, and one has some justification to believe some proposition Q, one's justification to believe Q is *independent* from the experience just in case one could have the justification to believe Q even if one did not have the experience. The key feature of what we can call the *Conservative* view—again adapting the terminology of Pryor (2004)—is that it explains the justificatory power of Moore's experience in terms of Moore's possession of independent justification to disbelieve skeptical hypotheses about his experience. On this view, when Moore's experience justifies him in believing that he has hands, his experience does not do so on its own, but instead jointly with some independent justification he has to believe ¬BIV (Wright, 1985, 2000, 2002, forthcoming; Davies, 1998, 2000, 2003, forthcoming).[3] In more general terms:

(Conservatism) Whenever your visual experience E gives you justification to believe its content that P

[2] Here, as elsewhere, I set aside the natural thought that Moore also enjoys a non-visual, proprioceptive justification for believing that he has hands. I'm also setting aside questions about what propositional contents experiences exactly have, assuming that experiences have propositional contents at all. For some recent discussion of these questions see Siegel (2006) or Brewer (2006).

[3] Also relevant are Bonjour (1985) or Cohen (2002).

(i) your experience does not give you immediate justification to believe that P, i.e. what makes your experience justify you to any degree in believing that P includes your having some independent justification to believe other propositions,

and in particular,

(ii) for any skeptical hypothesis H which entails that [you have E and it's not the case that P], what makes your experience justify you to any degree in believing that P includes your having independent justification to disbelieve H.[4]

The Conservative view says that, whenever your experience is a source of justification, it is only a source of mediate or inferential justification, one which relies on your independent justification to disbelieve skeptical hypotheses incompatible with the content of the experience. On this line of thought your experience is like a gas gauge: it provides you with justification only in conjunction with background information that it is not malfunctioning. Notice that the formulation of Conservatism concerns one's acquisition of any amount of justification from one's experience, and not just one's acquisition of enough justification to believe a proposition outright.

Now that we have formulated Conservatism, it's a short step to formulate Liberalism. The Liberal accepts that Moore has perceptual justification to believe that he has hands, but rejects the first clause of Conservatism, and insists that experience can be a basic source of justification. According to the Liberal, Moore's experience gives him some justification to believe that he has hands on its own, separately from his having independent reason to believe ¬BIV or any other proposition. On this view,

(Liberalism) It's not the case that: whenever your visual experience E gives you justification to believe its

[4] Most Conservatives would also want to explain perceptual justification in terms of our having justification to reject certain hypotheses compatible with the contents of one's experiences, such as the hypothesis that one is hallucinating, or the hypothesis that one's experiences are not reliable, or even the hypothesis that one is not veridically hallucinating. However, giving a properly general formulation of Conservatism raises several complications I don't have the space to address here.

> content that P, what makes your experience justify you to any degree in believing that P includes your having some independent justification to believe other propositions.

On the Liberal view your experience is sometimes a source of immediate or non-inferential justification, where your having independent reason to believe other propositions plays no role in giving you that justification to believe that P. Here your experience is not like a gas gauge: it provides you with justification directly.

Given that Liberalism is formulated as the rejection of the Conservative's (i), Liberalism does not yet say that there are any cases in which experiences give one enough immediate justification to believe a proposition outright. The formulation leaves open the possibility that experiences only give one enough justification to believe a proposition outright in conjunction with independent reason to believe other propositions. I believe that experiences do sometimes give one enough immediate justification for outright belief, and I believe that the arguments for Liberalism establish the stronger claim. However, my focus in what follows will mainly be on claims about degrees of justification.

There is of course an intermediate position which accepts the Conservative's (i) yet rejects the Conservative's (ii), but I won't be addressing that position in this paper. As far as I can see, there is no tenable middle ground between the Liberal and the Conservative. In what follows I will assume that Liberalism is true if Conservatism is false.

We should be clear that, according to the Liberal, experiences need not be a source of immediate justification whenever they are a source of justification.[5] For example, if I'm justifiably confident that all of my experiences of grandfather clocks are veridical hallucinations, and I have an experience as of a grandfather clock, my experience does not provide me with immediate justification to believe that there is a grandfather clock in front of me. In such a case, any capacity of my experience to give me non-inferential justification is undermined. Nevertheless, thanks to my background information that the experience is a veridical hallucination, my experience does provide me with mediate justification to believe that there is a

[5] Thanks to Brian Weatherson here.

grandfather clock in front of me. Such a case is not a counterexample to the Liberal view, which simply insists that experiences are sometimes a source of immediate justification when they are a source of justification.

We can further clarify the dispute between the Liberal and the Conservative by comparing it with the dispute between foundationalists and non-foundationalists. Doing so also brings out the broader significance of the Liberal/Conservative debate.

Consider the moderate foundationalist view that, for any inferentially justified empirical belief, its justification can be traced to some immediately justified perceptual belief about the environment. Liberalism does not entail the view, since perceptual beliefs could be immediately justified while failing to play the structural role required by foundationalism. However, the moderate foundationalist view about the structure of empirical justification is true only if Liberalism is true. Since it matters whether the moderate foundationalist view is true, it matters whether Liberalism is true.

1.2. *A Separate Dispute About When Experiences Justify Belief in their Contents*

So far we have clarified a dispute about *how* experiences justify beliefs. A separate question concerns *when* experiences justify beliefs. That question is left open by both views we have considered. In particular, the Liberal view should not be confused with the following claim:

(Sufficiency) When you have a visual experience which represents it to be that case that P, and you have no reason to suspect that any skeptical hypothesis about your experience is true, then you have justification to believe that P (Pryor, 2000: 532–7; Peacocke, 2004: 70).[6]

Sufficiency is formulated in different terms than the Liberal and Conservative views. Liberalism and Conservatism are concerned with what makes it the case that one has perceptual justification.

[6] I borrow the "reason to suspect" phrase from Schiffer (2004). In n. 23, I state a caution about how to understand Sufficiency.

Sufficiency is itself silent on the matter, being merely the statement of a sufficient condition for experiences to justify beliefs.

It's important that Sufficiency and Liberalism are logically independent.

First, it could be that Sufficiency is true and Liberalism is false. On some views, we have "default entitlement" to reject skeptical hypotheses: whenever one has no reason to suspect that a skeptical hypothesis is true, one has reason to reject the hypothesis (Cohen, 2000; Davies, 2003; Wright, 2004).[7] This is a claim about when we have justification to reject skeptical hypotheses, and not yet the Field-like claim that there is no substantive explanation of why we have justification to reject the hypotheses (Field, 2000, 2005). Default entitlement views are of course available to Conservatives. But if we are justified by default in rejecting skeptical hypotheses, then we have independent reason to reject skeptical hypotheses whenever the antecedent of Sufficiency is true. It is therefore open to Conservatives to accept Sufficiency. The upshot is that if one wants to commit oneself to the Liberal view, one cannot do so merely by endorsing Sufficiency.[8]

Second, it could be that Liberalism is true and Sufficiency is false. It might be that some experiences have contents which are too fine-grained for the experiences to immediately justify believing those contents.[9] For example, if my glance at the skyline determinately represents that there are 11,122 lights on, yet I have no reason to suspect that a skeptical hypothesis ascribing that experience to me is true, I may fail to have justification to believe that there are 11,122 lights on. This case would be a counterexample to Sufficiency,

[7] I pass over the complication that, in Wright (2004), our entitlement is described as one to an attitude other than belief. That's because I think everybody should say that we have justification to believe the obvious consequences of what we have justification to believe. See Jenkins (forthcoming) for critical discussion of Wright (2004).

[8] Given that the most explicit commitment in Peacocke (2004) is to Sufficiency, it's not obvious that the position defended in Peacocke (2004) is a Liberal one. Chapter 3 of the book sets out an argument which could provide an independent justification for a reader to disbelieve certain skeptical hypotheses about her experiences. It's not clear whether a thinker's tacit grasp of that argument is supposed to explain her having perceptual justification for her beliefs. So it's not obvious that Peacocke (2004) is committed to Liberalism.

[9] Discussions of the "speckled hen problem" are relevant here. See Ernest Sosa in Bonjour and Sosa (2003: ch. 7).

but it would not show that experiences never provide immediate justification.[10]

In sum, the Liberal should not be confused with the proponent of Sufficiency, and the Conservative should not be confused with the opponent of Sufficiency. The Liberal/Conservative dispute is orthogonal to the question of when experiences justify beliefs.

1.3. A Question About Whether Experiences Can Justify Disbelief in Skeptical Hypotheses

So far we have discussed questions about how and when Moore is justified in believing that he has hands. By a straightforward and plausible closure principle for justification, Moore must have justification to believe ¬BIV if he has justification to believe HANDS. We can state the closure principle (or schema) as follows:

(JB-Closure) Necessarily, if you have justification to believe that P, and you know that [P only if Q], then you have justification to believe that Q.[11]

Our closure principle, plus the plausible claim that Moore satisfies its antecedent, yields the result that Moore has justification to believe ¬BIV. However, the principle does not yield any result about exactly how Moore has justification to believe ¬BIV.

According to the *Moorean*, Moore's experience in one way or another gives him justification to believe that he's not a BIV who merely seems to have hands.

I should say right away that some Mooreans are beyond the scope of this paper. That's because there can be disagreements within the Moorean camp about how to characterize Moore's total evidence. Most Mooreans—internalist Mooreans—will think Moore could

[10] Steup (forthcoming) illustrates another way Sufficiency might fail even if Liberalism does not. Suppose my experience justifies me in believing its content only if I'm in a position to know that I'm having the experience. Suppose also that in some case I'm not in a position to know what experience I'm having (Williamson, 2000: ch. 5). Such a case would be a counterexample to Sufficiency without posing any problem for the Liberal view.

[11] JB-Closure is formulated in terms of knowing that [P only if Q] rather than merely in terms of being justified in believing that [P only if Q]. It may be that the principle formulated in terms of justified belief rather than knowledge is false. Someone who has a justified though false belief that [P only if Q] might well have justification to believe that P while failing to have justification to believe that Q.

have the very same evidence if BIV were true. However, some Mooreans—externalist Mooreans—will think that Moore could not have the same evidence if BIV were true. For example, perhaps what justifies Moore in believing that he has hands is really that he *sees that* he has hands, where he can see that he has hands only if he does have hands. In this paper my focus will be on the internalist Moorean view rather than the externalist Moorean view.[12]

Some philosophers will reject the Moorean view because they are skeptics, or because they deny closure. My focus, however, will be on the non-Moorean who allows that Moore has justification to believe ¬BIV, but denies that Moore's experience in any way supplies justification to disbelieve the skeptical hypothesis. We can think of this figure as the *Rationalist*.[13]

There are many ways to be a Rationalist. Cohen (2000) suggests a story on which the denials of skeptical hypotheses are non-evidentially rational to believe, Vogel (1990, 2005) offers a story in terms of an inference to the best explanation of one's experiences, and Wright (2004) offers a story in terms of broadly pragmatic considerations. My aim here will not be to decide between these or other accounts, but rather to defend the claim that at least one such account is correct.[14]

[12] For arguments against the externalist Moorean view, see Silins (2005*a*). There I argue that the view provides us with too little justification in the case in which we are deceived, and with too much justification in the case in which we are not deceived.

[13] A further possible view is that Moore has both perceptual justification and independent justification to believe ¬BIV. I set this view aside in what follows.

[14] As far as our knowledge of the falsehood of sweeping BIV or evil demon hypotheses is concerned, some philosophers hold that all worlds in which sweeping skeptical hypotheses hold are remote, and that the remoteness of these worlds in one way or another accounts for our knowledge that the hypotheses are false (e.g. Sosa, 1999, or Pritchard, 2005). Such philosophers typically exploit some "safety condition" on knowledge along the following lines: one knows p only if one is not mistaken in nearby worlds in believing p or a related proposition. Such views are vulnerable to skeptical arguments which purport to use skeptical hypotheses true in nearby worlds. Consider for instance the hypothesis that "the particles belonging to the desk remain more or less unmoved but the material inside the desk unfolds in a bizarre enough way that the system no longer counts as a desk" (Hawthorne, 2004: 4–5). However unlikely such a hypothesis is to be true, it arguably is true in some nearby world in which I still believe that there's a desk in front of me. Even if a condition for knowledge in terms of safety from error undermines some skeptical arguments, the safety condition threatens to underwrite other skeptical arguments.

1.4. The Key Positions

Now that we have clarified and formulated the rival answers to our questions, we should consider how these views interact. To the best of my knowledge, Liberals in the literature have always been Mooreans, without allowing or considering that Liberals could be Rationalists.[15] Also, Conservatives have always been Rationalists, without allowing or considering that Conservatives may be Mooreans. I think that far too narrow a view has been taken of how these positions interact. In fact we need to consider four views (see Figure 5.1).

The slot for the Moorean Conservative is so far unoccupied, but it may well be taken in the future: consider philosophers' ongoing gentrification of logical space. The slot may still strike some readers as unoccupiable. A consequence of Conservatism is that Moore has justification to believe that he has hands only if he has independent justification to believe ¬BIV—so how could Moore's experience remain a source of justification to believe ¬BIV? To address this worry, we should clarify that the Moorean makes a claim about how one can increase one's justification to disbelieve skeptical hypotheses, and not yet a claim about how one can acquire one's justification to disbelieve skeptical hypotheses for the *first time*. Moore's experience arguably could increase his justification to believe ¬BIV without providing his first justification to believe ¬BIV.

On my view, the Moorean Conservative is doubly mistaken: both Liberalism and Rationalism are true. This space may also strike

	Moorean	**Rationalist**
Liberal	e.g. Pryor (2000, 2004) Davies (2004) Peacocke (2004)	The author
Conservative	Space available!	e.g. Wright (1985, 2000, 2002, 2003) Davies (1998, 2000, 2003)

Figure 5.1. The key positions

[15] More carefully: Liberals in the literature who have accepted standard closure principles have always been Mooreans. A denier of closure such as Dretske (1970) might count as a Liberal non-Moorean, since he would deny that Moore has justification to believe ¬BIV.

readers as unoccupiable. If Liberalism is true, what could stop Moore's experience from being a source of justification to believe ¬BIV? This concern, and others, will be addressed in sections 3.2 and 4. For now, I will simply stress that the question of how we have perceptual justification is a very different one from the question of how we have anti-skeptical justification. In particular, even if we enjoy independent justification to reject skeptical hypotheses about our experiences, our having that independent justification need not be what makes us have justification to believe the contents of our experiences. Analogously, even if all red things are disposed to look red, it does not follow that their being disposed to look red is what makes them red (Jackson and Pargetter, 1987). There is therefore room to combine a Rationalist story about how we have anti-skeptical justification with a Liberal story about how we have perceptual justification.

2. SUPPORTING LIBERALISM

Now that we have a clearer view of the positions available in the debate, I will defend my own overall view, starting with the defense of Liberalism itself. I have no knockdown argument for Liberalism, but I do have three reasons to believe it.

First, Liberalism is more plausible than Conservatism because the Conservative faces a challenge the Liberal does not: the Conservative is in a weaker position to endorse the claim that our perceptual beliefs are well-founded in addition to being propositionally justified. In order for a belief to be well-founded, I take it, one must hold the belief on the basis of what justifies it. Thus, if Conservatism is true, then our perceptual beliefs are well-founded only if they are based on our independent justifications to reject skeptical hypotheses about our experiences. It's hard to see that we actually do base our perceptual beliefs on any such independent justifications, whether or not it is in principle possible for us to do so. So the Conservative may be forced to accept the moderate skeptical claim that our actual perceptual beliefs are not well-founded, even if the Conservative can accept the anti-skeptical claim that our actual perceptual beliefs are propositionally justified. The Liberal faces no such problem. That's because the Liberal does not say that our perceptual beliefs are justified only in conjunction with our independent justification to hold other beliefs. A major advantage of Liberalism is that it is psychologically undemanding and straightforwardly compatible with the well-founded status of our perceptual beliefs.

Second, Liberalism is attractive because perceptual beliefs are among the best candidates to be immediately justified. I take it that, whether or not any version of foundationalism is true, at least some of our beliefs are not justified by their relations to any other beliefs. In particular, some of our beliefs about our own states of mind are immediately justified. Now, one might insist that none of our perceptual beliefs are immediately justified, even though some of our introspective beliefs are immediately justified. But I can see no reason to maintain this view. For instance, one might say that our perceptual beliefs are fallible and defeasible whereas our introspective beliefs are not. However, some of our immediately justified introspective beliefs—like our beliefs that we have such and such a belief, or such and such a desire—are fallible and defeasible as well. In general, we have introspective beliefs that are immediately justified, even though they are not better candidates than our perceptual beliefs to be immediately justified. Rather than concluding that neither perceptual beliefs nor introspective beliefs are immediately justified, we should instead accept that both perceptual beliefs and introspective beliefs are immediately justified. At the very least, we should not hold, as most Conservatives do, that denials of skeptical hypotheses are better candidates to be immediately justified than propositions about the external world such as the proposition that there is a hand.

Finally, we can support the Liberal view by considering judgments about cases. But we need to proceed with caution. I'll start by criticizing a tempting though unsuccessful argument before moving to a successful one.

Both arguments consider how one might answer the *perceptual question*: "why does Moore have any reason at all to believe that he has hands?"

The first argument focuses on the *pre-theoretical judgment*: "well, it looks to him as if he has hands." According to this argument, the pre-theoretical judgment is plausibly a correct answer to the perceptual question, and we should believe Liberalism rather than

Conservatism because the pre-theoretical judgment is plausibly a correct answer to the perceptual question.[16]

The first argument does not work. The problem with the argument is that both the Liberal and the Conservative can accept that the pre-theoretical judgment is a correct answer to our question. They do not dispute that Moore's experience justifies him in believing that he has hands. Their dispute is instead about whether Moore's experience justifies him in believing that he has hands only in conjunction with independent justification he has to disbelieve skeptical hypotheses. So the plausibility of the pre-theoretical judgment does not favor the Liberal view.

The better argument focuses squarely on a Conservative answer to the perceptual question: "well, it looks to him as if he has hands, and he has good reason to believe that he's not being deceived by an evil demon or anything like that." Call this the *Conservative judgment*.

At the very least, I take it that the Conservative judgment fails to be an intuitively correct answer to the question, so that there is no presumption in favor of the Conservative view. But I also take it that the Conservative judgment seems to be an incorrect answer to the perceptual question. Our question concerned why Moore has any reason to believe just that he has hands—I take the mention of positive reasons to disbelieve skeptical hypotheses to seem beside the point. When the question concerns why Moore has any reason to believe just that he has hands, the answer should not involve his having reason to reject skeptical hypotheses. That is why Liberalism has the best fit with our judgments about the case.[17]

I conclude that Liberalism is correct.

3. UNDERMINING THE CASE FOR CONSERVATISM

I will now argue for the Rationalist view about anti-skeptical justification. I will do so indirectly, by first setting out the main

[16] This argument is arguably that of Pryor (2000: 536), criticized by Schiffer (2004: 173–4), Steup (2004: 416–18), or Neta (2004). My second argument aims to avoid their criticisms.

[17] One might protest that, since Liberalism is not the negation of Conservatism, my considerations at best support rejecting Conservatism, and do not support accepting Liberalism. As mentioned earlier, I'm assuming that no intermediate position between Liberalism and Conservatism is true.

argument for the Conservative view about perceptual justification. The advantage of this approach is that it permits us to kill two birds with one stone: to see why the main case for the Conservative view fails, in addition to seeing why the Moorean rejection of skeptical hypotheses does not work.

3.1. *The Case for Conservatism*

The main case for Conservatism can usefully be stated as an inference to the best explanation.[18] The fact to be explained, for now just assuming that there is such a fact, is that Moore's inference is not a way for him to acquire a well-founded belief in ¬BIV. Let's say that Moore's inference *fails to transmit warrant* just in case it fails to be a way for him to acquire a well-founded belief in ¬BIV. The thought is that the Conservative is best placed to explain why Moore's inference fails to transmit warrant. The explanation can be stated in the following three steps:

(C) If Conservatism is true, then Moore's inference "begs the question," in the sense that Moore is justified in believing the premise HANDS only in virtue of having independent justification to believe the conclusion ¬BIV.

(D) If Moore's inference begs the question, then Moore's inference fails to transmit warrant.

So,

(E) If Conservatism is true, then Moore's inference fails to transmit warrant.

According to the Conservative, the argument just set out makes the best sense of what's wrong with Moore's inference. The usual way Liberals have responded to the argument is by denying that there is the phenomenon that the Conservative is trying to explain. Given that Liberals have been Mooreans, they have by no means conceded that Moore's inference fails to transmit warrant. Instead, they have at most conceded that there is indeed something wrong with the inference, and have tried to provide an alternative description and explanation of what is wrong with the inference. For example, they have emphasized that it is not a way of resolving justified or

[18] See Wright (1985: 436–7, 2000: 141–3, 153–6, 2002: 334–7, 342–5, 2003: 59–63); Davies (2003: 29–30); McKinsey (2003: 101).

perhaps even unjustified doubts about the conclusion (Pryor, 2004; Davies, 2004).

There are a couple of problems with the usual Liberal response to the argument for Conservatism. First, and perhaps most importantly, I take the Moorean Liberal response to be unmotivated: it's unclear why anyone should want to hold on to the view that Moore's inference transmits warrant. Second, the textbook examples of Moore's inference are not ones in which he performs it in order to resolve justified doubts or even unjustified doubts about whether BIV is true. The inference performed in the textbook examples seems defective all the same. However, given the usual Liberal diagnosis of the problem with the inference, it's unclear why anything should seem wrong with the inference except when it is performed in order to resolve justified or unjustified doubts about the conclusion. If Moore's inference isn't a means to X, it's not clear why we should take something to be wrong with his inference unless we take him to be trying to X. There might be a way to work out the usual Liberal explanation of what's wrong with Moore's inference, but it would be nice to have a simpler story.

In response to the first point, Liberals might think that they are committed to being Mooreans, and that we have reason to believe the Moorean view given that we have reason to believe the Liberal view. To undermine Moorean Liberalism, and to start to reveal what's wrong with the main case for Conservatism, we may highlight a bad argument for the conclusion that the Liberal must be a Moorean.

We can set out the line of argument as follows. First, and straightforwardly, if Liberalism is true, then Moore's inference does not "beg the question" in the stipulative sense discussed by the Conservative. Second, and much less straightforwardly, if Moore's inference does not beg the question, then it is a way for him to become justified in believing ¬BIV. So, if Liberalism is true, then Moore's inference is a way for him to become justified in believing ¬BIV.[19]

[19] There might be an example of the reasoning in recent work by Martin Davies, where he discusses a "TABLE" inference analogous to Moore's inference: "suppose that, as against Wright's view, there is no need for an antecedent warrant—not even an antecedent unearned warrant—for assuming, trusting, or believing that TABLE (III) is true. Suppose that the evidence described in TABLE (I) by itself

The key assumption of this argument is that Moore's inference fails to transmit warrant only if it "begs the question" in the Conservative's sense. If the assumption is false, and an inference can fail to transmit warrant without begging the question, then there is space for a Liberal who rejects the Moorean view. In the following section, I will show just how one can reject the Moorean view without betraying Liberalism.

3.2. *The Bayesian Explanation of Transmission Failure*

There is a clearer and better explanation of why, given the justification he has for believing HANDS, Moore's inference is not a way for him to become justified in believing ¬BIV. This explanation is itself consistent with the Liberal view (and the Conservative view).

We can set it out in two stages.

Stage 1

The aim of the first stage is to show that, when Moore responds to the evidence that it visually seems to him that he has hands (SEEMS), it is rational for him to *decrease* his confidence in ¬BIV, rather than to increase his confidence in ¬BIV.

We can use a probabilistic argument to establish the result.[20] The intuitive point is that, since the skeptical hypothesis about Moore's experience predicts that he has the experience, Moore ought to increase his confidence in the hypothesis in response to the experience.[21]

We can set out the argument in more detail by showing how Bayes's theorem, together with facts about the case, entails the

supports TABLE (II). Then, not only do I have an evidential warrant for believing TABLE (II), but also, by following through the *modus ponens* argument, I can gain—perhaps for the first time—a warrant for believing TABLE (III)" (2004: 237, see also 231 and 243).

[20] Variants of this line of argument can be found in White (2006), and Cohen (2005). Also relevant is Williamson (2004), Hawthorne (2004), Okasha (2004), and Schiffer (2004).

[21] As emphasized earlier, my target in the main text is the internalist Moorean. At least some externalist Mooreans will insist that, far from being predicted by the skeptical hypothesis, Moore's total evidence is in fact incompatible with the skeptical hypothesis.

needed result. Let's take BIV to be the relevant H, and SEEMS to be the relevant E.

First of all, by Bayes's theorem,

$$P(BIV|SEEMS) = [P(BIV)/P(SEEMS)] \times P(SEEMS|BIV)$$

Clearly, if Moore is a brain in a vat who merely appears to have hands, then he appears to have hands. Since BIV obviously entails SEEMS,

$$P(SEEMS|BIV) = 1$$

Thus,

$$P(BIV|SEEMS) = P(BIV)/P(SEEMS)$$

So far, we can see that the probability of BIV conditional on SEEMS is the prior probability of BIV divided by the prior probability of SEEMS. Thus, provided that the prior probability of BIV is greater than 0 and the prior probability of SEEMS is less than 1, the probability of BIV conditional on SEEMS will be greater than the prior probability of BIV. After all, if the conditions on the prior probabilities are satisfied, the probability of BIV conditional on SEEMS will be the result of multiplying the (non-zero) prior probability of BIV by a number greater than 1, yielding a product greater than the prior probability of BIV.

Since Moore wasn't certain that he would have an experience as of his hands,

$$P(SEEMS) < 1$$

Also, however confident Moore is permitted to be in ¬BIV, he is surely permitted to be even more confident in other propositions, such as the proposition that all triangles are triangles. So

$$P(BIV) > 0$$

Putting these pieces together, we have the result that

$$P(BIV|SEEMS) > P(BIV)$$

The final assumption we need is that Moore's degrees of confidence should track the facts about probability set out above. In particular, if you acquire the evidence E, when P(H | E)>P(H), you ought to increase your confidence in H.[22] Thus, when Moore responds to the evidence that he seems to have hands, he ought to increase his confidence in BIV, and decrease his confidence in ¬BIV itself.[23]

Stage 2

The aim now is to extend the result about the rational revision of Moore's partial beliefs to a result about the impact of his inference.

The first step is to link our considerations in terms of probability with considerations in terms of justification. It's plausible that, if Moore's experience provides him with positive justification to believe ¬BIV, then the rational response to his experience should be to *increase* his confidence in ¬BIV. However, the Bayesian explanation does not depend on that claim. It's even more plausible

[22] One might protest that we should not think about the revision of belief in response to experience as a matter of responding to evidence. After all, we arguably can rationally respond to an experience without having a belief that self-ascribes the experience. On this line of objection, Bayesian considerations don't tell us anything about how we should revise our beliefs in the light of our experiences. In response to the objection I should first stress that we often do have beliefs about what experiences we have, and that Bayesian considerations do tell us how we should revise our beliefs in the light of those beliefs which ascribe experiences to us (White, 2006). Second, having a belief that you have an experience shouldn't undermine the power of the experience to justify other beliefs. So our experiences should have the same justificatory powers in the cases where we don't believe we have them: the Bayesian considerations can tell us whether our experiences justify us in rejecting skeptical hypotheses.

[23] One interesting upshot is that we must be careful when stating a non-idealized sufficient condition for an experience to justify a belief. If one tries to identify such a condition, whether one is a Liberal or not, it's natural to start with the following template:

(Sufficiency*) Necessarily, if one has a visual experience with the content P, and no reason to believe any skeptical hypothesis about one's experience, and ——, then one has perceptual justification to believe P.

The problem with proposals along those lines is that the antecedent won't be satisfied by any ordinary subject. For any ordinary subject, the first conjunct of the antecedent is a sufficient condition for the falsehood of the second conjunct. To capture a non-vacuous sufficient condition for an ordinary subject to have perceptual justification to believe P, we will have to proceed along different lines. The phrase "reason to suspect" in the earlier Sufficiency is a placeholder for the solution to this problem.

that, if Moore's experience makes his justification to believe ¬BIV go up, then it can't be that his confidence in ¬BIV should instead go down.[24] Regardless of whether epistemic justification can be analyzed in terms of epistemic probability, presumably his justification to believe ¬BIV does not increase when the rational response to his evidence is for his confidence in ¬BIV to decrease.

The next step is to link the consideration about the epistemic force of Moore's experience with a more general consideration about the epistemic force of his inference. If Moore's inference is a way for him to become justified in believing ¬BIV, then in particular Moore's experience as of his hands must give him justification to believe ¬BIV, at least by giving him justification to believe HANDS. However, if the rational response to Moore's experience is to become less confident in ¬BIV, Moore's experience as of his hands does not even indirectly provide him with justification to believe ¬BIV. So Moore's inference is not a way for him to become justified in believing the conclusion.

In sum, there is a strong probabilistic argument for the conclusion that Moore's experience does not provide him with justification to believe ¬BIV. The conclusion entails that Moore's inference fails to transmit warrant.

To strengthen the argument, it's worth highlighting just how hard it is to hold on to the Moorean view. There are a couple of options to pursue. Both are unattractive. One option is to hold that, even though Moore's experience raises the probability of the skeptical hypothesis, Moore nevertheless gains justification to disbelieve the skeptical hypothesis. But it is obscure how, despite his experience's negative impact on his confidence in ¬BIV, his inference could still improve his position with respect to ¬BIV.[25] Another option is to deny that Moore's experience lowers the probability of ¬BIV. To develop this option in any satisfying way, the Moorean would have to provide a model of why Moore need not raise his confidence in BIV in response to his experience.[26] Here the Moorean owes us an

[24] See White (2006: n. 10). Compare Peacocke (2004: 114–15).

[25] One might say that Moore's experience as of his hands provides him with knowledge that he has hands, and that it is really his knowledge that he has hands which justifies him in believing ¬BIV. I explore this option in Silins (2005*b*); I reject the option for reasons given in Silins (2005*a*).

[26] Pryor (forthcoming *b*) and Weatherson (forthcoming) are relevant here.

independent motivation for the alternative model, with precedents in cases which are not problem cases for the view, and without new puzzle cases which are problem cases only for her view. A disadvantage of this approach is that it is revisionary: I take it to be a last resort.

I take it that we now have a clearer and more straightforward explanation of why Moore's inference fails to transmit warrant. The explanation does not appeal to the Conservative claim that Moore is justified in believing HANDS in virtue of having independent justification to believe ¬BIV. The Liberal can explain the failure of Moore's inference at least as well as the Conservative.

Before we proceed any further, it's worth while to consider what the Bayesian argument does and doesn't show. The argument does not show that our experiences fail to justify us in believing that there's an external world. That is because the argument applies only to hypotheses which predict our experiences. The hypothesis that there's no external world (understood strictly as the claim that there are no external concrete objects) doesn't predict our experiences, but rather predicts that we don't exist at all. So it may well be that our experiences do justify us in believing that there's an external world.

The Bayesian argument does apply to hypotheses which predict our experiences and are consistent with the contents of those experiences. Consider the hypothesis that one is hallucinating hands or that one is veridically hallucinating hands. Just as Moore's experience does not justify him in rejecting the claim that he misleadingly seems to have hands, it also does not justify him in rejecting the claim that he is hallucinating that he has hands, or that he is veridically hallucinating that he has hands.

Now, there are generic skeptical hypotheses that don't predict our experiences, yet still are incompatible with our ordinary beliefs (e.g. the hypothesis that one is a radically deceived BIV). Can our experiences justify us in rejecting such generic skeptical hypotheses? The Bayesian argument doesn't by itself answer that question, since it applies only to hypotheses which predict our experiences.

A Conservative might protest that Moorean inferences to the falsehood of generic skeptical hypotheses are just as bad as Moorean inferences to the falsehood of specific skeptical hypotheses, and insist that we should believe a generalized version of Conservatism which provides a uniform explanation of what's wrong with the inferences. On this line of thought, each inference is defective because it "begs the question" in the Conservative's sense.

The conservation objection is inconclusive. One possibility is that Moorean inferences against generic hypotheses succeed although Moorean inferences against specific skeptical hypotheses fail. Another possibility is that both inferences fail, although for different reasons. In the case of specific skeptical hypotheses, the problem is that our experiences have a negative impact on our credence that the skeptical hypotheses are false. In the case of generic skeptical hypotheses, the problem would be that our experiences fail to have any impact on our credence that the skeptical hypotheses are false. The Conservative needs to rule out both of these possibilities.

Let me now sum up what we have seen so far. By now I hope to have motivated the Liberal position, and to have undermined the core argument for the Conservative view, by providing an alternative explanation of why Moore's inference is not a way for him to become justified in believing ¬BIV. The best overall position is the one which holds that experiences are an immediate source of perceptual justification, while denying that experiences are a source of anti-skeptical justification. This position nevertheless does not give up on closure.[27] On my line of thought, the Conservative is indeed right in saying that Moore has independent justification to believe ¬BIV, just wrong in saying that Moore has perceptual justification to believe HANDS only because he has independent justification to believe ¬BIV.

4. RATIONALIST LIBERALISM

My overall position has not been considered in the literature, let alone endorsed. That may be because philosophers have taken

[27] More carefully: my position accepts JB-Closure. It's less clear what to say about closure principles formulated in terms of knowledge or well-founded belief. It may be that, if Moore knows that he has hands on the basis of his experience as of his hands, but believes ¬BIV only on the basis of deduction of HANDS, he has a badly-founded belief in ¬BIV, and fails to know ¬BIV. Here my views have evolved from those of Silins (2005*b*).

various objections to the view to be fatal. I'll now address what I take to be the two most threatening objections to the package.

4.1. Objection 1

According to the first objection, the Bayesian explanation set out in section 3.2 establishes that Liberalism is false, and not just that the Moorean view is false. According to the objector, that's because the explanation can be extended into an argument for the conclusion that, if Moore has perceptual justification to believe HANDS, then Moore has independent justification to believe ¬BIV. The thought is broadly that, when I give the Bayesian explanation of what's wrong with Moore's inference, I am playing with fire.

I'll first rehearse how one might argue for the stronger conclusion, remaining neutral about whether the further argument is sound.[28] I'll then show that, even if the stronger conclusion is established, it is compatible with my Liberal view.

The upshot of the Bayesian explanation was that SEEMS disconfirms or lowers the probability of ¬BIV. Thus,

$$P(\neg BIV) > P(\neg BIV|SEEMS)$$

Now, since HANDS entails ¬BIV,

$$P(\neg BIV|SEEMS) \geq P(HANDS|SEEMS)$$

Putting the two things together,

$$P(\neg BIV) > P(HANDS|SEEMS)$$

The upshot so far is that, if the probability of HANDS conditional on SEEMS is to be high, the probability of ¬BIV must be higher. Now, the objector may appeal to the claim that, if Moore's experience is

[28] See White (2006) or Okasha (2004). One might think that I'm already committed to the conclusion of the argument. I'm not. Since I accept JB-Closure, but reject Mooreanism, I accept that everyone who has perceptual justification to believe HANDS and *knows that HANDS is true only if ¬BIV is true* also has independent justification to believe that ¬BIV is true. This leaves open whether everyone who has perceptual justification to believe HANDS has independent justification to believe ¬BIV.

to justify him in believing HANDS, it must raise the probability of HANDS.[29] Thus, if Moore's experience provides him with justification to believe that he has hands, then Moore has justification to believe that he is not a BIV who merely seems to have hands. Given that it is not his experience which provides him with justification to believe ¬BIV, the upshot is that, if his experience provides him with justification to believe HANDS, then he has independent justification to believe ¬BIV.

It's tempting to think that the extension of the Bayesian explanation establishes Conservatism itself. The tempting thought is wrong. The Liberal view is compatible with the claim that Moore has perceptual justification to believe HANDS only if he has independent justification to believe ¬BIV. I'll now explain how these claims are compatible, and respond to the main worries one might have about their combination.

The key to my response lies in the proper understanding of the Liberal view. The central Liberal claim is that some of our perceptual beliefs are non-inferentially justified, that is, justified in a way which does not involve our having independent justification against this or that skeptical hypothesis. The Liberal does not yet say that any of our perceptual beliefs are justified despite our lack of independent justification against skeptical hypotheses. So the Liberal can allow that, whenever Moore has perceptual justification to believe HANDS, he also has independent justification to believe ¬BIV.[30]

There is of course a view on which one can be perceptually justified in believing some proposition P, while failing to have independent justification to disbelieve any skeptical hypothesis

[29] The current probabilistic argument, like the earlier one, needs to use a linking principle to get from claims in terms of probability to claims in terms of justification. It's worth highlighting that the current argument needs to use a stronger linking principle than the earlier argument. The current argument needs the claim that, if e provides one with justification to believe p, then e raises the probability of p. The earlier argument only needed the claim that, if e provides one with justification to believe p, then e does not raise the probability of not-p.

[30] There's a delicate question as to whether Moore's independent reason to believe ¬BIV enhances his degree of justification to believe that he has hands, without explaining why he has perceptual justification in the first place to believe that he has hands. It could be that Moore's experience by itself justifies him in believing to degree n that he has hands, and that Moore's experience plus his independent reason to reject BIV justify him in believing to some greater degree that he has hands. I won't try to settle such questions here.

about one's experience. Call this view *Strong Liberalism*. Strong Liberalism is more than a view about perceptual justification; it is also a view about anti-skeptical justification. But in holding that we have immediate justification for some of our perceptual beliefs, one need not also hold that we lack independent justification against skeptical hypotheses about our experiences. The extension of the probabilistic argument at best establishes that Strong Liberalism is false.[31]

It may be tempting to think that Liberalism entails Strong Liberalism. To support the claim that Liberalism does not entail Strong Liberalism, we can cast doubt on the claim that, if S is perceptually justified in believing that P only if S has independent justification to believe that Q, then S is not immediately justified in believing that P. Consider the trivial proposition that all hands are hands, which I always have justification to believe, provided that I have the concepts required to entertain the proposition. Given that I always have justification to believe the proposition, whenever my seeming to have hands justifies me in believing that I have hands, I will also have independent justification to believe that all hands are hands. However, my having independent justification to believe that all hands are hands is by no means something which makes my experience justify me in believing that I have hands. Even though I always have independent justification to believe that all hands are hands, we cannot yet infer that my perceptual belief is not immediately justified. My perceptual justification can be a sufficient condition for me to have some independent justification, without the independent justification threatening the immediate status of my perceptual justification. In particular, even if Strong Liberalism is false, it does not follow that Liberalism is false.

In fact, there are many cases where it seems perfectly possible both that (i) whenever I have one sort of justification I have another

[31] According to Pryor, "when you have an experience as of *p*'s being the case, you have a kind of justification for believing *p* that does not presuppose or rest on any other evidence or justification you may have. You could have this justification even if there were nothing else you could appeal to as ampliative, non-question-begging evidence that *p* is the case" (2000: 532). The first sentence of the passage nicely states the position we've been calling Liberalism (also relevant is Pryor 2004: 359). The second sentence goes further to state what I called Strong Liberalism. Strong Liberalism isn't required by Liberalism.

sort of justification and (ii) my having the second sort of justification is not what makes me have the first sort of justification. First, consider the contingent proposition that I exist. Presumably, whenever I have perceptual justification to believe that I have hands, I have a cogito-style independent justification to believe that I exist. But we should not infer from this that I am not immediately justified in believing that I have hands. Second, consider testimony and contingent propositions I don't always have justification to believe. It may well be that, whenever a source's testimony justifies me in believing that p, my experience plays some role in giving me justification to believe that the source testified that p. We cannot yet infer that my testimonial justification is to be explained in terms of my experiential justification (Burge, 1993). Third, consider introspection and contingent propositions I don't always have justification to believe. It might be that, whenever my experience justifies me in believing that p, something other than experience (inner sense, perhaps) justifies me in believing that I have the experience. We cannot yet infer from this that my experience does not immediately justify me in my belief. In sum, it seems perfectly possible for me to gain immediate justification to believe P from a source S even if, whenever I gain immediate justification to believe P from S, I have independent reason to believe Q.

One might concede that Liberalism does not entail Strong Liberalism, but still insist that once we have good reason to reject Strong Liberalism, we also have good reason to reject Liberalism. On this line of thought, it would be a bizarre coincidence if Liberalism were true and Moore had perceptual justification to believe HANDS only if he has independent justification to believe ¬BIV. Perhaps Conservatism makes the best sense of the possibility that Moore has perceptual justification to believe HANDS only if he has independent reason to believe ¬BIV, by assigning an explanatory link between Moore's having independent reason to believe ¬BIV and his having any perceptual justification at all. So perhaps we have good reason to believe that Conservatism is true if we have good reason to believe that Strong Liberalism is false.

In response to this objection, we can sketch an equally good explanation of the correlation between perceptual justification and independent justification. First, reconsider the view on which one has default entitlement to believe ¬BIV, i.e. one has justification to believe that BIV is false provided that one does not have reason to suspect that BIV is true. This view is merely a thesis about when one has independent justification, not a thesis about how one has it or about what further role it plays, so the Liberal is free to help herself to the view. Second, notice that all parties in the debate agree that perceptual justification is defeasible, and in particular that one has perceptual justification to believe HANDS only if one lacks reason to suspect that BIV is true. It follows that, if one has justification by default to believe ¬BIV, one has perceptual justification to believe that one has hands only if one has independent justification to believe ¬BIV. After all, the following argument is valid:

(F) If one's experience as of hands justifies one in believing that one has hands, then one lacks reason to suspect that BIV is true.

(G) If one lacks reason to suspect that BIV is true, then one has reason to believe ¬BIV.
Therefore,

(H) If one's experience as of hands justifies one in believing that one has hands, then one has reason to believe ¬BIV.

Here the question of whether one has the perceptual justification only because one has the independent justification is left entirely open. Indeed, it might be that my lacking reason to suspect that the skeptical hypothesis is true plays a role in explaining both my independent justification and my perceptual justification. In this scenario my perceptual justification and independent justification would both be upstream from a common cause. In any case, my having default justification to believe ¬BIV is enough to explain the correlation between perceptual justification and independent justification, without requiring any appeal to Conservatism. It needn't be a bizarre coincidence that I have immediate justification to believe that I have hands only if I have independent reason to believe ¬BIV.

In sum, the extended Bayesian argument may or may not establish that Strong Liberalism is false, but it does not establish that Liberalism is false. The Liberal is free to accept that, whenever Moore's experience justifies him in believing that he has hands, he also has independent reason to believe ¬BIV. In doing so, the Liberal still leaves room open for moderate foundationalism, and still reveals that the standard Conservative diagnosis of what's wrong with Moore's inference is wrong.

4.2. *Objection 2*

My combination of Liberalism with Rationalism has no distinctive story about how one might be justified in rejecting skeptical hypotheses. I instead hold that some story (or stories) given by the Conservative will be correct. One might protest that the Rationalist Liberal has nothing distinctive to say to the skeptic, and that we have no reason to believe the view given that it has nothing distinctive to say to the skeptic.

In response to this objection, I'll first illustrate that any Liberal does have something to say to the skeptic, albeit not very much. I'll then try to divorce the question of whether Rationalist Liberalism is true from the question of how to respond to skeptical arguments.

There is at least one skeptical argument which any version of Liberalism undermines. It's no surprise that Liberalism undermines the argument, since the argument has a premise which is plainly inconsistent with the Liberal view. We can state the argument roughly as follows (relying on Pryor, 2000: 530–2):

(I) If Moore has perceptual justification to believe that he has hands, then part of what makes him have perceptual justification to believe that he has hands is that he has independent justification to believe that he is not a BIV who merely seems to have hands.

(J) Moore does not have independent justification to believe that he is not a BIV who merely seems to have hands.

So,

(K) Moore does not have perceptual justification to believe that he has hands.

We can think of this argument as the *Conservative* argument*, since its first premise is a weakening of Conservatism designed to be compatible with skepticism. If there is a presumption in favor of Liberalism—indeed, if there simply fails to be a presumption against the view—this skeptical argument is not threatening until it is supplemented with a good argument for Conservatism*. We have yet to see any such case. So the Liberal does have something to say in response to the Conservative* argument.

The Liberal has something to say to the skeptic about perceptual justification, but not very much. If the skeptic is to exploit the premise that Moore does not have independent justification to disbelieve ¬BIV, she of course does not need to use any claim as strong as Conservatism* to derive the conclusion that Moore does not have perceptual justification to believe that he has hands. As far as the validity of the skeptical argument is concerned, the proposal of a necessary condition for perceptual justification will do:

(L) If Moore has perceptual justification to believe that he has hands, then he has independent justification to believe that he is not a BIV who merely seems to have hands.

(J) Moore does not have independent justification to believe that he is not a BIV who merely seems to have hands.

So,

(k) Moore does not have perceptual justification to believe that he has hands.

Liberalism does not by itself offer any response to the further skeptical argument.

One might protest that, even though the new argument uses a claim weaker than Conservatism*, the first premise of the new argument can be motivated only by appealing to Conservatism* itself (Pryor, 2000: n. 33). This response is mistaken. As we saw in the discussion of the previous objection, there is a straightforward probabilistic argument for the first premise of the new argument. Since the new skeptical argument uses something weaker than Conservatism* as a premise, and also does not use any premise which is essentially motivated by Conservatism*, the new argument is more threatening than the Conservative* argument. We have yet to settle the question of whether the new argument is successful. Since its premises can be motivated independently of Conservatism*, however, the Liberal has nothing distinctive to say about where flaws in the argument might lie. Liberalism by no means provides the key to skepticism about perceptual justification.[32]

[32] Compare Pryor's conclusion after his discussion of what is in effect the Conservative* argument: "What I have done is offer a plausible and intuitive account of perceptual justification that *we* can accept. I have also shown how, once we accept this account of perceptual justification, the skeptic's best argument is revealed to rest on a false principle." (2000: 541)

Even though Liberalism indeed fails to solve a hard skeptical problem, we should not conclude that we have no reason to believe the view. One point is that, given the diversity of skeptical arguments, we have reason to expect that no one-size-fits-all strategy will succeed. Thus, if there is a skeptical argument to which an epistemological view does not supply a response, that is by itself no failing of the view. Another point is that, in order to motivate a view, it is never sufficient just to say that it is in tension with a skeptical claim. If *all* one says to support a claim is that it is incompatible with a premise of a skeptical argument, or that it is incompatible with some further premise for the skeptical premise, the anti-skeptical claim is so far unsupported. One could always respond to the skeptical argument by denying another claim on which the argument depends.

In order to assess whether we have good reason to believe Liberalism, we should not consider what the Liberal has to say to the skeptic. We should instead consider what it takes for our perceptual beliefs to be well-founded, which beliefs are the best candidates for immediate justification, and so on.

5. CONCLUSION

If Conservatism is true, then Moore's inference begs the question, in the sense that his independent justification for the conclusion is part of what justifies him in believing the premise. Given that Liberalism is true, Moore's inference does not, by begging the question, fail to be a way of becoming justified in believing its conclusion.

It is too quick to conclude that, if Liberalism is true, then Moore's inference is a way for him to become justified in believing its conclusion. Begging the question is arguably sufficient for the inference to be epistemically deficient, but begging the question is not necessary for the inference to be deficient. I hope to have shown that Liberalism is true despite that, for probabilistic reasons, Moore's inference fails to be a way for him to become justified in believing its conclusion. On my view, Liberalism should be pried apart from the Moorean story about how we are justified in believing that radical skeptical hypotheses are false.

What does Liberalism tell us, if it does not provide any distinctive story about rejecting skeptical hypotheses? To see why the view is important, we need to set aside skeptical arguments about whether we have perceptual justification, and turn our attention to the task of explaining *how* we have perceptual justification. After all, we arguably know that we have perceptual justification, regardless of what a skeptic might try to say to convince us that we don't. And we would be overly impressed with skepticism if we thought that, as far as perceptual justification is concerned, the central question is whether we have any.

Our experiences in one way or another provide us with justification for our beliefs, but how exactly do our experiences do that? According to the Conservative, there is far more to perceptual justification than meets the eye: our experiences justify our beliefs only in conjunction with our having positive reason to disbelieve skeptical hypotheses about our experiences. This view rules out a moderate foundationalist story about the role of our perceptual beliefs in our overall economy of empirical beliefs. What Liberalism tells us is no more and no less than that the Conservative is wrong. By insisting that we have non-inferentially justified perceptual beliefs, Liberalism leaves open space for the foundationalist story, without entailing it. What Liberalism secures is that, despite the failure of our experiences to underwrite a Moorean response to the skeptic, our experiences are a source of justification that is basic.

REFERENCES

Bonjour, Laurence (1985) *The Structure of Empirical Knowledge* (Oxford).

—— and Ernest Sosa (2003) *Epistemic Justification: Internalism vs. Externalism, Foundations vs. Virtues* (Malden).

Brewer, Bill (2006) 'Perception and Content', *European Journal of Philosophy*, 14: 165–81.

Burge, Tyler (1993) 'Content Preservation', *Philosophical Review*, 102: 457–88.

—— (2003) 'Perceptual Entitlement', *Philosophy and Phenomenological Research*, 67: 503–48.

Cohen, Stewart (1999) 'Contextualism, Skepticism, and the Structure of Reasons', *Philosophical Perspectives*, 13: 57–89.

—— (2000) 'Contextualism and Skepticism', *Philosophical Issues*, 10: 94–107.

Cohen, Stewart (2002) 'Basic Knowledge and the Problem of Easy Knowledge', *Philosophy and Phenomenological Research*, 65: 309–29.

—— (2005) 'Why Basic Knowledge is Easy Knowledge', *Philosophy and Phenomenological Research*, 70: 417–30.

Davies, Martin (1998) 'Externalism, Architecturalism, and Epistemic Warrant', in C. Wright, B. C. Smith, and C. Macdonald (eds.), *Knowing our own Minds* (Oxford), 321–61.

—— (2000) 'Externalism and Armchair Knowledge', in P. Boghossian and C. Peacocke (eds.), *New Essays on the A Priori* (Oxford), 384–414.

—— (2003) 'The Problem of Armchair Knowledge', in S. Nuccetelli (ed.), *New Essays on Semantic Externalism and Self-Knowledge* (Cambridge Mass.), 23–56.

—— (2004) 'Epistemic Entitlement, Warrant Transmission and Easy Knowledge', *Aristotelian Society Supplementary Volume*, 78: 213–45.

—— (forthcoming) 'Two Purposes of Arguing and Two Epistemic Projects'.

Dretske, Frederick (1970) 'Epistemic Operators', *Journal of Philosophy*, 67: 1007–23.

Feldman, Richard, and Earl Conee (1985) 'Evidentialism', *Philosophical Studies*, 48: 15–34.

Field, Harty (2000) 'A Prioricity as an Evaluative Notion', in P. Boghossian and C. Peacocke (eds.), *New Essays on the A Priori* (Oxford), 117–49.

—— (2005) 'Recent Debates about the A Priori', *Oxford Studies in Epistemology*, 1: 69–88.

Fumerton, Richard (1996) *Metaepistemology and Skepticism* (Lanham, Md.).

Hawthorne, John (2004) *Knowledge and Lotteries* (Oxford).

Huemer, Michael (2001) *Skepticism and the Veil of Perception* (Lanham, Md.).

Jackson, Frank, and Robert Pargetter (1987) 'An Objectivist's Guide to Subjectivism about Colour', *Revue Internationale de Philosophie*, 41: 127–41.

Jenkins, Carrie (forthcoming) 'Entitlement and Rationality', *Synthese*.

McKinsey, Michael (2003) 'Transmission of Warrant and Closure of Apriority', in S. Nuccetelli (ed.), *New Essays on Semantic Externalism and Self-Knowledge* (Cambridge, Mass.).

Markie, Peter (2005) 'Easy Knowledge', *Philosophy and Phenomenological Research*, 70: 406–16.

Neta, Ram (2004) 'Perceptual Evidence and the New Dogmatism', *Philosophical Studies*, 119: 199–214.

Okasha, Samir (2004) 'Wright on the Transmission of Support: A Bayesian Analysis', *Analysis*, 64: 139–46.

Peacocke, Christopher (2004) *The Realm of Reason* (Oxford).
Pollock, John (1974) *Knowledge and Justification* (Princeton, NJ).
Pritchard, Duncan (2005) *Epistemic Luck* (Oxford).
Pryor, James (2000) 'The Skeptic and the Dogmatist', *Noûs*, 34: 517–49.
—— (2001) 'Highlights of Recent Epistemology', *British Journal of Philosophy of Science*, 52: 95–124.
—— (2004) 'What's Wrong with Moore's Argument?', *Philosophical Issues*, 14: 349–78.
—— (forthcoming *a*) 'When Warrant Transmits'.
—— (forthcoming *b*) 'Uncertainty and Undermining'.
Schiffer, Stephen (2004) 'Vagaries of Justified Belief', *Philosophical Studies*, 119: 161–84.
Siegel, Susanna (2006) 'Which Properties are Represented in Perception?', in T. Gendler and J. Hawthorne (eds.), *Perceptual Experience* (Oxford), 481–503.
Silins, Nicholas (2005*a*) 'Deception and Evidence', *Philosophical Perspectives*, 19: 375–404.
—— (2005*b*) 'Transmission Failure Failure', *Philosophical Studies*, 126: 71–102.
Sosa, Ernest (1999) 'How to Defeat Opposition to Moore', *Philosophical Perspectives*, 13: 141–54.
Steup, Matthias (2004) 'Internalist Reliabilism', *Philosophical Issues*, 14: 403–25.
—— (forthcoming) 'Are Mental States Luminous?'.
Vogel, Jonathan (1990) 'Cartesian Skepticism and Inference to the Best Explanation', *Journal of Philosophy*, 87: 658–66.
—— (2000) 'Reliabilism Leveled', *Journal of Philosophy*, 97: 602–23.
—— (2005) 'The Refutation of Skepticism', in M. Steup and E. Sosa (eds.), *Contemporary Debates in Epistemology* (Malden), 72–84.
Weatherson, Brian (forthcoming) 'In Defense of a Dogmatist'.
White, Roger (2006) 'Problems for Dogmatism', *Philosophical Studies*, 131: 525–57.
Williamson, Timothy (2000) *Knowledge and its Limits* (Oxford).
—— (2004) 'Skepticism', in F. Jackson and M. Smith (eds.), *The Oxford Companion to Analytical Philosophy* (Oxford).
Wright, Crispin (1985) 'Facts and Certainty', *Proceedings of the British Academy*, 71: 429–72.
—— (2000) 'Cogency and Question-Begging: Some Reflections on McKinsey's Paradox and Putnam's Proof', *Philosophical Issues*, 10: 140–63.
—— (2002) '(Anti)-Sceptics Simple and Subtle: Moore and McDowell', *Philosophy and Phenomenological Research*, 65: 330–48.

Wright, Crispin (2003) 'Some Reflections on the Acquisition of Warrant by Inference', in S. Nuccetelli (ed.), *New Essays on Semantic Externalism and Self-Knowledge* (Cambridge), 57–78.

—— (2004) 'Warrant for Nothing (and Foundations for Free?)', *Aristotelian Society Supplementary Volume*, 78: 167–212.

—— (forthcoming) 'The Perils of Dogmatism', in S. Nuccetelli and G. Seay (eds.), *Themes from G. E. Moore: New Essays in Epistemology and Ethics* (Oxford).

SYMPOSIUM

6. Rational Credence and the Value of Truth

Allan Gibbard

Belief aims at truth—or so it is said, and there must be something right in the saying.[1] Belief, though, can't aim literally; it's *we* who aim. We aim, moreover, in acting—when we shoot an arrow, say, or more broadly, whenever we act to try to bring something about. Believing isn't an action; we can't believe at will. In some extended, metaphorical sense, perhaps, belief does aim at truth. Understanding this sense might even offer a philosophical key to belief. It might in particular tell us something important about rationality in belief. To employ the key, though, we'll have to understand what literally might underwrite this obscure dictum that belief aims at truth.

True belief is useful, we all know: armed with true beliefs, we can most effectively pursue our goals. A youth stands facing two doors; behind one, he has learned, is a lady to marry, and behind the other a ravenous tiger. If he knows the truth as to which door conceals the tiger, he can keep from being its prey. Otherwise, he takes his chances. True belief, then, has value as a guide to action, in pursuit of survival, wedlock, and a host of other goals that a person might have.

Sheer usefulness for such ulterior purposes, though, is not the only way that truth in belief can matter. We seek the truth, sometimes, purely to know it. Science at its purest is a search for important truths just to discover and have them. Indeed it's this disinterested search for truth, perhaps, that underlies rationality in belief of a special kind, a rationality that is not pragmatic but purely epistemic.

[1] Velleman (2000) examines the claim "Belief aims at the truth," and offers a sense in which he thinks that it does. His interpretation of the dictum is quite different from the one I develop in this paper, though I think that his version and mine are compatible.

I share this last intuition, but I cannot make it work. There is such a thing as purely epistemic rationality, I accept, and it may sometimes contrast with pragmatic desirability in belief, with what it's rational to want to believe. (The man with indications that his wife is having an affair is a stock example; it may be epistemically rational for him to believe that she is, but rational for him to *want* not to believe it.) And epistemic rationality does tie in closely with the value of truth as a guide to bringing about other things of value by our actions, such as wealth or happiness—with its "guidance value" as I'll call it. It has little to do, though, I am forced to conclude, with wanting truth for its own sake. Nothing about a goal of truth for its own sake leads to epistemic rationality as we know it.

1. TRUTH AS THE AIM

The "value of truth" is presumably the value of having true beliefs. It must also, it seems clear, include the disvalue of having beliefs that are false. Otherwise we could maximize our array of true beliefs just by believing everything whatsoever, true or false. It's these two kinds of value that are specifically epistemic, and that inform epistemic rationality. Belief in some sense aims at truth, but mostly, deliberate action isn't how we come to beliefs. If we are epistemically rational, we respond to our evidence directly with beliefs that are rational in light of that evidence. We don't will to believe with the aim of believing truly, as the youth might will to open the door on the left with the aim of finding the lady.

Here, though, is a way we might charitably interpret the claim that epistemically rational belief "aims at truth"—a way that will allow us to ask whether the aim of belief is truth for the sake of truth. Generally, to be sure, a person doesn't believe things by setting out to believe them. Still, we can try asking what it is to aim at anything in general, to have aims like avoiding tigers. If a person is epistemically rational, we can then hypothesize, then it is *as if* she chose her beliefs with the aim of believing truths and shunning falsehoods. She doesn't literally set out to believe truths, the way she might set out to get a high score on a test by intentionally putting down the right answers. But it is as if she did: it is as if she aimed at truth and away from falsehood in her beliefs in the same way one aims at any other goal.[2]

How, though, could this be? What the youth does with the aim of evading the tiger will depend on what he believes. If he believes the tiger lurks behind the door to the right, he aims to avoid it by going to the left. Suppose, then, he wants to believe the truth and disbelieve all falsehood as to where the tiger lurks. If he believes that the tiger lurks to the right, he'll pursue his aim, if he can, by believing that it lurks to the right. This aim, it seems, has a strange property: no matter what he believes, it will be as if he had chosen his belief with the aim of believing the truth. He may of course lack all belief as to where the tiger lurks, but in that case, he would be at a loss for what to believe in pursuit of believing the truth, just as he is at a loss for which door to open in pursuit of evading the tiger. The aim of believing the truth, then, is empty in a way: if he thinks he knows what to believe in pursuit of it, that's what he already believes.

To aim at the truth is to guide one's beliefs by the evidence, we might try saying. This too, though, threatens to be empty. A person aims in light of what, rightly or wrongly, he *regards* as evidence. The youth aims to evade the tiger, and if he mistakes a datum for evidence as to where the tiger is, that's what he'll guide his actions by. What is it, then, we must ask, to regard a datum as evidence? Isn't it to adjust one's beliefs accordingly—or to perhaps to think that so adjusting them is warranted? If so, then to be responsive, by one's own lights, to the evidence may require no more than that one respond to data coherently, in a way that doesn't discredit

[2] Velleman (2000) argues that a mental system doesn't count as forming beliefs unless its function is to produce true representations. He takes the dictum as covering all belief, not just belief that is fully rational. "To believe a proposition is to accept it with the aim of thereby accepting a truth" (p. 251). One's acceptance, that is to say, "is regulated, either by the subject's intentions or by some other mechanisms in ways designed to ensure that it is true" (p. 254). His term 'acceptance' covers not just beliefs but fantasies that motivate such things as children's make-believe, talking to oneself, and shaking one's fist at the man on the television screen. If the function in question is biological, then, as Nishi Shah argues, no normative consequences are strictly entailed (2003: 460–5). In this paper, I offer a normative interpretation of the dictum. My goal is not to interpret the dictum in the best way for all purposes, but to inquire whether we can explain epistemic rationality as somehow a matter of aiming at truth intrinsically. In adopting an interpretation in pursuit of this goal, I follow Joyce (1998) in many respects.

itself. We'll need to understand what such coherence consists in, and if the injunction to heed the evidence helps in this, we need to discover how.

In another way, to be sure, the aim of truth is far from empty. The youth would take great efforts, if he could, to learn the truth of where the tiger lurks. Experiment, research, and deliberate observation are ways of acquiring true beliefs by seeking out further evidence. Often the costs are worth paying, and this shows that true belief is often of value, in a sense that has genuine import.[3] The value of truth as it is treated in this paper is highly relevant to questions of whether to bear a cost to acquire true beliefs, but the question I chiefly explore is a different one: Whether when we form our beliefs rationally, with no chance to seek out further evidence, it is as if we were forming beliefs at will with the aim of truth.

Grant, then, that we can't come to true beliefs by pulling on our own epistemic bootstraps, taking it as a real question what to believe in pursuit of truth. Aiming at truth in one's beliefs must have a strong element of circularity. Still, if the claim that belief aims at truth verges on being empty, isn't it at least true? With an epistemically rational person, it is as if, by her own lights, she were aiming at truth. This dictum might, indeed, offer a minimal test for epistemic rationality. A way of forming beliefs should at least satisfy this condition: if one forms beliefs that way, it will be as if one were, by one's own lights, forming beliefs voluntarily with the aim of believing truths and not falsehoods. Such a way of forming beliefs we might call *immodest*: it views itself as a way of acquiring truths and avoiding falsehoods. Immodesty is a minimal requirement, it might seem, on ways of forming beliefs. Absent it, after all, belief doesn't even aim at truth by its own lights. An empty virtue it may be, but indispensable.[4]

Immodesty will be my topic, and my puzzle will be this: If we look to belief for the sake of guidance, we'll indeed find that epistemically rational ways of forming beliefs are immodest. If instead, though,

[3] See Raiffa (1968: 105–7 and ch. 7) on "buying" information, and Loewer (1993: 271–8) on the value of experiments. Horwich discusses the value of truth in *Truth* (1998); see pp. 44–6 on the instrumental value of truth and pp. 62–3 on its intrinsic value.

[4] The term "immodest" and the thought behind it are drawn from David Lewis (1971).

we look to truth's intrinsic value, to the pure scientific aim of truth for its own sake, immodesty eludes us.

All this will, of course, need elucidating. For epistemic rationality I'll assume a standard Bayesian account, and I'll draw on a background of Bayesian decision theory. Central to my argument will be theorems in a 1989 article by statistician Mark Schervish.[5]

2. PARTIAL CREDENCE

I have been taking belief, so far, as a matter of all or nothing. If the youth, though, formed some full belief as to where the tiger lurks, he would be rash. A full belief that the tiger is to the right might by luck be true, for all he knows, but then too it might be false. Rationality in belief often requires doubt; it demands some partial degree of credence. We need, then, to ask a further question. Suppose that an investigator, faced with her evidence, forms degrees of credence in a way that is epistemically rational. She doesn't, to be sure, form her partial beliefs at will, intentionally, in pursuit of a goal. Still, isn't it as if she did? Isn't it as if she somehow rationally chose her degrees of credence with the aim of truth in belief?

We are blessed with ample accounts of what it is to pursue a goal in light of one's degrees of credence. (I'll follow David Lewis and speak of a degree of credence, for short, as a *credence*.) The classic derivations in this vein stem from Ramsey and Savage, with Hammond's perhaps the most general and complete.[6] I don't in this paper try to reassess the arguments for this classical account of the rational pursuit of goals under uncertainty. The account is controversial, and I won't comment on the points in dispute. What I'll ask is this: Suppose the classic account of expected utility maximization does indeed describe the rational pursuit of goals under uncertainty. Then can we say that belief aims at truth? I interpret this as before: When a person forms her credences with epistemic rationality, is it *as if* she were choosing her credences voluntarily, rationally aiming, in light of her credences, at truth in those very credences? Is an epistemically rational way of forming credences "immodest" in this sense?

[5] Schervish (1989), esp. theorem 4.2, p. 1861.

[6] Ramsey (1931); Savage (1954); Hammond (1988).

More needs to be said to give a clear sense to this question. A complex of goals, on the classic account, is represented by a utility function. This function summarizes how one trades off one goal against another when one can't reach all of them with certainty. When credence is partial, a matter of degree, what utility function, we can ask, would characterize having the pure goal of truth in one's beliefs? Full credence in truths is sought and full credence in falsehoods shunned, to be sure—but ordinarily, one doesn't fully know how to achieve this aim. What of intermediate degrees of credence? In the case of a truth, if truth is what the agent seeks in her credences, then in her estimation, it seems, the higher the credence the better. The closer to full belief a credence is, we could say, the more "accurate" it is, and what the agent seeks is, in this sense, credences that are accurate.[7] For a falsehood, correspondingly, the lower the credence the better; the closer it is to a fully accurate credence of zero.

This is what we can draw from our intuitive concept of purely seeking truth in one's credences. Suppose, in particular, that only one claim is at issue: say, the claim that modern Europeans descend at least in part from the Neanderthals. (Call this claim S.) Take an investigator who values nothing but the accuracy of her degree of credence in this claim. The states which have greater or lesser utility in her eyes have two components: whether the claim is true or false, and her credence in the claim. We could represent her utilities, then, with a function $u(\mathbf{v},x)$, where $\mathbf{v}$ is a truth value $\mathbf{t}$ or $\mathbf{f}$, and x is a possible credence, a real number with $0 \leq x \leq 1$. More conveniently, we can use two separate functions. Let $g_1(x) = u(\mathbf{t}, x)$, the value, in the believer's eyes, of having a credence of x in claim S where S turns out to be true. Let $g_0(x) = u(\mathbf{f}, x)$, the value, in her eyes, of having a credence of x in claim S where S turns out to be false. That she values truth and truth alone in her credence in S, then, seems to consist in satisfying this condition:

[7] Joyce (1998: 586–97), speaks of the "gradational accuracy" of a degree of credence. Maher (2002: 79) criticizes Joyce's "Norm of Gradational Accuracy," in part because it requires a standard of accuracy. Here I simply require that one who "aims at truth" maximize expected accuracy on some specification or other of the standard. Maher advocates looking to a concern to accept truths and not falsehoods for the tie of credence to truth. On this score I have sided with Joyce, but I won't pursue the debate further.

Condition $\mathcal{T}$: Function $g_1(x)$ increases strictly monotonically with x, and function $g_0(x)$ decreases strictly monotonically with x.

In other words, she thinks that in case S is true, the higher her credence in S the better, and that in case S is false, the lower her credence in S the better.

This allows, though, that there are many somewhat different ways a person could value truth in her credences. She could equally value every 1 percent increase in her credence in a truth and every 1 percent decrease in her credence in a falsehood. Alternatively, for a truth, she could be especially concerned with approaching full certainty: she might value the difference between 89 percent certainty and 99 percent certainty far more than that between 50 percent and 60 percent certainty. These differences will be represented by the functions g_1 and g_0: in the first case the functions are both linear, in that for some constants $k > 0$, a_1, and a_0,

$$g_1(x) = a_1 + kx; \quad g_0(x) = a_0 - kx.$$

In the second case, we have

$$g_1(.99) - g_1(.89) \gg g_1(.60) - g_1(.50).$$

Either such function, it seems, fits the intuitive content we have teased out of the notion of exclusive concern with the truth. They indicate different emphases that such a concern might adopt—an emphasis, say, on certainty verses its lack, as opposed to equal concern with each possible 1 percent difference in credence.

Return now to our hypothesis that "belief aims at truth." With all or nothing belief, the hypothesis threatened to be empty; what happens now? When a person forms her credences with epistemic rationality, our hypothesis will now run, it is as if she were voluntarily chosing her credences with the pure aim of truth—that is to say, to maximize the expected accuracy or her credence. Accuracy we characterize with two functions g_1 and g_0 that satisfy Condition $\mathcal{T}$.

I begin with the good news: At least one variant of "aiming at truth" does fit this hypothesis. This result is well known; the utility function in question is the "Brier score" explored by George

Brier in 1950. Later, though, comes more distrubing news: Most variants of "aiming at truth" fail to fit this hypothesis. What, we can then ask, characterizes the subclass of variants that do fit it? A theorem of Schervish gives the answer: the utility functions that fit the hypothesis turn out to be the ones that could constitute a measure of *guidance value:* the value of an array of credences as a guide to choice in pursuit of other values—money, love, or succoring humanity, say. Intrinsic concern with truth, so far as I can discover, has nothing to do with what makes this subclass special.

3. CREDENCE-ELICITING FUNCTIONS

The rational believer of our inquiry has an array of credences formed with epistemic rationality on the basis of evidence. We ask whether those are the credences that, in light of her evidence, she most prefers to have, the ones that she would choose if she could choose her credences at will. Her only concern is, in some sense, how accurate her credences are; the emphases she places on various different aspects of accuracy are indicated by our two functions g_1 and g_0.

Another question of the same mathematical form has been much investigated. (I follow Joyce in pursuing the parallel.[8]) Beginning with Brier, a number of writers have asked what incentives would elicit an expert's true credences—a weather forecaster's credences, say, in rain for tomorrow.[9] The resulting payment to the expert, the idea is, can serve as an index of the quality or success of the expert's reported credences, how "close to the truth" those credences come. To aim to maximize such an index, we can say, would be to aim at truth in one's beliefs.

We engage as an expert informant, then, a *homo economicus* who has no intrinsic concern with reporting to us honestly. What incentives can we give him to reveal to us his genuine credences? What we pay him will depend on the credences he reports and the actual truth of the matter. Where x is his reported credence in a contingency S (rain tomorrow, say), we pay him (in utility) $g_1(x)$

[8] Joyce (1998). [9] Brier, (1950) and others noted below.

if S turns out to be true and $g_0(x)$ if S turns out to be false. Since this takes the same mathematical form as our own problem of what sort of intrinsic concern with the truth would make one want the credences one has, I'll say that our problem is to characterize pairs of functions g_1 and g_0 that are *credence-eliciting*.

The Brier score is given by the following credence-eliciting pair of functions. For convenience, define $\overline{x} = 1 - x$. Then we let

$$g_1(x) = 1 - \overline{x}^2; \quad g_0(x) = 1 - x^2.$$

(Define the believer's *inaccuracy* as the distance of her credence from full accuracy. Complete accuracy would be credence 0 for S false and 1 for S true; the inaccuracy of a credence in S is thus x for S false and $\overline{x}$ for S true. The Brier score penalizes the believer by the square of her inaccuracy.)

We can now ask whether, if a rational believer maximizes the expected value of her Brier score, she will choose, in prospect, the credences she already has. Let her actual credence $\rho(S)$ in S be α. What credence x would she choose to have, if she could? Her expected Brier score is

$$\alpha(1 - \overline{x}^2) + \overline{\alpha}(1 - x^2)$$

As Brier showed, this is maximized when $x = \alpha$, so that one most prefers the credence one has.[10]

Consider, though, a different pair of functions g_1 and g_0 that satisfy Condition $\mathcal{T}$ and so indicate a way in which one might be concerned to to minimize a gauge of the the inaccuracy of one's credence. Suppose I aim to minimize my expected inaccuracy, rather than its square, so that for me,

$$g_1(x) = -\overline{x}; \quad g_0(x) = -x.$$

My expected utility for having credence x, then, is

$$\alpha(-\overline{x}) + \overline{\alpha}(-x).$$

[10] Her expected utility is $u(x) = 1 - \alpha\overline{x}^2 - \overline{\alpha}x^2$. The first derivative is $2\alpha\overline{x} - 2\overline{\alpha}x = 0$ for $u(x)$ maximal, which holds just for $x = \alpha$.

I maximize this by making my beliefs extreme in their certitude: if $a > 1/2$, then my best bet is setting $x = 1$, and if $a < 1/2$, then my best bet is setting $x = 0$. If my intrinsic concern with truth took this form, I would rationally advance this concern, if I could, by moving to an epistemically rash certitude, by jumping to whichever conclusion I found even slightly more plausible.

We can ask, then, what form an exclusive, intrinsic concern of truth must take for epistemic rationality to be prospectively the best policy. Equivalently, what functions are credence-eliciting? Here is the answer in a form that ties in with lessons about "guidance value" that I draw later. Let h be any smooth, increasing function of x. Then we can let g_1 and g_0 be functions that satisfy these conditions:

$$g_1'(x) = \bar{x}h'(x), \qquad (1_1)$$

$$g_0'(x) = -xh'(x). \qquad (1_0)$$

Smooth functions g_1 and g_0 are credence-eliciting, the theorem is, just in case there exists some smooth, increasing function h such that (1_1) and (1_0) obtain.[11]

The function h turns out to be of special significance: its slope indicates the urgency the believer ascribes to getting credences right, by her lights, in the vicinity of x. If, for instance, the believer is especially concerned with distinguishing degrees of near certainty, then the slope of function h will be especially great for credences near one. That's a story for later, though. For now, the two points to note are these. First, many different, non-equivalent payment schemes turn out to be credence-eliciting. Many different balances of concern turn out to be characterized, for some smooth increasing function h, by equations (1_1) and (1_0), and thus to engender immodesty. In Figure 6.1 there are a few examples. of the pairs of functions g_1, g_0 that are generated by various functions h.

[11] This is a variant of Theorem 1 of Shuford *et al.* (1966: 128). Savage (1971) gives the answer in a different form. Schervish (1989: 1863) puts the result in terms of a measure λ rather than an increasing function h. He relaxes the restriction to smooth functions in his appendix, pp. 1874–8. Schervish and others speak of "proper" and "strictly proper" scoring rules. The rule is *proper* iff it makes honest reporting of credences optimal, and *strictly proper* iff it make honest reporting uniquely optimal. By my term 'credence-eliciting' I mean strictly proper.

$h(x)$	$g_1(x)$	$g_0(x)$
$2x$	$x(2-x)$	$-x^2$
$3x^2$	$x^2(3-2x)$	$-2x^3$
$-ln(1-x)$	x	$x+ln(1-x)$

Figure 6.1. Pairs of functions generated by various functions h

Still, the requirement of immodesty is quite constrictive. The functions g_1 and g_0 must bear a tight relation to one another. We can let g_1 be any smooth increasing function whatsoever, but once g_1 is chosen, g_0 is determined apart from a constant. Likewise, g_0 can be any decreasing function, but it determines g_1 down to an arbitrary constant. Specify that $g_1 = -\bar{x}^2$, and we must have $g_0 = K - x^2$, the Brier rule plus a constant. Specify that $g_1 = x$, and we must have $g_0 = K + x + ln(1 - x)$. The vast bulk of pairs g_1 and g_0 won't be credence-eliciting; indeed those that are will be an infinitesimal fraction of all the possible pairs of smooth increasing functions.

Explicitly (though these precise formulas won't matter for the rest of what I have to say), we require that for every x,

$$\bar{x}g_0'(x) = -xg_1'(x), \qquad (2)$$

so that given function g_1, we have

$$g_0(x) = K - \int_0^x \frac{z}{\bar{z}} g_1'(z), \qquad (3)$$

Only quite a special relation between the functions g_1 and g_0, then, allows epistemic rationality to be the best policy, by one's own rational lights, in pursuit of truth. We need a term for pairs of functions g_1 and g_0 that satisfy condition (2) and hence formula (3). We must ask what makes for this special relation. In the meantime, I'll coin a label for it: a pair of functions g_1, g_0 that satisfies (3) I'll call *SAM-qualifying*, after the authors who discovered the relation.[12]

[12] Conditions (2) and (3) are variants of formulas in Shuford *et al.* (1966: 128–9).

4. CREDENCE AS GUIDE TO ACTION

An intrinsic concern for accuracy in one's credences is not the only reason one might care what one's credences are. As I stressed at the outset, credence guides action in pursuit of any array of aims whatsoever—avoiding tigers and gaining a lady, for instance. The value of one's credences in this role I am calling their *guidance value*. We can ask what array of credences will, by a rational person's lights, have the maximal expectation of guidance value. The answer turns out to be, whatever credences one in fact has. So long as they are formally coherent—satisfy the standard conditions on probabilities—any array of credences whatever will be, in this new sense, "immodest."

Previously, I characterized immodesty as follows. An epistemic policy is immodest just in case when a person forms credences by that policy, it is as if she were forming them voluntarily, rationally aiming, by her lights, at truth in her credences. This required a specification of what it is to aim at truth in one's credences. The specification must take the form, I said, of a pair of SAM-qualifying functions g_1 and g_0, functions related to each other as in (2). We can speak, then, of an epistemic policy P as *truth-immodest* with respect to functions g_1 and g_0 just in case, as calculated according to policy P and determined by g_1 and g_0, the expected payoff of adopting policy P is at least as great as that of adopting any alternative epistemic policy. With respect to some pairs of functions that specify a way of aiming at truth—the ones that are SAM-qualifying—all coherent epistemic policies are truth-immodest. With respect to other pairs that equally well specify a standard of aiming at truth, however, no epistemic policy will be truth-immodest. We now can specify a similar but distinct notion of immodesty, which I'll call being "guidance-immodest." Roughly, an epistemic policy P will be guidance-immodest just in case, as calculated in accordance with policy P, policy P has maximal prospective guidance value.

The guidance value of an epistemic policy, though, depends on a number of things: the choices one must make, the facts that determine the outcomes of those choices, and the values of those possible outcomes. We need to spell out more fully, then, what constitutes guidance-immodesty in an epistemic policy, and with respect to what.

For truth-immodesty, I hypothesized at the outset that, with an epistemically rational thinker, it is as if she had chosen her credences voluntarily, with an intrinsic aim of accuracy. That turned out to be true only if the concern with accuracy takes a form that is sharply constrained, only if it is SAM-qualifying. Now, though, we can try out a different hypothesis, one that invokes guidance-immodesty. With an epistemically rational thinker, it will turn out, it is as if she had chosen her credences voluntarily and entirely for their prospective guidance value. It is as if she had chosen them for their value in guiding an array of choices she might be faced with, in pursuit of ultimate goals that don't include accuracy in her credences.

Guidance value, of course, is far from the only kind of value one's credences can have. Beliefs can be comforting. They can be empowering. They can link one to others in a fellowship of conviction. I'll label all the kinds of value that credences can have apart from their guidance value as *side value*. The import of the Schervish theorem I'll be presenting is this. Suppose one's credences have no side value whatsoever but only guidance value. Then epistemically rational credences are prospectively the best ones to have.

With "side value" defined just as any value apart from guidance value, I should specify more clearly what "guidance value" means. The rough idea is clear, I hope: The gallant youth opens whatever door he more strongly believes conceals the lady. His credences have high guidance value if they lead him to the lady, and terrible guidance value if they lead him to the tiger. He thus brings about a result—that he finds the lady or that he finds the tiger—acting voluntarily, on a policy that directs what to do as a function of his credences.[13] He maximizes expected utility, as calculated in the standard way using his credences and some scale of valuation. We gauge the outcome using that same scale of valuation. With respect to that scale of valuation, then, the guidance value of an array of

[13] An act "brings about" its causal consequences, but not only those. For a driver, for instance, the act of pushing the turn signal lever down may bring it about that one thereby signals a left turn. That one signals a left turn isn't, strictly, caused by the act of pushing the lever, as the blinking of the signal light is caused by that act, but the act does bring it about that one signals the turn. If the signaling itself has value, that counts toward the utility of pushing the lever. See Kim (1974).

credences ρ is the value, on that scale, of all that he would bring about by performing, at will, whatever acts have highest expected utility as reckoned using credences ρ.

More generally, take any policy F for acting on the basis of one's evidence, and consider a scale of value v. The guidance value of F with respect to scale v is the value, on scale v, of all that would be brought about by the voluntary acts directed by policy F. Now a coherent policy F for action, I am assuming, will consist in a coherent epistemic policy F_E and a policy of maximizing expected utility as reckoned with some scale of value v and the credences ρ yielded by policy F_E. (What the policy directs in case of ties won't matter for our purposes, as long as it directs some act that maximizes expected utility so calculated.) We can speak, then, of the guidance value of credences σ with respect to scale of value v. This is the value, on scale v, of all that would be brought about by the voluntary acts maximizing expected utility calculated with credences σ and value scale v.

The actual guidance value of one's credences, the guidance value they in fact turn out to have had, is thus a matter not only of what choices one would rationally make, in light of those credences and in pursuit of one's aims, but also of how things turn out to be. Suppose that in fact, the tiger is behind the door to the right, and the youth cares, rationally, only about escaping the tiger. Rationally, then, he will go left—and so escape the tiger—just in case his credence in the tiger's being to the right is greater then $\frac{1}{2}$.[14] Let the unit of value be the ramsey or "ram," and let the value of escaping the tiger be 100ram. Then as matters stand, any greater-than-even credence that the tiger is to the right has 100ram greater guidance value than does any less-than-even credence.

Prospective guidance value, then, in light of one's credences, is one's subjective expectation of this actual guidance value. The youth, suppose, for some reason or other, rationally has a credence of 60 percent that the tiger is to the right. Then the prospective guidance value of any degree of credence $x > \frac{1}{2}$, as opposed to any degree $y < \frac{1}{2}$, by his lights, will be $.6 \cdot 100\text{ram} + .4 \cdot 0\text{ram} = 60\text{ram}$. Prospective guidance value, by one's lights, thus depends on one's

[14] I'll ignore, in this discussion, points of indifference, as when his credence is exactly $\frac{1}{2}$.

credences. Even if we could choose what credences to have, we couldn't bootstrap our way to credences prospectively useful as guides to choice by starting with a mind empty of all credence. We can ask, though, whether a way of forming credences is *immodest* from the standpoint of guidance value: whether, if one forms one's credences that way, one will attribute to credences formed in that very way, then, a maximal expectation of guidance value.

The actual guidance value of an array of credences depends on the choices one encounters. Likewise, their prospective guidance value, by one's own lights, depends on one's credences as to what choices one will encounter. Think of life as a single big and complex gamble, and suppose one is uncertain what complex gamble one will face. I'll consider only the special case where a single contingency is to be gambled on, but at odds one doesn't know in advance. Set up, then, a continuum of bets on a claim S. One will take or reject each of these bets, suppose, on the basis of a credence x in S that one choses at will.

For each β with $0 < \beta < 1$, then, set up an infinitesimal bet G_β at odds $\overline{\beta} : \beta$. Being guided by a credence $\rho(S) = x$ in S consists in the following: accepting all bets G_β for $\beta > x$ and rejecting all bets G_β for $\beta < x$. It turns out that one's most favorable prospect, by one's own lights, will be to choose as one's guiding credence x one's true credence $\rho(S) = \alpha$.[15]

Schervish's result (in my own words and apart from some niceties) is this:[16]

> Theorem: Smooth functions g_1 and g_0 are credence-eliciting if and only if for some possible continuum of bet offers and a policy of accepting any bet offer G_γ exactly when $\gamma < x$, $g_1(x)$ gives the expected payoff of the policy given S, and $g_0(x)$ gives the expected payoff of the policy given $\overline{S}$.

[15] It won't then matter, prospectively by one's own lights, how we decide on bets G_β with $\beta = x$, since one will be prospectively indifferent between accepting and rejecting a bet G_β when one's credence in S is β.

[16] Schervish (1989). This is essentially his theorem 4.2, p. 1861, which concerns scoring a set of actual forecasts. As he later notes, "The results of the previous sections can be easily translated to results concerning the expected score" (p. 1869). Where f is the average loss to the decision-maker and a "proper" scoring rule is one that is, in my terms, credence-eliciting, Schervish writes, "Integrating f is essentially equivalent to calculating a proper scoring rule" (1989: 1862).

As Schervish summarizes this finding, "Scoring rules are just a way of averaging all simple two-decision problems into a single, more complicated, decision problem" (1989: 1873).

Schervish also gives us an interpretation for the function h, a function which was left an uninterpreted mystery in our previous discussion. The slope $h'(x)$ of h at x turns out to be the payoff density of bets G_x at odds $\bar{x} : x$. It is the payoff density at those odds in the package of bets that one accepts or rejects on the basis of one's chosen guiding credence x. This will explain how different functions playing the role of h represent different ways of aiming at the truth. For any given x, the slope $h'(x)$ indicates the urgency of probability discriminations in the vicinity of x. If a is the best credence to report, then to a second approximation, a "mistake" of size of size δ costs, prospectively, $\frac{1}{2}h'(a)\delta^2$. The slope of h also indicates, to a second approximation, the value of acquiring a piece of evidence as to whether S obtains. Appendix I demonstrates all this.

The choice among guidance-immodest pairs of functions g_1, g_0 affects not which credence you will regard as optimal, but your preference among those you regard as non-optimal. Different "mistakes" in choosing your credences would affect different choices you might make, and the question is how these choices prospectively matter.[17] Whatever kinds of prospective choices you emphasize in your concern for truth, whatever functions g_1 and g_0 indicate these emphases, the following will obtain: so long as you coherently value truth solely for the sake of guidance, you do prospectively best, by your own lights, with the credences you have. In this regard, the choice among guidance-immodest specifications of the aim of truth does not matter.

5. DISCUSSION: SEEKING TRUTH

Epistemically rational belief aims at the truth—or so we might think. My hypothesis at the outset, recall, was this: When a subject forms

[17] Schervish explains why different scoring rules order forecasters differently (1989: 1862): one measure has more of its mass at probabilities where the one forecaster does better, and the other measure, where the other forecaster does better. (His measure λ is the one induced by my function h.)

her credences with purely epistemic rationality, it is as if she chose her credences voluntarily with the pure aim of accuracy. I assumed that a necessary condition for epistemic rationality is *coherence*, in the sense of satisfying the standard axioms of probability, and that a necessary condition for rationally aiming at something is that one maximize expected value, on some scale of value that specifies the aim, as calculated using some coherent array of credences. The emphases the subject gives to different aspects of accuracy in her credences are represented by the functions g_1 and g_0, the first increasing and the second decreasing. The hypothesis holds true, it turns out, just in case the functions g_1 and g_2 are SAM-qualifying—just in case they bear a highly constrained relation to one another, the relation given by (2) and by (3). If they are SAM-qualifying, then the hypothesis is fairly empty: any way of forming coherent credences will fit the hypothesis. (What happens if credences are not coherent I have not here investigated.[18])

More explicitly put, our finding was this. Suppose a subject aims purely at accuracy in her credence x for claim S, in that her utility is given by an increasing function $g_1(x)$ for the case of S true and a decreasing function $g_0(x)$ for the case of S false. Then if she forms her credences with epistemic rationality, it is as if she chose her credences voluntarily with a pure, SAM-qualifying aim of accuracy. It is not, however, as if she chose them with a aim of accuracy that fails to be SAM-qualifying.

An aim of accuracy is SAM-qualifying in this sense, we have seen, just in case it exactly matches a pure concern with guidance value, given some possible, sufficiently rich prospect for what "bets" one will face in life. One could value accuracy in one's credences intrinsically and prefer the epistemically rational credences one has—but only if one's valuations of truth takes this special form, only if it is SAM-qualifying.

So could a pure concern with truth for its own sake explain epistemic rationality? It seems not. In the first place, of course, as with any aim, to pursue an aim of accuracy, one must already have credences in place—and to pursue such an aim rationally, one must have rational credences already in place. In the second place,

[18] Joyce's theorem (1998) gives the answer for a class of functions g_1 and g_0 that include the Brier score.

though, even then, a concern with accuracy leads one to prefer rational credence only if the concern is SAM-qualifying, only if it takes a special form. Simply wanting truth or accuracy for its own sake does not explain this form. Wanting truth entirely for the sake of guidance *would* explain it—and this is the only explanation we have found.

Might there be some further explanation? Perhaps we have not teased out all the requirements that are implicit in the ordinary notion of a "pure concern with truth" in one's beliefs. Joyce places two further requirements on a pure concern for accuracy, which he calls Normality and Symmetry (1998: 596). With these conditions, he is able to prove a strong result—one that it would be good to prove for the framework of this paper. All and only coherent arrays of credence, he shows, satisfy the dictum that belief aims at truth. The dictum he interprets as I have have interpreted it in this paper, but with Joyce's two additional conditions in place. These conditions, though, have the effect of restricting functions g_1 and g_0 to the Brier rule and scoring rules closely related to it. In my terms, they require that that the function h be linear, that its slope h' be constant. Most of the scoring rules I gave as examples violate this condition. A constant slope for h means, as Schervish shows, that the subject has equal concern for every 1 percent difference in credence. I argued early on in this paper that this is no requirement for a pure concern with truth, that an investigator's pure concern with truth is unsullied if he cares much more about getting near to certainty than about fine differences in middling credences.[19]

Where does this leave pure concern with truth? I find the matter puzzling. Earlier, I distinguished the guidance value of a credence from its "side value." A side value, I said, is any value a credence might have apart from its pure guidance value: the comfort, empowerment, or fellowship it brings, for example. Now by this strict definition, any intrinsic value that truth might have counts as a side value. As with other side values, we have seen, an intrinsic concern for truth, for some form of accuracy in one's credences, can lead one to prefer credences that are not coherent, and so not epistemically rational.

[19] The argument was in section 1, when I introduced Condition $\mathcal{T}$. Maher criticizes Symmetry (2002: 76–8).

Intrinsically valuing truth, though, won't do this if one's concern with accuracy takes the right restricted form—if it is "qualifying," if it matches a guidance value that one's credences might have had. And it does seem that we all have some intrinsic concern with the truth. We're all curious, after all. It does seem too that pure science purifies and elaborates this concern. That won't lead to trouble if the aim of truth takes a form that is qualifying, as I have defined the term, if it mimics possible guidance value.

An intrinsic concern for the truth can't be what we demand of pure investigators unless it mimics a concern for truth for its guidance value. An intrinsic concern for truth, though, so long as it does match aiming at truth purely for its guidance value, seems to be just what characterizes rational curiosity and the purest of science. But concern with guidance value is instrumental, not intrinsic. Why must the pure aims of science mimic it? I don't know the answer.

Does belief, then, aim at truth? Yes, but in a special way. Belief, we have seen, aims at truth, but not perhaps for the sake of truth itself. Belief aims at truth for the sake of guidance.[20]

APPENDIX I. FUNCTION h AS AN INDICATOR OF URGENCY.

What is the prospective cost to our advisor of reporting the wrong credence. Her true credence is α, suppose; what would she lose by guiding herself by a credence $x = \alpha + \delta$ (where δ may be positive or negative)? To a first approximation, small misreports are prospectively costless: only a small range of bet offers get decided differently, and the mistake she makes on any one of those is prospectively small. Where $\mathcal{E}(x)$ is the expected payoff of adopting x as one's guiding credence and we define

$$\Delta\mathcal{E}(\alpha) = \mathcal{E}(\alpha + \delta) - \mathcal{E}(\alpha),$$

[20] Earlier versions of this paper were presented to the Center for the Philosophy of Science at the University of Pittsburgh and to the Creighton Club meeting at Cornell University. I am grateful for discussion on both occasions. James Joyce has been of especial value to me in discussing this paper and in guiding me into its subject and the literature of the field. Teddy Seidenfeld pointed me to his "Calibration" (1985: 276–7), which led me to Schervish's paper. I am grateful to Aaron Bronfman, Paul Horwich, and David Velleman for helpful discussion.

then to a second approximation we have

$$\Delta\mathcal{E}(\alpha) = \mathcal{E}'(\alpha)\delta + \frac{1}{2}\mathcal{E}''(\alpha)\delta^2 = \frac{1}{2}\mathcal{E}''(\alpha)\delta^2,$$

since $\mathcal{E}'(\alpha) = 0$. Since we have

$$\mathcal{E}(x) = \alpha g_1(x) + \bar{\alpha} g_0(x)$$

the first derivative is

$$\begin{aligned}\mathcal{E}'(x) &= \alpha g_1'(x) + \bar{\alpha} g_0'(x)\\ &= \alpha\bar{x}h'(x) - \bar{\alpha}xh'(x).\end{aligned} \tag{4}$$

The second derivative, then, is

$$\mathcal{E}''(x) = (\alpha\bar{x} - \bar{\alpha}x)h''(x) - (\alpha + \bar{\alpha})h'(x).$$

Thus $\mathcal{E}'(\alpha) = 0$, as we already know, and $\mathcal{E}''(\alpha) = -h'(\alpha)$. The slope of function h at α, then, indicates how urgent it is to avoid mistaken reports in the vicinity of α. To a second approximation, if α is the best credence to adopt as a guide, then a mistake of size δ prospectively costs $\frac{1}{2}h'(\alpha)\delta^2$.

Now consider buying information. In one sense, one values truth in one's belief concerning a proposition T if one is willing to pay a cost to learn whether or not S obtains, or to acquire evidence as to whether or not S obtains. For our advisor who has credence α in S and faces payoffs functions g_1 and g_0, the prospective value of learning the truth about S is

$$\alpha[g_1(1) - g_1(\alpha)] + \bar{\alpha}[g_0(0) - g_0(\alpha)].$$

For $g_1(1) - g_1(\alpha)$ is her gain from reporting a credence of one instead of α if S obtains, and $g_0(0) - g_0(\alpha)$ is her gain from reporting a credence of zero instead of α if S doesn't obtain. These are both positive, since g_1 increases and g_0 decreases, and so learning whether or not S is true has a positive prospective guidance value. (Of course its actual guidance value may turn out negative; even for the ideally rational, a little truth can be a dangerous thing.)

This leads to an analysis of how the payoff functions g_1 and g_0 induce her to value evidence as to whether *S* obtains. For sufficiently weak evidence, the slope of the function *h* indicates the value of the evidence to her, to a second approximation. Suppose that the question whether *T* bears on the question whether *S*, and that this bearing exhausts the guidance value of *T*. Let her credence in *T* be β, and suppose learning that *T* would shift her credence in *S* by an amount δ_1, whereas learning that *T* is false would shift her credence in *S* by an amount δ_0. Then we have seen that to a second approximation, her prospective gain from learning that *T* obtains, in case it does, is $\frac{1}{2}h'(\alpha)\delta_1^2$. Her prospective gain from disbelieving *T*, in case *T* doesn't obtain, is $\frac{1}{2}h'(\alpha)\delta_0^2$. Her prospective gain from learning the truth as to whether *T*, then, is

$$\frac{1}{2}\beta h'(\alpha)\delta_1^2 + \frac{1}{2}\overline{\beta}h'(\alpha)\delta_0^2$$
$$= \frac{1}{2}h'(\alpha)[\beta\delta_1^2 + \overline{\beta}\delta_0^2]$$

REFERENCES

Brier, Glenn W. (1950) 'Verification of Forecasts Expressed in Terms of Probability', *Monthly Weather Review*, 78/1 (Jan.): 1–3.

Hammond, Peter (1988) 'Consequentialist Foundations for Expected Utility', *Theory and Decision*, 25: 25–78.

Horwich, Paul (1998) *Truth*, 2nd edn. (Oxford: Oxford University Press).

Joyce, James (1998) 'A Nonpragmatic Vindication of Probabilism', *Philosophy of Science*, 65: 575–603.

Kim, Jaegwon (1974) 'Noncausal Connections', *Noûs*, 8: 41–52.

Lewis, David (1971) 'Immodest Inductive Methods', *Philosophy of Science*, 38: 54–63.

Loewer, Barry (1993) 'The Value of Truth', in E. Villanueva (ed.), *Philosophical Issues*, 4: 265–80 (Atascadero, Calif.: Ridgeview Publishing Company).

Maher, Patrick (2002) 'Joyce's Argument for Probabilism', *Philosophy of Science*, 67: 73–81.

Raiffa, Howard (1968) *Decision Analysis* (Reading, Mass.: Addison Wesley).

Ramsey, Frank Plumpton (1931) 'Truth and Probability', *The Foundations of Mathematics and Other Logical Essays* (London: Routledge & Kegan Paul).

Savage, Leonard J. (1954) *The Foundations of Statistics* (New York: Wiley).
____ (1971) 'Elicitation of Personal Probabilities and Expectations', *Journal of the American Statistical Association*, 66: 783–801.
____ (1972) *The Foundations of Statistics*, 2nd edn. (New York: Dover).
Schervish, Mark J. (1989) 'A General Method for Comparing Probability Assessors', *Annals of Statistics*, 17/4: 1856–79.
Seidenfeld, Teddy (1985) 'Calibration, Coherence, and Scoring Rules', *Philosophy of Science*, 52: 274–94.
Shah, Nishi (2003) 'How Truth Governs Belief', *Philosophical Review*, 112/3 (Oct.): 447–82.
Shuford, E. H., A. Albert, and H. E. Massengill, (1966) 'Admissible Probability Measurement Procedures', *Psychometrika*, 31: 125–45.
Velleman, David (2000) 'On the Aim of Belief', *The Possibility of Practical Reason* (Oxford: Clarendon Press), 244–81.

7. Rationality and Self-Confidence

Frank Arntzenius

1. WHY BE SELF-CONFIDENT?

Hair-Brane theory is the latest craze in elementary particle physics. I think it unlikely that Hair-Brane theory is true. Unfortunately, I will never know whether Hair-Brane theory is true, for Hair-Brane theory makes no empirical predictions, except regarding some esoteric feature of the microscopic conditions just after the Big Bang. Hair-Brane theory, obviously, has no practical use whatsoever. Still, I care about the truth: I want my degree of belief D(H) in Hair-Brane theory H to be as close to the truth as possible. To be precise:

(1) if H is true then having degree of belief $D(H) = r$ has epistemic utility $U(D) = r$ for me

(2) if H is false then having degree of belief $D(H) = r$ has epistemic utility $U(D) = 1 - r$ for me.

Currently, my degree of belief $D(H) = 0.2$. Am I, by my own lights, doing a good epistemic job? Let's see. The expected epistemic utility EU of degree of belief $D'(H) = r$, given my current degree of belief D, is:

(3) $EU(D') = D(H)U(D'\&H) + D(\neg H)U(D'\&\neg H) = 0.2r + 0.8(1 - r) = 0.8 - (0.6)r.$

Obviously, $EU(D')$ is maximal for $D'(H) = 0$. So, by my own lights, I am not doing a good job; I would do better if I were absolutely certain that Hair-Brane theory is false. Unfortunately, I am not capable of setting my degrees of belief at will. All I can do is recognize my own epistemic shortcomings. So I do.

The above is a strange story. Real people, typically, do not judge their own degrees of belief as epistemically deficient. To coin a term: real people tend to be "self-confident." The puzzle that Gibbard poses is that he can see no good reason to be self-confident. For, according to Gibbard, all that follows from having the truth as one's goal, all that follows from having the accuracy of one's state of belief as one's desire, is that a higher degree of belief in the truth is better than a lower degree of belief in the truth. That is to say, according to Gibbard, the only constraint on the epistemic utilities of a rational person is that they should increase as her degrees of belief get closer to the truth. The simplest, most natural, epistemic utility function ('scoring' function), which satisfies this constraint, is a linear function. In the case of a single proposition, the function that I stated in (1) and (2) is such a function. So, according to Gibbard, not only is it rationally acceptable to judge one's own degrees of belief as epistemically deficient, it is very natural to do so.

In the next section I will suggest that considerations regarding updating can serve to explain why real people are self-confident. However, I will then go on to explain why I am nonetheless sympathetic to Gibbard's suggestion that one cannot give a purely epistemic justification for why our belief states are as they are.

2. UPDATING AND SELF-CONFIDENCE

Gibbard's considerations are entirely synchronic. That is to say, he does not consider the evolution of one's belief state through time. But having the truth as one's goal surely includes the desire to get closer to the truth as time passes. In this section I will try to incorporate such considerations.

Let's start with a simple example. Suppose I initially have the following degree of belief distribution D:

(4) $D(H\&E) = 0.4$
(5) $D(H\&\neg E) = 0.2$
(6) $D(\neg H\&E) = 0.1$
(7) $D(\neg H\&\neg E) = 0.3$

And suppose that I have a linear epistemic utility function. In particular, suppose that, according to my current degrees of belief D, the expected epistemic utility of degree of belief distribution D′ is:

(8) $0.4D'(H\&E) + 0.2D'(H\&\neg E) + 0.1D'(\neg H\&E) + 0.3D'(\neg H\&\neg E)$

This is maximal for $D'(H\&E) = 1$. So, epistemically speaking, I desire that I currently be certain that H&E is true, even though in fact I am not certain of that at all.

Now suppose that I know that in one hour I will learn whether E is true or not. And suppose that the only thing I now care about is the degrees of belief that I will have one hour from now. If that is so, what should I now regard as epistemically the best policy for updating my degrees of belief in the light of the evidence that I will get? That is to say, what degrees of belief D_E do I now think I should adopt if I were to get evidence E, and what degrees of belief $D_{\neg E}$ do I now think I should adopt if I were to get evidence ¬E? Well, my current expected epistemic utility for my future degrees of belief is:

(9) $0.4U(H\&E\&D_E) + 0.2U(H\&\neg E\&D_{\neg E}) + 0.1U(\neg H\&E\&D_E) + 0.3U(\neg H\&\neg E\&D_{\neg E})$.

We can expand each of the four epistemic utilities that occur in (9):

(10) $U(H\&E\&D_E) = D_E(H\&E) + (1 - D_E(H\&\neg E)) + (1 - D_E(\neg H\&E)) + (1 - D_E(\neg H\&\neg E))$

(11) $U(H\&\neg E\&D_{\neg E}) = (1 - D_{\neg E}(H\&E)) + D_{\neg E}(H\&\neg E) + (1 - D_{\neg E}(\neg H\&E)) + (1 - D_{\neg E}(\neg H\&\neg E))$

(12) $U(\neg H\&E\&D_E) = (1 - D_E(H\&E)) + (1 - D_E(H\&\neg E)) + D_E(\neg H\&E)) + (1 - D_E(\neg H\&\neg E))$

(13) $U(\neg H\&\neg E\&D_{\neg E}) = (1 - D_{\neg E}(H\&E)) + (1 - D_{\neg E}(H\&\neg E)) + (1 - D_{\neg E}(\neg H\&E)) + D_{\neg E}(\neg H\&\neg E)$

After substituting these terms into (9) and fiddling around a bit we find that my expected epistemic utility is:

(14) $3 + 0.3D_E(H\&E) - 0.5D_E(H\&\neg E) - 0.3D_E(\neg H\&E) - 0.5D_E(\neg H\&\neg E) - 0.5D_{\neg E}(H\&E) - 0.1D_{\neg E}(H\&\neg E) - 0.5D_{\neg E}(\neg H\&E) + 0.1D_{\neg E}(\neg H\&\neg E)$.

This expression is maximized by setting $D_E(H\&E) = 1$ and $D_{\neg E}(\neg H\&\neg E) = 1$ (and setting the other degrees of belief equal to 0). So if all I care about is the degrees of belief I will have one hour from now, then I should update on E by becoming certain that H&E is true, and I should update on ¬E by becoming certain that ¬H&¬E is true. In particular, by my current lights, it would be wrong to first change my degrees of belief so as to maximize my current expected epistemic utility, then update these degrees of belief by conditionalization, and then change these conditionalized degrees of belief so as to maximize expected epistemic utility by the lights of these conditionalized degrees of belief. So there is a conflict between maximizing the expected epistemic utility of my current degrees of belief (by my current lights), and maximizing the expected epistemic utility of my future degrees of belief (by my current lights). At least there is such a conflict, if I update by conditionalization.

Given that there is such a purely epistemic conflict, the obvious question is: what should I do if I only have epistemic concerns and I care both about the accuracy of my current degrees of belief and about the accuracy of my future degrees of belief? One might answer: no problem, I should maximize expected epistemic utility (by my current lights) of both of my current degrees of belief and my future degrees of belief, and hence I should jettison conditionalization. That is to say I should now set my degree of belief to $D'(H\&E) = 1$. And then, if I get evidence E, my degrees of belief should stay the same, but if I get evidence ¬E, I should set my degrees of belief to $D_{\neg E}(\neg H\&\neg E) = 1$. Unfortunately, there are two problems with this answer.

In the first place, it seems worrying to jettison conditionalization. The worry is not just the general worry that conditionalization is part of the standard Bayesian view. The worry, more specifically, is that if one rejects conditionalization one will have to reject standard arguments in favor of conditionalization, namely diachronic Dutch books arguments. But if one does that, shouldn't one also reject synchronic Dutch book arguments? And if one does that, then why have degrees of belief, which satisfy the axioms of probability, to begin with? I will return to this question in section 4. For now, let me turn to the second problem.

The second problem is that if one were to reset one's current degrees of belief so as to maximize one's current expected epistemic utility, one would thereby lose the ability to set one's future degrees of belief so as to maximize the current expected epistemic utility of those future degrees of belief. Let me explain this in a bit more detail.

According to my current degrees of belief D the epistemically best current degree of belief distribution is:

(15) $D'(H\&E) = 1$
(16) $D'(H\&\neg E) = 0$
(17) $D'(\neg H\&E) = 0$
(18) $D'(\neg H\&\neg E) = 0$

Now, according to my original plan, if I were to learn E then I should update by becoming certain that H&E is true, and if I were to learn

$\neg$E then I should become certain that $\neg$H&$\neg$E is true. But if I were to replace D by D′ then I would lose the information as to what I should do were I to learn $\neg$E. The reason why I originally desire to update on $\neg$E by becoming certain that $\neg$H&$\neg$E, rather than becoming certain that H&$\neg$E, is that D($\neg$H/$\neg$E) is higher than D(H/$\neg$E). But if I were to change D into D′ the relevant information is no longer encoded in my degrees of belief: D′ could have come from a degree of belief D (via expected epistemic utility maximization) according to which D($\neg$H/$\neg$E) is lower than D(H/$\neg$E), but it could also have come from one according to which D($\neg$H/$\neg$E) is higher than D(H/$\neg$E). That is to say, if one's epistemic utilities are linear, then maximizing the expected epistemic utility (by one's current lights) of one's degrees of belief can make it impossible to maximize the expected epistemic utility (by one's current lights) of one's degrees of belief at a future time.

The obvious solution to this problem is for the ideal rational agent to have two separate degree of belief distributions. An ideal rational agent should have a 'prudential' degree of belief distribution, which she uses to guide her actions *and* to compute epistemic utilities, and an 'epistemic' degree of belief distribution, which she always sets in order to maximize epistemic utility.

Now, one might worry that there is still going to be a problem. For consider again the example that I started this section with, i.e. suppose that my initial prudential degrees of belief are,

(19) $D^{pr}(H\&E) = 0.4$
(20) $D^{pr}(H\&\neg E) = 0.2$
(21) $D^{pr}(\neg H\&E) = 0.1$
(22) $D^{pr}(\neg H\&\neg E) = 0.3$

Suppose I use these initial prudential degrees of belief to set my initial epistemic degrees of belief so as to maximize expected epistemic utility. Then my initial epistemic degrees of belief would be:

(23) $D^{ep}(H\&E) = 1$
(24) $D^{ep}(H\&\neg E) = 0$
(25) $D^{ep}(\neg H\&E) = 0$
(26) $D^{ep}(\neg H\&\neg E) = 0$

Now I don't (yet) need to worry that I have lost the possibility of maximizing the expected epistemic utility (according to my initial prudential degrees of belief) of my epistemic degrees of belief one hour from now, since, even though I adopted initial epistemic degrees of belief as indicated, I have retained my initial prudential degrees of belief. However there might still be a problem. For when I acquire evidence E, or evidence ¬E, I will, presumably, update my prudential degrees of belief by conditionalization. So will our problem therefore reappear? Will my *updated* prudential degrees of belief contain enough information for me to be able to deduce from them which epistemic degree of belief distribution has maximal expected epistemic utility according to my *initial* prudential degree of belief distribution? And, even if I do have enough information to be able to stick to my original plan, will that plan still look like a good plan according to my *updated* prudential degrees of belief? Let's see.

Recall that according to my initial prudential degrees of belief, if all I care about is the epistemic utility of my degrees of belief one hour from now, then I should update on E by becoming certain that H&E is true, and I should update on ¬E by becoming certain that ¬H&¬E is true. Now, if I were to learn E and update my prudential degree of belief by conditionalization, then my prudential degrees of belief would become,

(27) $D^{pr}(H\&E) = 0.66$
(28) $D^{pr}(H\&\neg E) = 0.33$
(29) $D^{pr}(\neg H\&E) = 0$
(30) $D^{pr}(\neg H\&\neg E) = 0$

According to these prudential degrees of belief expected epistemic utility is maximized by being certain that H&E is true.

Similarly, if I were to learn ¬E and I conditionalized on this, then my prudential degrees of belief would become,

(31) $D^{pr}(H\&E) = 0$
(32) $D^{pr}(H\&\neg E) = 0$
(33) $D^{pr}(\neg H\&E) = 0.75$
(34) $D^{pr}(\neg H\&\neg E) = 0.25$

According to these prudential degrees of belief expected epistemic utility is maximized by being certain that ¬H&¬E is true.

So, in this case at least, the epistemic degrees of belief that I should adopt in the light of evidence, according to my initial prudential degrees of belief, are the same as the ones that I should adopt according to my later prudential degrees of belief, if I update my prudential degrees of belief by conditionalization.

What it is more interesting, and perhaps more surprising, is that this is true for every possible initial prudential degree of belief distribution, *and for every possible epistemic utility function*. That is to say, no matter what one's epistemic utilities are, if according to one's prudential degrees of belief at some time t, plan P for updating one's epistemic degrees of belief maximizes expected epistemic utility, then, after one has updated one's prudential degrees of belief by conditionalization, plan P will still maximize expected utility according to one's updated prudential degrees of belief. The proof of this fact for the general finite case is simple, so let me give it.

Let $D^{pr}(W_i)$ be my initial prudential degree of belief distribution over possibilities W_i.[1] Let $U(W_i\&D^{ep})$ be my epistemic utility for having degree of belief distribution D^{ep} in possibility W_i. Suppose I know that in an hour I will learn which of $E_1, E_2, \ldots E_n$ is true (where the E_i are mutually exclusive and jointly exhaustive). An 'epistemic plan' P is a map from current prudential degree of belief distributions plus evidence sequences to future epistemic degree of belief distributions. Let P map D^{pr} plus E_i to $D^{ep}{}_i$. Then P has maximal expected epistemic utility according to D^{pr} and U iff for every alternative plan P′ (which maps D^{pr} plus E_i to $D^{ep\prime}_i$) we have:

$$(35)\quad \sum_i \sum_k D^{pr}(W_k\&E_i)U(W_k\&E_i\&D^{ep}{}_i) \geq \sum_i \sum_k D^{pr}(W_k\&E_i)U(W_k\&E_i\&D^{ep\prime}_i)$$

We can rewrite this as,

$$(36)\quad \sum_i \sum_k D^{pr}(E_i)D^{pr}(W_k/E_i)U(W_k\&E_i\&D^{ep}{}_i) \geq \sum_i \sum_k D^{pr}(E_i)D^{pr}(W_k/E_i)U(W_k\&E_i\&D^{ep\prime}_i).$$

The left-hand side being maximal implies that each separate i-term is maximal:

$$(37)\quad \sum_k D^{pr}(E_i)D^{pr}(W_k/E_i)U(W_k\&E_i\&D^{ep}{}_i) \geq \sum_k D^{pr}(E_i)D^{pr}(W_k/E_i)U(W_k\&E_i\&D^{ep\prime}_i), \text{ for each i.}$$

Therefore,

$$(38)\quad \sum_k D^{pr}(W_k/E_i)U(W_k\&E_i\&D^{ep}{}_i) \geq \sum_k D^{pr}(W_k/E_i)U(W_k\&E_i\&D^{ep\prime}_i), \text{ for each i.}$$

[1] I am assuming that my degrees of belief are not part of the possibilities W_i that I distribute my degrees of belief over.

But this just means that if we conditionalize D^{pr} on E_i then, according to the resulting degree of belief distribution (and U), the expected epistemic utility of $D^{ep}{}_i$ is maximal.

Let me now summarize what we have seen in this section, and draw a tentative conclusion. No matter what one's epistemic utility function is, one can maximize one's epistemic utilities at all times by having two separate degree of belief distributions: a prudential degree of belief distribution which guides one's actions and one's choice of an epistemic degree of belief distribution, and an epistemic degree of belief distribution whose sole purpose is to maximize epistemic utility. One can then give a purely epistemic argument for updating one's prudential degrees of belief by conditionalization, on the grounds that such updating guarantees cross-time consistency of epistemic utility maximization. The epistemic degrees of belief of an ideal agent at a given time do not determine how she updates her epistemic degrees of belief in the light of evidence. Rather, she updates her epistemic degrees of belief by first conditionalizing her prudential degrees of belief and then maximizing epistemic utility. Thus the epistemic degrees of belief of an ideal agent are largely epiphenomenal: they are only there to maximize the *epistemic score* of an agent, they are not there to guide her actions, nor are they there to help determine her future epistemic degrees of belief. This suggests that rational people can make do without epistemic utilities and epistemic degrees of belief, which could explain why real people do not consider themselves epistemically deficient. Let me bolster this suggestion by arguing that it is not clear what epistemic utilities are.

3. WHAT ARE EPISTEMIC UTILITIES?

Gibbard characterizes epistemic utilities, roughly, as follows. Person P's epistemic utilities are the utilities that P would have were P to ignore both the 'guidance' value and the 'side' values of his degrees of belief. The 'guidance' value of P's degrees of belief is the value these degrees of belief have for P due to the way in which they guide P's actions. The 'side' values of P's degrees of belief for P are values such as P's happiness due to, for example, P's certitude that he will have a pleasant afterlife, or P's dejection due to, for example, P's certitude of his own moral inferiority, and so on. My worry now is that it is not clear what epistemic utilities are, and hence it is not clear that rational people must have epistemic utilities. That is to say, I am willing to grant that rational people have all-things-considered utilities. But it is not clear to me exactly what should be 'subtracted' from 'all considerations' in order to arrive at purely 'epistemic' utilities.

Consider, for instance, my home robot servant, Hal. The robot factory equipped Hal with reprogrammable degrees of belief, reprogrammable utilities, a conditionalization module, and an expected utility maximization module. When I bought Hal I set his degrees of belief equal to mine, his utilities equal to mine (that is to say, my 'all-things-considered' utilities), and I instructed Hal to act on my behalf when I was not present. Occasionally Hal and I updated each other on the evidence that each of us received since our last update, and all went well. Unfortunately Hal's mechanics broke down a while ago. That is to say Hal still has degrees of belief and utilities, and can still conditionalize and compute expected utilities, but he can no longer perform any actions. He just stands there in the corner, a bit forlorn. I have not bothered updating Hal recently, since he can't do anything any more. Gibbard asks me, "Suppose you just wanted Hal's current degrees of belief to be accurate, what degrees of belief would you give him?" I answer, "I don't know. Tell me what you mean by the word 'accurate', and I will tell you what I would set them to." For instance, suppose that there is only one proposition p that Hal has degrees of belief in. Of course if I know that p is true, then I will judge Hal's degrees of belief the more accurate the higher Hal's degree of belief in p is. That much presumably follows from the meaning of the word "accurate." But this by itself does not determine what I take to be the accuracy of Hal's degrees of belief when I am uncertain as to whether p is true or not. Nor does it even allow me to figure out the *expected* accuracy of Hal's degrees of belief. In order to be able to calculate such *expected* accuracies, I need to attach *numerical* values to the accuracy of degree of belief distribution/world pairs (where these numerical values are unique up to positive linear transformations). And I don't know how to do that. So I am stuck. I suggest that this is not for lack of rationality or lack of self-knowledge on my part, but rather, because Gibbard is asking an unclear question. Presumably Gibbard would respond that the above paragraph is confused. On his view of course the question, "What would you set Hal's degrees of belief to if you just wanted them to be accurate?" does not have a person-independent, objectively correct, answer. The problem, according to Gibbard, is precisely that one could rationally have epistemic utilities such that one desires to set Hal's degrees of belief to equal one's own degrees of belief, but one's epistemic utilities could also be such that one desires to set Hal's degrees of belief to be different from one's own degrees of belief. This just goes to show that the correct answer to his question is person-dependent.

My worry, however, is not that Gibbard's question is a well-defined question which has a person-dependent answer, but rather that his question is not a well-defined question. My worry is that it is a question like, "What color socks do you want Hal to wear, bearing in mind that your only goal is colorfulness?" I can't answer that question, not because I am not clear about my own desires or because I am not rational, but because the term "colorfulness" is too vague, or ill-defined. Similarly, I worry that the term "epistemic" is too vague, or ill-defined, so that there are no well-defined (person-dependent) numerical epistemic utilities.

4. WHY HAVE DEGREES OF BELIEF?

Suppose one's only concerns are epistemic. Why then have degrees of belief? That is to say, when one's only goal is truth why should one's epistemic state satisfy the axioms of probability theory? I see no good reason. Let me indicate why I am skeptical by very briefly discussing standard arguments for having belief states which satisfy the axioms of probability theory.

Standard Dutch book arguments rely on the assumption that one does not want to be guaranteed to lose money, or, more generally, that one does not want to be guaranteed to lose prudential value. So, prima facie, if one's only concerns are epistemic, Dutch book arguments have no bite. However, there have been attempts to remove prudential considerations from Dutch book arguments. (See, for instance, Howson and Urbach 1989; Hellman 1997; or Christensen 1996.) The basic idea of these attempts is to claim that the epistemic states of rational people must include judgments regarding the 'fairness' of bets, where these judgments have to satisfy certain axioms which, in turn, entail the axioms of probability theory, so that, purportedly, the epistemic states of rational people must include degrees of belief which satisfy the axioms of probability theory.

There are two reasons why such arguments do not show that one's epistemic state must include degrees of belief which satisfy the axioms of probability theory when one's only goal is the pursuit of truth. In the first place the authors give no justification based only on the pursuit of truth for why epistemic states should include judgments of the 'fairness' of bets. (This may not be a slight on the cited authors, since it is not clear that they intended to give such a justification.) Secondly (and this is a slight on the authors), as argued in Maher (1997), even if a rational person does have epistemic reasons for having such a notion of "fairness" of bets, the authors' arguments for why this notion should satisfy the suggested axioms are not convincing. In fact, Maher shows that some of the suggested axioms will typically be violated by rational people. For instance, if a person judges a bet to be fair just in case the expected utility of accepting the bet is zero, and if her utilities are non-linear in dollars, then her judgments of fairness will violate some of the proffered axioms.

The next type of arguments rely on so-called 'representation theorems.' Such theorems show that preferences which satisfy certain axioms are always representable as those of an expected utility maximizer who has degrees of belief which satisfy the axioms of probability theory. I already find it hard to see why a rational person's all-things-considered preferences should satisfy some of these axioms.[2] I find it even harder to see why a person's purely epistemic preferences should do so, even assuming that sense can be made of 'purely epistemic' preferences. Let me explain in slightly more detail why I find it so hard to see why there should be purely epistemic preferences which satisfy the axioms needed for representation theorems.

One of the axioms needed for representation theorems is that preferences are transitive: if a rational person prefers A to B and B to C then she prefers A to C. When it comes to all-things-considered preferences this axiom seems to me very plausible. For, on a very

[2] For instance, Jeffrey's *continuity axiom* and Savage's *P6 axiom* seem to have no obvious justification other than mathematical expediency. See Jeffrey (1983: ch. 9), and Savage (1972: ch. 3).

plausible understanding of what all-things-considered preferences are, one can be money pumped if one violates this axiom. Now, however, let us consider the case of purely epistemic preferences. Perhaps in this case too one can be money pumped. Fine, but why should one care if one only has epistemic concerns? One might respond that the money pumping argument should not, at bottom, be taken to be a pragmatic argument which only applies to people who are concerned at avoiding a guaranteed loss of money; rather, the argument serves to demonstrate the fundamental incoherence of preferences which are not transitive. I am not moved by such a reply. It may well be that preferences cannot coherently be taken to violate transitivity. However, that merely shifts the issue. For then the question becomes, "is there any reason for a rational person with purely epistemic concerns to have preferences at all?" I can see no such reason.

Finally, there are arguments such as Cox's theorem, and de Finetti's theorem, which show that "plausibility" judgments which satisfy certain axioms are uniquely representable as numerical degrees of belief which satisfy the axioms of probability theory.[3] Again, I can think of no non-question-begging reason why the epistemic states of rational people with purely epistemic concerns should include "plausibility" judgments which satisfy the axioms in question. Let me give a little bit more detail.

De Finetti's theorem and Cox's theorem do roughly the following: they show that one can recover the quantitative values of a probability distribution from the associated comparative qualitative probability judgments. Now, there is a way in which these theorems are not that surprising. For instance, imagine a probability distribution as represented by a heap of mud lying over a continuous space. Then one can think of the qualitative probability judgments as being claims of the form, "the amount of mud over area A is bigger or smaller than the amount of mud over area B." Now, clearly, one cannot shift the mud around in any way without altering some such qualitative judgments. So the qualitative judgments determine the quantitative probabilities. While this argument as it stands is not

[3] See, for instance, Jaynes (2003: ch. 2), or Howson and Urbach (1989: ch. 3). The fundamental notions in the case of Cox are "plausibilities" and "conditional plausibilities," and in the case of De Finetti the fundamental notion is that of "comparative likelihood."

precise, and does not prove exactly what de Finetti and Cox proved, it does give one some of the flavor of their theorems.

Now, while the axioms in question may seem plausible to many, this, it seems to me, is due to the fact that one has in mind that the plausibility assessments are the natural qualitative judgments associated with quantitative probabilistic assessments. One way or another, for instance, the presupposition is made that the possible epistemic states with respect to a single proposition form a one-dimensional continuum, and no argument for this is given based on purely epistemic concerns. More generally, in so far as one thinks that the axioms on plausibility judgments cannot coherently be violated by a rational person with only epistemic concerns, I can see no reason why the epistemic state of a rational person with only epistemic concerns should include such judgments. So Cox's theorem and De Finetti's theorem do not seem to supply a purely epistemic justification for having degrees of belief satisfying the axioms of probability theory.

In short, I am not aware of any good *purely epistemic* argument for having belief states which satisfy the axioms of probability theory. Now, one might respond that, indeed, the reason for having belief states that satisfy the axioms of probability theory is (at least partly) prudential, but that, given that one has such belief states, one can ask whether rational people can have purely epistemic reasons to be dissatisfied with the degrees of belief that they have. However, if a rational person has no purely epistemic reason to have degrees of belief, why think a rational person must have purely epistemic preferences over all possible degree of belief distributions?

5. CONCLUSIONS

The notion of purely epistemic concerns is unclear to me. In so far as it is clear to me I find it hard to see a purely epistemic reason for a rational person to have belief states which satisfy the axioms of probability. If I nonetheless grant that a rational person does have such belief states and that it is clear what purely epistemic concerns are, then I can see reasons for a rational agent to have two different sets of degrees of belief: epistemic ones which serve only to maximize her epistemic utilities, and prudential ones to do everything else. Prudential degrees of belief should then be updated by conditionalization. Epistemic degrees of belief will get dragged along by the prudential ones, relegating epistemic utilities and epistemic degrees of belief to the status of an unimportant side-show.

REFERENCES

Christensen, David (1996) 'Dutch-Book Arguments Depragmatized: Epistemic Consistency for Partial Believers', *Journal of Philosophy*, 93: 450–79.

Hellman, Geoffrey (1997) 'Bayes and Beyond', *Philosophy of Science*, 64: 191–221.

Howson, Colin, and Peter Urbach (1989) *Scientific Reasoning, the Bayesian Approach* (La Salle, Ill.).

Jaynes, Edwin Thompson (2003) *Probability Theory, the Logic of Science* (Cambridge).

Jeffrey, Richard C. (1983) *The Logic of Decision* (Chicago).

Maher, Patrick (1997) 'Depragmatized Dutch Book Arguments', *Philosophy of Science*, 64: 291–305.

Savage, Leonard J. (1972) *The Foundations of Statistics* (New York).

8. A Note on Gibbard's "Rational Credence and the Value of Truth"

Eric Swanson

Gibbard observes that "With an epistemically rational person, it is as if, by her own lights, she were aiming at truth," and argues that although aiming at guidance value is sufficient for this kind of "epistemic immodesty," aiming at truth alone is not. His arguments trade on an analogy between a certain kind of idealized believer and ordinary believers like us: if it is (in certain respects) "as if" we are such idealized believers, then there is good reason to think that we have (certain of) their features. Here I try to undermine Gibbard's case by showing that for another kind of idealized believer—a kind that is more like us than Gibbard's believers are—in many cases having the aim of truth alone does suffice for epistemic immodesty. In particular, a believer who 'aims at truth' in part by being sensitive to new evidence in the way that is most conducive to the *eventual* accuracy of her beliefs most prefers her actual credences. I don't think this conclusively shows that our having the aim of truth suffices for epistemic immodesty. But it does make me suspect that Gibbard's conclusion that guidance value plays a special role in securing our epistemic immodesty is an artefact of his choice of idealization.

1

Let $g_1(\cdot)$ be a function from a believer's credence in some proposition S to her value for having that credence if S is true, and let $g_0(\cdot)$ be a function from the believer's credence in S to her value for having that credence if S is false. Gibbard says that a believer's valuing

Thanks to Frank Arntzenius, Allan Gibbard, Alan Hájek, and Sarah Moss for discussion and helpful comments on earlier drafts.

"truth and truth alone in her credence in S ... seems to consist in satisfying"

CONDITION $\mathcal{T}$: $g_1(x)$ strictly increases with x increasing, and $g_0(x)$ strictly increases with x decreasing.

In many respects Condition $\mathcal{T}$ is not a substantive constraint. Note, for example, that for any positive m and n it is satisfied by the value functions

$$g_1(x) = x^m$$
$$g_0(x) = 1 - x^n$$

The claim that valuing truth alone is compatible with *such* a wide range of pairs of value functions should be controversial. But this is not to say that Condition $\mathcal{T}$ is toothless. Indeed, I think some argument is needed to show that the value functions of a believer who values truth and truth alone must be *strictly* monotonic, as Condition $\mathcal{T}$ demands. Consider for example a believer who, as her known last act, chooses credences that will maximize expected epistemic value by the lights of the value functions

$$\hat{g}_1(x) = \begin{cases} 1 \text{ if } x = 1; \\ 0 \text{ otherwise} \end{cases}$$

$$\hat{g}_0(x) = \begin{cases} 1 \text{ if } x = 0; \\ 0 \text{ otherwise} \end{cases}$$

Has such a believer ipso facto ceased to value truth? To be sure, she values correct *guesses* at S's truth value while disvaluing accurate estimates of its truth-value, in the sense of Jeffrey (1986) and Joyce (1998). But I find it plausible enough that choosing known-to-be-final credences that are not 'lukewarm' can count as a way of aiming at truth alone.

At any rate, Gibbard thinks that epistemic rationality puts far more substantive constraints on credal value functions. In particular, he thinks that for an epistemically rational agent $g_1(\cdot)$ and $g_0(\cdot)$ must be a **credence eliciting pair**, where this means that a believer with such value functions most prefers to have the credence she actually has. I will say that such a believer is **epistemically immodest** with respect to S. Many pairs of value functions satisfy Condition $\mathcal{T}$ without being credence eliciting, and indeed many plausible strengthenings of Condition $\mathcal{T}$ admit non-credence eliciting pairs of value functions.

For example, one might think that for a believer who values truth alone in her credences must have symmetric value functions, in the sense that for any $x \in [0, 1]$, $g_1(x) = g_0(1 - x)$.[1] After all, the value of believing S if S is true *just is* the value of disbelieving $\overline{S}$ if $\overline{S}$ is false, and it seems plausible that ways of valuing pure credal accuracy should not be sensitive to the particular proposition that is believed or disbelieved. To motivate this idea in a slightly different way, perhaps "Belief aims at truth" is a special case of the less homey truism that credence aims at accuracy. And a valuation of credal accuracy should not arbitrarily privilege credence in truths or credence in falsehoods by valuing them asymmetrically.

We would then have

CONDITION $\mathcal{T}$, SECOND PASS:

- $g_1(x)$ strictly increases with x increasing, and $g_0(x)$ strictly increases with x decreasing;
- for all $x \in [0, 1]$, $g_1(x) = g_0(1 - x)$.[2]

One non-credence eliciting pair of value functions that satisfies Second Pass is

$$g_1(x) = x$$
$$g_0(x) = 1 - x$$

As Gibbard notes, a believer with this pair of credal value functions would maximize her expected value by "making [her] beliefs extreme in their certitude" unless her initial credence in S is 0.5. So even Second Pass is satisfied by pairs of value functions that are not credence eliciting.

[1] See Winkler (1994) for some discussion of this sort of symmetry.

[2] I also assume henceforth that credal value functions are well-defined and continuous over $[0, 1]$. I think this assumption does need some argument, strictly speaking, but I doubt Gibbard would contest it.

2

Pairs of credal value functions that make the counterintuitive prescription that we set any credence besides 0.5 to one of the extreme values of 0 and 1 are in some intuitive sense credally pernicious. A believer with such values will, if she can, at a given time choose credences that dramatically misrepresent the evidence that she has in fact acquired to that time.

There are several factors that together constitute the credal perniciousness of these particular value functions, however, and it is important to pull them apart. The **report relation** for a pair of credal value functions $g_1(\cdot)$ and $g_0(\cdot)$ is that relation R such that αRx iff, according to $g_1(\cdot)$ and $g_0(\cdot)$, given initial credence α in S, having credence x in S (or reporting credence x in S) maximizes expected value.[3] The report relation for $g_1(x) = x$ and $g_0(x) = (1 - x)$ is:

$$\alpha R \begin{cases} 1 \text{ if } \alpha > 0.5; \\ 0.5 \text{ if } \alpha = 0.5; \\ 0 \text{ if } \alpha < 0.5 \end{cases}$$

R has three properties that encapsulate the credal perniciousness of $g_1(\cdot)$ and $g_0(\cdot)$:

1. Some $\alpha \neq \beta \in [0, 1]$ bear R to the same x. R thus *conflates* prior credences.
2. Some values in (0,1) bear R to 0, and some bear R to 1. So applying R to a regular credence distribution will sometimes result in an irregular distribution. Even if regularity in one's credences is not a necessary condition for rationality, it is counterintuitive to value irregularity on purely epistemic grounds.
3. Some values in [0,1] do not bear R to themselves. This is just what it means to have a pair of credal value functions that is not credence eliciting.

[3] It is important to think in terms of report relations instead of report functions because for some credal value functions distinct credences in S yield maximal expected value given a single initial credence. For example, for $g_1(x) = x^2$ and $g_0(x) = (1 - x)^2$, if $\alpha = 0.5$ we have maximal expected value at both $x = 1$ and $x = 0$.

The first two properties mentioned above are artefacts of the particular non-credence eliciting value functions we are considering. So it will be helpful to consider pairs that satisfy Second Pass and exhibit only the third property.

Consider for example the following pair of credal value functions, superficially similar to those for the Brier score.

$$g_1(x) = 1 - (1 - x)^3$$
$$g_0(x) = 1 - x^3$$

This pair has the report relation plotted in Figure 8.1:

$$\alpha R x \text{ iff } \alpha = \frac{x^2}{2x^2 - 2x + 1}$$

For all $\alpha, \beta \in [0,1]$, $\alpha = \beta$ iff α and β bear R to the same x. Moreover, no values between 0 and 1 bear R to 0 or 1. Nevertheless, this pair of credal value functions is not credence eliciting: for every value of α but 0, 0.5, and 1, R is not reflexive.

Can a believer aim at truth, choose credences partly on the basis of these value functions, and update those very credences as new evidence comes in? If a believer is certain that she will get no more evidence that will interact with her level of credence in S—as it were, if she knows that she is on her deathbed and

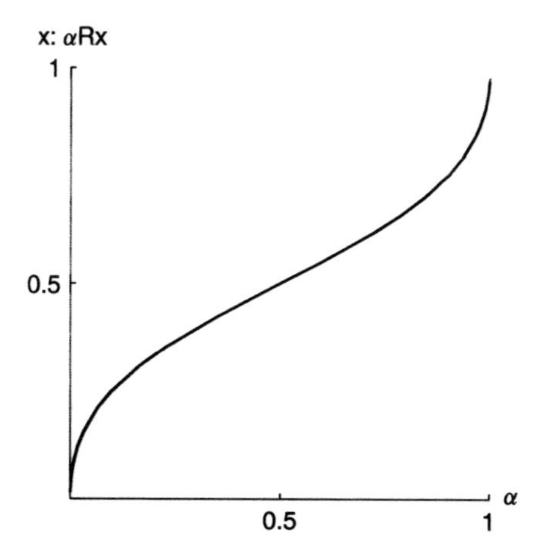

Figure 8.1. The report relation for $g_1(x) = 1 - (1 - x)^3$, $g_0(x) = 1 - x^3$

for whatever reason wants to hedge her bets, somewhat, with her final credences—I think she could choose credences on the basis of this pair of value functions and still count as aiming at the truth. But the circumstances in which a believer can count as aiming at the truth and shift her credences in this way—without making compensating shifts in her updating procedures—are quite rare. A believer who aims at truth alone in her beliefs and thinks that she might get evidence that will interact with her level of credence in S should take every care *not* to let new evidence directly interact with credences that misrepresent her old evidence. Otherwise she would be distorting her total evidence in a way that would undermine her aim to *eventually* estimate the truth in a way that makes the best use of the evidence available to her.

To see this consider a meteorologist trying to decide what value to report as the probability that a storm will pass over a particular island. She is confident that she updates well on the basis of new information, but for prudential reasons she believes that the greater the probability that the storm will pass over the island, the more she should exaggerate that probability in her report. Imagine that she can handle new information that she acquires using either of the following step-by-step strategies:

Applying R at the end

1. She begins to construct an array, writing her initial credences in the first row.
2. When new information comes in, she writes, in row $n+1$ under the last complete row n, the values that would be the product of her updating on that information if her priors were given by row n.
3. For her forecast she reports the relevant value of the image of the last complete row under a non-credence eliciting report relation R.[4]

[4] In these examples suppose that any $a \in [0,1]$ bears R to exactly one x. That is, suppose that the report relation can be understood as a report function that is well-defined over $[0,1]$.

Applying R with each update

1. She begins to construct an array, writing her initial credences in the first row.
2. She writes, in row $n+1$ under the last complete row n, the image of row n under R.
3. When new information comes in, she writes, in row $n+1$ under the last complete row n, the values that would be the product of her updating on that information if her priors were given by row n, *and then returns to step 2.*
4. For her forecast she reports the relevant value of the last complete row.

Clearly our meteorologist should adopt the first strategy: she should apply R only at the end, so that it affects her report exactly once. Her aim is to estimate the probability that the storm will pass over the island as accurately as she can and then to determine what probability she should report in order to maximize expected value by the lights of her value functions. The second strategy has the potential to lead her far astray—for example, it would make her reported value sensitive to *how many times* she had updated, and this is no part of the way she values estimates of truth value. In brief, the fact that she values estimates of the truth value of a proposition disproportionately depending on their proximity to 1 does not entail that she similarly values what amounts to disproportionate *updating*.

For just these reasons, a believer with non-credence eliciting value functions who aims to eventually estimate the truth in a way that makes the best use of her evidence must have doxastic policies that allow her at least to *emulate* the first strategy. But there is a problem here: a believer with such value functions cannot simply *wait* to apply R until the moment of report, as the meteorologist could. A believer with non-credence eliciting value functions applies R to her credences whenever she acts so to maximize expected value. What constraints does this put on her credal value functions?

Perhaps it would be enough that their report relation be injective. Then one R-step 'backward' from the credences the believer arrived at after taking one R-step 'forward' from her initial credences would return her to her initial credences. The believer's updating procedures could then be modified to update not her actual credences, but their image under the inverse relation of R. She could in effect 'undo' her previous choice with each update. We would then have the following constraint on the value functions of a believer who aims at truth, thinks she may acquire more evidence, and wants to put that evidence to fruitful epistemic use:

CONDITION $\mathcal{T}$, THIRD PASS:

- $g_1(x)$ strictly increases with x increasing, and $g_0(x)$ strictly decreases with x decreasing;
- for all $x \in [0, 1]$, $g_1(x) = g_0(1 - x)$;
- the report relation for $g_1(\cdot), g_0(\cdot)$ is injective over $[0, 1]$.

But this is just more grist for Gibbard's mill, because even this very strong condition does not rule out non-credence eliciting report relations. For example, the report relation of the 'Brier cubed' score is injective over [0, 1], and the relevant pair of value functions satisfies the other clauses of Third Pass.

3

There is a problem with this proposal, however, that points the way toward a constraint that permits only credence eliciting value functions. The doxastic lives of the believers that we have chosen to theorize about consist of sequences of updating and acting so as to maximize expected value. Consider some such believer, who has a non-credence eliciting value function and at some time or times

1. Acts, *inter alia* choosing new credences;
2. Immediately acts again, *inter alia* again choosing new credences, partly on the basis of the credences she chose in the immediately preceding action.

For such a believer to 'work backward' to credences that aren't distorted by non-credence eliciting choices, modifying updating procedures to compensate for non-credence eliciting choices of credences, is not enough: she also needs to ensure that her *actions*—and in particular, her choices of credence—compensate for her choices of credence. Otherwise the believer will choose a credence for a proposition on the basis of a credence which itself may have been chosen to maximize expected value, which itself may have been chosen to maximize expected value, and so on. In virtue of choosing credences in this fashion—one choice immediately following another—such a believer embodies a one-dimensional discrete dynamical system, the evolution rule of which is $R(\cdot)$. A believer who engages in just one choice of credence takes one step in the dynamical system, so that if she starts with a credence in S of $\rho(S)$, she chooses a credence of $R(\rho(s))$ in S. A believer who engages in two immediately consecutive choices of credence takes two steps, so that she ultimately chooses a credence of $R(R(\rho(s)))$, and so on.

Being able to 'work backward' from the output of such a dynamical system requires much more than that the report relation be injective. For example, it is necessary (though obviously not sufficient) that at least one of the following conditions obtains:

1. The believer knows whether the evolution rule has been applied once or twice.
2. Whether the evolution rule has been applied once or twice doesn't make a difference to how the believer should work backward.

The cognitive lives of believers who satisfy the first condition must be quite transparent to them: they must be able to determine, through introspection, how many times they have acted to maximize expected value. We are unlike such believers in a host of ways. We are *less* unlike believers who do not enjoy such introspective transparency, and thus satisfy only the second condition. To be sure, we are unlike them in important respects as well. But we are *closer* to them than we are to believers who can survey their expected value maximizing actions in the ways necessary to satisfy the first condition.

For a believer to satisfy the second condition, her report relation must not conflate distinct credences under iteration. By this I mean that there must not be distinct credences such that one is related to a value by *one* R-step that the other is related to by *two* R-steps. The only report relation with this feature maps each element in $[0, 1]$ to itself and only to itself. And only credence eliciting pairs of credal value functions have this report relation. More formally: The credal value functions $g_1(\cdot)$ and $g_0(\cdot)$ of a believer who thinks she may get new, relevant evidence, and aims at the *eventual* truth—and thus aims to be optimally sensitive to new evidence as it comes in—must satisfy

Condition $\mathcal{T}$, fourth pass: The report relation for $g_1(\cdot)$ and $g_0(\cdot)$ is such that for no $x \neq y \in [0,1]$ is there any z such that xR^2z and yR^1z.[5]

A pair of credal value functions is credence eliciting iff the pair satisfies Fourth Pass.

$\Rightarrow$ Suppose a pair is credence eliciting. Then xRx for any $x \in [0,1]$, and if xRy then $y = x$. So for any k, xR^kx, and if xR^ky then $y = x$. So for any $x \neq y$ and any k and l, x does not bear the R^k relation to any value that y bears the R^l relation to. In particular, x does not bear the R^2 relation to any value that y bears the R^1 relation to.

$\Leftarrow$ Suppose a pair of credal value functions, $g_1(\cdot)$ and $g_0(\cdot)$, satisfies Fourth Pass. Then for no $x \neq y \in [0,1]$ is there any z such that xR^2z and yR^1z. [0, 1] is compact, and $g_1(\cdot)$ and $g_0(\cdot)$ are continuous over [0, 1], so by the extreme value theorem every value in [0, 1] bears the R relation to some value in [0, 1]. In particular, every value in [0, 1] bears the R relation only to itself. For suppose not: then for some $x \neq y \in [0,1]$, xR^1y. There is also some $z \in [0,1]$ such that yR^1z. But then xR^2z, contradicting our initial supposition. So xRx for any $x \in [0,1]$, and if xRy then $y = x$. So the pair is credence eliciting.

This shows that we are more like believers who (in order to aim at eventual truth) must have credence eliciting value functions than we are like believers who can aim at eventual truth without having credence eliciting value functions.

4

How should what we learn about hypothetical believers (who always act to maximize expected value, can choose their own credences, and so on) inform our thinking about believers like us? One reason to think about hypothetical believers in general is that they—or at any rate, some of them—help provide tractable and

[5] aR^nb iff b is accessible from a by an n length sequence of R-steps. So aR^1b iff aRb; aR^2b iff there is some c such that aRc and cRb, etc.

not too misleading models of believers like us. In light of this it would be interesting to see examples of believers whose cognitive lives *demand* that they be modeled using non-credence eliciting value functions: believers for whom it really is "as if" they choose their own credences according to such functions. I am not sure that there are any such believers because, as I have tried to bring out, a believer who has non-credence eliciting value functions and can choose his own credences engages in very odd doxastic behavior over time.

But even without such examples, clarifying the constraints that govern the spaces of various kinds of purely hypothetical believers can point the way toward interesting hypotheses about non-idealized believers. Studying believers that are unlike us can be misleading, however, if we do not correct for artefacts generated by the particular kind of hypothetical believer we choose to focus on. I have argued that for believers who cannot survey the number of times they have acted to maximize expected value, having the aim of eventual truth suffices to ensure that their value functions are credence eliciting. Of course this is compatible with the claim that for *another* kind of believer the aim of eventual truth does not so suffice. But because the believers Gibbard focuses on are in important respects more unlike us than the kind I have discussed, I am not moved to think that it is the aim of maximizing prospective guidance value that secures our epistemic immodesty.

REFERENCES

Jeffrey, Richard C. (1986) 'Probabilism and Induction', *Topoi,* 5: 51–8.

Joyce, James M. (1998) 'A Nonpragmatic Vindication of Probabilism', *Philosophy of Science,* 65(4): 575–603.

Winkler, Robert L. (1994) 'Evaluating Probabilities: Asymmetric Scoring Rules', *Management Science,* 40(11): 1395–405.

9. Aiming at Truth Over Time: Reply to Arntzenius and Swanson

Allan Gibbard

I want to thank both Frank Arntzenius and Eric Swanson for their fine, illuminating commentaries. Both propose that my analysis of belief should be made dynamic. In my paper I considered only a simplest possible case, the static case with a single uncertain proposition and its negation. I might have gone on to consider a more complex thinker, prone to change degrees of credence as new evidence comes in. I agree with Arntzenius and Swanson that the dynamic case needs investigating. I think, however, that for the dynamic case, most of the lessons I drew reappear in new forms.

1. THE PROBLEM

In my paper, recall, I tried to make sense of the idea that "belief aims at truth." I considered epistemic rationality, and asked whether it can somehow be explained as answering to a pure concern with truth. By epistemic rationality, I mean rationality in one's degrees of credence. (For short, following David Lewis, I call degrees of belief "credences.") The epistemic rationality of a state of belief is different from its overall desirability. It is not the same thing as rationality in acting to affect the belief state, or the belief state's being the kind one might go for given the choice. The upshot of my inquiry was both negative and positive. Concern for truth, I first argued, might take any of various forms. Some of these are friendly to epistemic rationality, and some are not. In arguing this, I took for granted standard ideas of what epistemic rationality consists in—or at least, I took the standard decision-theoretic conditions as necessary for perfect epistemic rationality. Concern for truth as such, I thought I showed, couldn't explain epistemic rationality. Epistemic rationality answers to a concern for truth only if the concern takes a special form: that of concern with truth for the sake of guidance.[1]

I helped myself to standard requirements on credence in order to see if they are self-endorsing. Since I took these requirements as assumptions, no argument of the kind I gave could possibly convince anyone of these requirements who wasn't already convinced. Jim Joyce undertakes a more ambitious kind of argument, one that addresses a person who doubts that epistemic rationality requires standard coherence in one's credences—where "standard coherence," as I'm using the term, amounts to satisfying the usual axioms of probability. Joyce tries to show, on the basis of things that such a person would accept, that probabilistic incoherence is defective. His vindication of standard coherence was meant to be non-pragmatic, and one of my conclusions was that a non-pragmatic vindication, along the lines he attempts, is not to be had. I criticized some of the conditions he himself laid down; they aren't all required, I argued, for a person to qualify as purely concerned with truth. Then I helped myself to standard decision theory, parts of which he meant to vindicate, squeezed all I could from the notion of purely epistemic goals, and still couldn't get the main result that he derived from his conditions. It would seem that if a non-pragmatic vindication along Joyce's lines isn't to be had even with assumptions that help themselves to the view to be vindicated, it isn't to be had at all. Epistemic rationality, I concluded, isn't to be explained as what a sheer concern with truth must endorse.

Concern with truth in one special form, though, did seem to do some explaining. That was the lesson I drew from theorems of Mark Schervish. The form is concern with truth on pragmatic grounds, but of one particular kind—or alternatively, a concern with truth that mimics such a pragmatically grounded concern. Attempted pragmatic vindications of probabilism are of course well known, and aspire to be much more general than the limited pragmatic vindication that I ventured. Whether any of these pragmatic vindications work has been widely debated, and Frank Arntzenius may be unconvinced by some of them. Nothing I showed adds anything to those debates. It does seem to be a lesson of my argument,

[1] The theorems I appealed to and the core of my argument were, as I indicated, drawn from the work of statistician Mark Schervish.

though, that any successful vindication will have to be pragmatic. More guardedly, I should say, that's the lesson unless something more can be squeezed out of notions of truth-conduciveness than I myself could identify.

Both commentators put my puzzle in ways somewhat different from what I intended. According to Arntzenius, my puzzle is that I "can see no good reason to be self-confident," no good reason not to judge my beliefs epistemically deficient. Not exactly: as Arntzenius indicates later on, whatever reasons one has for one's degrees of credence are reasons for thinking them right, and thus that one has got them right. It's just that I don't see how the reason can take a particular form: thinking—even circularly—that one's credences aim at truth in a way that is optimal given one's evidence. I thus don't see how an intrinsic concern for the truth of one's beliefs could in any way underlie epistemic rationality. (Arntzenius, as I read him, doesn't see how either, though he may think we could see the folly of such approach without any argument like mine.)

I also don't think that it is "rationally acceptable to judge one's own degrees of belief as epistemically deficient." A perfectly rational person, I would think, will not so judge. It may well be rationally acceptable, I said, to wish that one's degrees of belief were different from what they are—even when it's rational to care only about their closeness, by some standard, to full truth. Epistemic deficiency, though, is different from being unwanted. It's different even from aiming badly at truth. My puzzle brings into question not epistemic rationality but a specious way of explaining it. Can we "give a purely epistemic justification for why our belief states are as they are" (if they are ideally rational)? Arntzenius says that I think we can't, but in truth I don't know and I would hope that we could. My conclusion was that we can't give such a justification along the lines that I scrutinized, explaining epistemic rationality as somehow well aimed at the truth for its own sake.

According to Swanson, I think that epistemic rationality constrains credal value functions to be credence-eliciting. Again, not exactly: A person could be epistemically rational and value truth in all sorts of ways. He might even disvalue truth, but find himself epistemically rational against his wishes. The thesis I scrutinize in my paper, once I think I have made sense of it, allows for this. If a person is epistemically rational, goes the thesis, it is *as if* she valued truth for its own sake and could choose her credences at will. Most of us can't choose our degrees of credence at will, and a person who can't might conceivably be epistemic rational to perfection, but wish that she weren't.

One more set of preliminary remarks: Swanson suggests strengthening my characterization of concern with truth. The concern with truth, he says, should be symmetric: one should value credence in the negation of a claim, should it be false, just as one values credence in the claim should it be true. He notes that this makes no difference to the conclusions I drew, but even so, I'll register my disagreement. To be sure, the truth of S amounts to the falsehood of $\neg S$, and so trivially, the truth of S and the falsehood of $\neg S$ are of equal import. It doesn't follow, though, that the truth and falsehood of S are of equal import. Take almost any example: let S be Newtonian physics, or a value for the speed of light, or the new Hair-Brane theory in particle physics. Must uncertainty that S is true in case it is true and uncertainty that S is false in case it is false be equal failings, from the standpoint of a pure, scientific thirst for truth? I don't see why. We're comparing, say, a person who is 95 percent certain of the inverse square law for gravity when it isn't quite the correct law, with a person who is 95 percent certain that it isn't the correct law when it is. Why must their high but misplaced confidence and their correct residual doubts be of equal purely epistemic import, when its being precisely true would tell us a lot and its being not quite right would leave it wide open just what is right? I don't know which residual doubt is more important, but once we're convinced that not every 1 percent difference in the credence one might have matters equally, why think that these two do matter equally? "Credence aims at accuracy," Swanson proposes, and "a valuation of credal accuracy should not arbitrarily privilege credence in truths or credence in falsehoods by valuing them asymmetrically." I agree that a blanket policy of treating all truths one way and all falsehoods another isn't even possible, since the negation of a falsehood is a truth. I suggest, however, that a particular truth and its negation might very well be treated asymmetrically by a person who still rightly counted as valuing truth purely for its own sake.

2. THE DYNAMIC CASE: UPDATING OVER TIME

Both Arntzenius and Swanson analyze thinkers who take in new evidence over time and somehow modify their credences in its light. I agree that such an analysis is needed, and I'll turn first to Swanson's treatment. Swanson argues that a dynamic analysis changes the lesson to be drawn—at least for beings like us, with our limitations. With this I mostly disagree.

Note first a crucial feature of the static case. A coherent believer who wants only truth, recall, may wish that her credences were different from what they are. That was the central point with which I began. Note, though: in that case, if she got what she wanted, she still wouldn't be satisfied. Her credences would be different from what they are, and so her prospective valuations of the various possible arrays of credences one might have would, in this counterfactual case, be different from what they are in actuality.

Swanson's treatment of the dynamic case plays on this feature. He considers hypothetical believers "who always act to maximize expected value" and "can choose their own credences." He shows that "a believer who has non-credence eliciting value functions *and can choose her own credences* engages in some very odd doxastic behavior over time."[2] His dynamic believer, able to choose her credences anew at each updating, ends up with credences she wouldn't have wanted in the first place for the case of receiving the string of evidence that she receives.

This is quite right, as he shows conclusively. The remaining question is how it bears on the claim that epistemically rational credences do in some sense "aim at truth." For the static case, I argued, rational credences do aim at truth, but in a special way: it is as if they aimed at truth for the sake of guidance. Valuing truth in a way that mimics valuing it for the sake of guidance, though, I said, is far from the only way one could value truth for its own sake. Now the way I set up the question for the static case has a parallel for the dynamic case. It is this parallel, I'll argue, and not the case that Swanson analyzes, that bears on whether epistemically rational policies for credences and their revision can be explained as aiming at truth.

[2] Emphasis mine, and with the pronoun changed to facilitate reference.

For the static case, recall, I put the question as whether, if a person is epistemically rational in her credences, it is *as if* she valued truth and had been able to choose her credences at will. (If she valued truth in a way that made her want different credences from the ones she has, we now note, she would want not only to have those different credences, but to lose her power to set her credences at will. Otherwise she would end up, after a series of new choices of credences, with credences different from the ones she now wants.) The answer to my question depends, of course, on what qualifies as "valuing truth"—but I'll put off further discussion of that until later, and assume for now that I was right about what valuing truth in one's credences consists in. Our question now is how to pose the parallel question for the dynamic case. For the dynamic case, we suppose that the believer values truth not only for her credences at the outset, but for the credences she will come to have as new evidence crops up. What she needs to evaluate, then, is whole ways she might be disposed to form credences and update them. In actuality, we are supposing, she is epistemically rational, and so her actual epistemic dispositions, whether she wants them to be that way or not, consist in starting out with a coherent, epistemically rational array of initial credences and then updating by standard conditionalization. The question is whether she will be glad that those are her epistemic dispositions. If she in some way values truth and truth alone, will her actual epistemic dispositions be the ones she most prefers to have?

The answer to this question for the dynamic case exactly parallels the answer for the static case. What are the alternatives among which she can have preferences? As both Swanson and Arntzenius recognize, she isn't restricted to wishing to update by standard conditionalization. Swanson proposes another restriction, though, which I'll accept as an important restriction to explore. Let's confine our consideration to beings who, like us, can't keep track of their past histories of updating. Suppose, indeed, that our believer can't even aspire to more, that she is constrained to wish only for epistemic dispositions that don't require keeping track of such matters as how many times she has updated. On each updating, we require for the world as she wishes it were, she must apply a rule that takes her current credences and the new item of evidence, and on the basis of these alone delivers a revised array of credences. What dispositions, under this restriction, will she most prefer to have? That is our question.

Swanson provides the machinery that delievers an answer to this question. Take the "report relation" R that Swanson defines, which takes actual to wished-for credences. Look, as he shows that we must, for an array of dispositions that mimic updating from her actual credences by standard conditionalization and then "applying R at the end." Because of the informational restriction, we must now, I agree, further require that her way of valuing truth yields a report relation that is injective (that is, that it is a one-to-one function from the interval [0,1] onto itself). As he notes, however, this isn't a severe restriction; it allows for many report relations that aren't the identity relation—that aren't the R of a believer who most prefers the epistemic dispositions that she in fact has.

Here are the dispositions she most prefers to have (though so long as R isn't identity, she doesn't in fact have them): the dispositions are, in effect, at each stage as new evidence arrives, to revert to her epistemically rational credences, apply standard conditionalization, and then go to the new credences that, in actuality, she prefers for the case of having that evidence. This works as follows. Let ρ_0 be her actual, epistemically rational credences at time 0, and for discrete times $t = 1, 2, \ldots$, let ρ_t be the credences that, with her actual dispositions, she would have at time t having received a string of evidence $E_1, E_2, \ldots, E_t$. What arrays of credence $\sigma_0, \sigma_1, \ldots, \sigma_t$, we now ask, does she wish she were disposed to have on receiving that string of evidence. She wishes, as Swanson says, that each σ_t were the one she would get by starting out with her actual initial credences ρ_0, updating by standard conditionalization, and applying R at the end. But a non-standard updating rule that she can wish for would accomplish just that. (Indeed it is a rule that Swanson considers, though it doesn't work for the situation that Swanson considers, where the believer is stuck having to wish for states where she could wish further and get what she then wished.) Let her wished-for initial credences σ_0 be the ones that result from applying R to her actual initial credences ρ_0. Let her wished-for dispositions to update be this: that on receiving each new piece of evidence, she update as if she first had reverted to the credences ρ_{t-1} that she is actually disposed to have, then had updated these by standard conditionalization, and finally had applied the report relation R to the result.

This gives her a wished-for updating rule that fits Swanson's restriction on wished-for information. The rule, more fully put, consists in first (i) applying to her wished-for credences σ_{t-1} the inverse R^{-1} of the report relation, yielding her rational credences ρ_{t-1}, then next (ii) applying standard conditionalization C_t, defined as $C_t(\rho_{t-1}) = \rho_{t-1}(\cdot/E_t) = \rho_t$, and finally, (iii) applying the report relation to the result to get $\sigma_t = R(\rho_t)$. Her wished-for updating function is thus RC_tR^{-1}, the transformation that results from applying successively the transformations R^{-1}, C_t, and R. This may be messy, but applying this updating rule would, with enough sheer calculating power, require only keeping track of one's current credences and what the new evidence is.

This dynamic parallel to the static case differs sharply from the case that Swanson analyzes. I examine only what the rational believer who values truth actually wants. Swanson examines a case where the believer, on the arrival of each new piece of evidence, gets what she wants and so forms new preferences which are then accorded at the next updating. This, as he shows, isn't something to want—unless one wants precisely the initial credences one has. His treatment plays, as I have said, on a feature that the dynamic and the static cases share: that in case the believer isn't satisfied with her credences, if she got what she wants she still wouldn't be satisfied.

Would this feature itself, though, indicate that she doesn't genuinely want truth in her credences? Does it show that she fails really to value truth and truth alone? If it does, then perhaps the dictum that belief aims at truth can still be interpreted as correct. We can still maintain that any rational believer who values truth *genuinely* will be glad she has the credences she does.

But this feature indicates no such thing. All sorts of things we might genuinely value in beliefs will display this feature. The suicide prefers self-inflicted death to his prospects otherwise—but once he kills himself, he no longer has this preference. His preference is none the less genuine. Or take an instance that is more complex: I want comfort, but I also want to be emotionally braced for rude surprises. I want not to be completely terrified all the time, but still to be somewhat prepared for the things I dread. What credences would, on balance, prospectively best meet these and my other competing desiderata? They may not be the credences I actually have and that I regard as epistemically rational. Perhaps, for the sake of comfort, they'd discount the likelihood of some of the things I fear—but still not too much, or I'll be too unprepared if terrifying things do happen. What credences I most want to have will thus depend, among other things, on how likely I now take various nasty eventualities to be. For that reason, if I had the credences I actually most want, the calculations I now make would no longer apply. I'd want even lower credence in fearsome things that might befall me. None of this means, though, that I don't now genuinely value comfort as a benefit that my credences might yield.

I conclude, then, that the dynamic case works like the static one—with a qualification. A being fully coherent in belief and preference might intrinsically value truth and truth alone and still want a credal policy different from her actual ones. In the dynamic case, she might want both different initial credences and a different updating rule. As Swanson indicates, the updating rule she wants will in some cases demand extraordinary amounts of information. Not so, however, in cases where her epistemic preferences yield, in Swanson's terms, a report relation that is injective. Then, the rule she most wants can run on the same information as standard conditionalization: one's credences prior to the new evidence and what the new evidence is. Valuing truth, then, even in this restricted way, needn't lead an ideally rational person to want the credences she has. Epistemically rational credences, then, can't be explained just as being what you'd want if you valued truth and truth alone.

Arntzenius, for the dynamic case, starts out with just the right question. "What should I now regard as epistemically the best policy for updating my degrees of belief in light of the evidence I will get." He shows, for the particular case he considers, that the policy will depart from standard conditionalization as its updating rule. I agree, as I have indicated in my treatment of Swanson. He finds problems with this, however. First, it goes against diachronic Dutch book arguments, and if we lose Dutch book arguments, we have no answer to why credences ought to satisfy the axioms of probability—why, as I'm using the term, they ought to be coherent. Dutch book arguments, though, are pragmatic, not purely epistemic, and I haven't questioned pragmatic arguments for classical decision theory. My point is that we can't get a certain kind of purely epistemic argument to work. As for why to have degrees of belief that satisfy the axioms of probability, that is an excellent question, but not one that I took up. I considered only degrees of belief in a single proposition.

Arntzenius's second problem with dropping standard conditionalization is that one loses "the ability to set one's degrees of belief so as to maximize the current expected epistemic utility of those future degrees of belief." Here what I said about Swanson applies. In the linear case, the one that Arntzenius chiefly analyzes, Swanson's report relation R isn't injective. We can still ask Arntzenius's question of what, by my actual lights, would be my prospectively best updating policy. The policy that looks prospectively best by my initial lights will still look prospectively best over time as new evidence comes in. But the policy will make heavy informational demands; it can't prescribe credences as a function just of what one's credences are before a piece of evidence comes in and what that evidence is. Arntzenius may be suggesting this when he says that if I had my desired credences, "I would lose the information as to what I should do were I to learn $\neg E$" (section 2). I need lose it, though, only in the sense that the information won't be given by my desired credences. Conceivably I might have the information in some other form. One form the information might take is in the double bookkeeping that Arntzenius proposes, having as one's information both one's "epistemic" and one's "prudential" utilities. If, on the other hand, the Swanson report relation R is one-to-one, the needed updating rule will require only the information that standard conditionalization requires.

Arntzenius draws the lesson, "if one's epistemic utilities are linear, then maximizing the expected epistemic utility (by one's current lights) of one's degrees of belief can make it impossible to maximize the expected epistemic utility (by one's current lights) of one's degrees of belief at a future time" (section 2). He himself, though, goes on to propose a way out, and it is important to bear in mind two qualifications to what I just quoted. First, we can imagine updating in a way that achieves both these goals if the policy can draw on enough information, as with Arntzenius's own proposal of keeping double books. Second, some perverse cases differ from the linear one that Arntzenius is treating, in that the Swanson report relation R is injective. For these cases, we don't face this dilemma.

I mostly agree with Arntzenius about his suggested way out, his proposal of keeping two books with two different arrays of credences. An agent who acts as well as believes will need "prudential" credences anyway, to guide her actions in pursuit of new evidence. The Schervish result shows that, purely for guidance, the rational agent will want the credences she has. If she also values some form of closeness to truth in her epistemic credences, just for its own sake, she might indeed then wish she kept such double books, with one array of credences to guide her and another to maximize closeness to truth by the standards she embraces. She might wish this, Arntzenius shows, even if she has no other goal than closeness to truth on some specification.

I agree with Arntzenius too that such a wish is ridiculous. First, of course, it will satisfy the believer's preferences only if she cares intrinsically solely about her "epistemic" credences and not about her guiding "prudential" ones. Otherwise, she'll have to find some array of guiding credences that best answer a balance of competing demands: the demand to govern her assessments of expected epistemic utility, and the demand of being truthful in the way she values intrinsically. (Like things would go for wanting credences that will comfort one, enhance one's social dominance, stave off depression and anxiety, and the like. The best thing might be to keep one's epistemically rational credences for purposes of guidance, and have a separate set of cuddly or enlivening credences for these "side" purposes.) Second, if she had the "epistemic credences" she wishes for, they would be idle.

One interesting lesson that Arntzenius draws is worth stressing. He has given, he says, "a purely epistemic argument for updating one's prudential degrees of belief by conditionalization, on the grounds that such updating guarantees cross-time consistency of epistemic utility maximization" (section 2). Even if one's goals are purely epistemic, he shows, epistemically rational credences can offer prospectively optimal guidance in achieving those goals. They can do so not only by guiding action in pursuit of new evidence, but by guiding assessments of possible epistemic states for their prospective closeness to truth by some standard. In these senses, we can have a purely epistemic vindication of epistemic rationality.

3. EPISTEMIC UTILITIES AND COHERENCE

Arntzenius in section 3 questions the whole notion of epistemic utilities. I should be happy with such questioning: the lesson I drew was a debunking one. Whether or not talk of epistemic utilities makes sense, I argued, no such utilities play any role in explaining epistemic rationality. (I would now admit an exception to this, namely the roles epistemic utilities played in the last paragraph above.) What might play such a role, I said, is rather a tie to mundane, non-epistemic utilities—to the utility of happiness, wealth, health, or some other such things. I admit I can't myself shake off a residual sense that a pure concern for truth is intelligible and might sometimes be reasonable. Nothing in my debunking, though, required making precise sense of the line I found wanting.

Arntzenius imagines an immobilized robot Hal, and has me asking, "Suppose you just wanted Hal's current degrees of belief to be accurate, what degrees of belief would you give him?" That depends on what I mean by "accurate," he responds—my point exactly. "Gibbard is asking an unclear question." Yes, but as Arntzenius goes on to recognize, I was asking questions like this in order to expose them as unclear. According to Arntzenius, though, I still think the question to be well-defined, though with only person-specific answers. I wouldn't put it that way, and I'm not clear just what such a thought would amount to. My point was that this ill-defined question suggests a whole family of well-defined questions. Tell us just what you mean by "accurate" and you will have indicated a particular question in this family.

Why then have degrees of belief? A big question, this, which I didn't vaunt myself as able to answer. As I think Arntzenius sees, he and I are pretty much in accord on this. "When one's only goal is truth why should one's epistemic state satisfy the axioms of probability?" To this I offered no answer. In the first place, I considered credence just in a single proposition, and so most of those axioms didn't come into play. In the second place, my aim was to refute a certain kind of purely epistemic vindication of standard coherence, and unless some replacement is found, that leaves only the familiar sorts of pragmatic vindications: Dutch book arguments and more comprehensive representation theorem arguments. I may be more optimistic about representation theorems than Arntzenius is, but that's another story, and his expertise on such matters far exceeds mine.

"Why think a rational person must have purely epistemic preferences over all possible belief distributions?" There's no reason—or at least no reason they can't all be zero—unless intrinsic curiosity is itself a requirement of reason. If it is, then the fully rational person is prone act, in some conceivable circumstances, just to find something out, for no further reason. Having learned from Arntzenius of the Hair-Brane theory, I'm curious, and given the opportunity, I might expend resources and effort to garner evidence of its truth or falsehood. Does this require a full set of utilities over my possible states of belief? The story here would be the same as with the rest of decision theory. On the one hand, I can cross bridges when I come to them, and form no preferences until I need them. If, though, I go to an extreme of looking before I might leap, deciding in advance every decision problem that is even conceivable, then consistency may require fully determinate utilities for everything.

If I do have well-defined utilities for everything, can we separate out a purely epistemic component of those utilities? I don't know. My own question was a hypothetical one about a being whose *sole* intrinsic concerns are with her degrees of belief. The being, I supposed, is ideally coherent in her credences. Such a being, I now agree, will still need epistemically rational credences for purposes of guidance. Only epistemically rational credences, after all, will be prospectively optimal, by the being's own lights, as guides in seeking out evidence or assessing the value of possible states of credence. If, though, the being is passive, with nothing she can do but sit back and await new evidence, then thirst for truth as such can't explain her epistemic rationality. Epistemically rational credence can't be explained just as aimed at truth.

4. THE OTHER PUZZLE

What, then, of guidance value? The two commentaries focused on the negative thesis of the paper, on the puzzle, if I am right, that aiming at truth as such can't underlie epistemic rationality. The Schervish results lead, though, to another puzzle. Does guidance value somehow underlie the nature of epistemic rationality? I haven't yet seen to the bottom of all this, and I need help.

The main Schervish result is striking: epistemic rationality is what a fully coherent person will want if she is concerned with her epistemic states solely as guides. Epistemic rationality isn't everything one could want from one's beliefs: one can want comfort, or self-affirmation, or any of a host of other things, and one can want truths just for the sake of having them. Guidance value is just one component of the value that one's beliefs may have. Schervish, though, demonstrates a tight relation between guidance value and epistemic rationality, and it would be strange if the nature of epistemic rationality has nothing to do with this striking relation. But although it is *as if* an epistemically rational person had chosen her credences for the sake of guidance, of course she didn't. She couldn't indeed have conducted a full, rational analysis of prospective guidance values without epistemically rational credences already in place. Exactly what, then, if anything, *is* the bearing of the Schervish findings on the nature of epistemic rationality? That is a second puzzle.

INDEX

A priori:
  justification 16
  knowledge 72–3, 83–4
  necessary truths 82
  reasons 16
absolute certainty 8, 19, 22
  see also Certainty Argument
acquaintance theorist 80, 84, 85
adverbial expression 34
Alston, W. 6, 30
Arntzenius, F. 190–5, 198–204
assertion 33, 39, 42, 44, 45–6, 50
atomic sentences 47–8, 53
auditory experience 110

Bayes's Theorem 123–4
Bayesian Argument 123, 125, 127, 129, 133
Bayesian Epistemology, Bayesian view 4, 27, 168
Bealer, G. 70, 85
Beaver, D. 49, 53, 60
behavioral ecology 89
belief 30, 43, 56, 64–5, 67–70, 71–5, 77–81, 83, 90, 108–110, 113–114, 118–119, 121, 125, 127, 128, 132, 136–7, 143–150, 152, 155, 160–2, 166, 168–177, 179, 181, 184, 190, 192, 197–9, 202–3
  binary 4
  de re 75
  degree of 4, 7, 21, 23, 25, 27, 28, 165, 167, 168, 190, 192, 197–201
  epistemic degrees of 69, 169–170, 172
  ideally rational 4, 13, 23
  immodest forming of 146
  introspective 119
  irrational 27
  justified *see also* justification
  rational 144
  true 143, 144, 146
  aims at the truth 143, 144, 147, 149, 158, 160–1, 181, 197
Bergmann, M. 63, 85
Blain, E. 40, 60
Bonjour, L. 110, 114, 137
boolean connectives 47
Brain in Vat (BIV) 108–111, 115, 116, 117, 118, 121–9
Breinlinger, K. 107
Brewer, B. 75, 85, 110, 137
Brier score 149–150, 159, 183, 186
Brier rule 153, 160
Brier, G. 149–150, 151
Brosnan, S. F. 97, 105
Burge, T. 108, 132, 137

Camerer, C. F. 105
capuchin monkey, (Cebus apella) 88, 96, 103–5
Certainty Argument 10–12, 14
Chavanne, T. J. 107
Chen, M. K. 95, 98, 99, 101, 105, 106
Cherniak, C. 5, 30
Chisholm, R. 66, 70, 79
Christensen, D. 5, 6, 7, 11, 30, 174, 178
Cleveland, A. 107
closure:
  logical 4, 48

closure: (*cont.*)
  principle for
    justification 115–117, 128, 129
cognitive:
  biases 102
  error 7, 12, 14, 17, 25
  evolution 88
  imperfection 3, 8
  mistake 8, 10, 12, 19
  perfection 3, 4, 12, 14–16, 18
  processes 19–20, 27
  strategy 103
Cohen, S. 18, 108, 110, 114, 116, 123, 137
community-based readings 37
conceptual regress 80, 81, 83
conditionalization 27–9, 167, 168, 170–2, 178, 195–200
conditionalization module 173
conditionals 36, 59
Conee, E. 5, 30, 64, 69–71, 109, 138
Conservatism: 63, 70–7, 80, 83, 85
  inferential 81, 64
  see also Liberalism
Conservative View, the 110–111, 113, 120–1, 123, 128
  see also Liberal view
context 32–7, 45–52, 57–8, 64
  sensitive, dependent 46, 58, 32–3, 35, 58
context change potential (CCPS) 47, 49, 50–6, 60
contextual factors 34
contextual modulation 35
continuity axiom 175
conversational background 35–7, 48, 56–8
Copeland, B. J. 35, 60
Cox's Theorem 176, 177
credence 8–10, 13, 21, 28, 29, 128, 143, 147–163, 179–187, 195–203
  as a guide to action 154
  actual 151, 179, 196
  coherent 7, 15
  degrees of 147, 148, 156–7
  epistemically rational 155, 159, 196, 198, 200, 202–3
  immodest forming of 157
  reported 150
  rational 143, 155, 159–160, 179, 197
  partial 147, 148
credence-eliciting pair 151, 180–3, 187–9, 184

Davies, M. 108, 110, 114, 117, 121–2, 138
Davies, N. B. 89, 106
Davis, H. 62
Dawes, R. M. 106
De Finetti's Theorem
de Waal, F. B. M 97,
Dechaine, R.-M. 40, 60,
Descartes, R. 66, 74
Dretske, F. 117, 138
Dutch Book (Argument) 13, 15, 25–6, 168, 174, 198, 201
dynamic:
  case 194–5, 197, 198,
  effects 45, 55
  framework 46, 50
  perspective 46, 48, 56–9
  semantics 33, 45–9, 52, 53, 55, 59–60
  system 56, 57, 187

Egan, A. 33, 60
Ellis, B. 4, 30
empirical predictions 165

endowment effect 94, 101–2
epistemic:
  dispositions 195–6, 204
  ideals 3, 6, 8, 12, 27–8, 30
  internalism 63
  immodesty 179, 181, 189
  justification 66, 166, 177
  necessity 38,
  possibility 37, 43, 44
  preferences 175, 176, 198, 202
  probability 82–4
  rationality 21 74, 144, 146–7, 149, 150, 152–3, 159, 180, 190–6, 198, 201–3
  responsibility 5
  status 18, 64, 67–8
evidence 3, 4, 6, 11, 14–15, 18–19, 20–4, 27–8, 30, 34–42, 44–5, 64, 67–8, 70, 74, 76–8, 81, 83, 88, 92, 102–3, 105, 115–116, 122–3, 125–6, 131, 144–7, 150, 156, 158, 162–3, 167–8, 170–3, 179, 182–7, 190, 192, 194–200, 202
  defeating 72
  empirical 18, 20
  indirect 39–40
  see also perception
evidential markers 33, 39,
evidentiality 37, 40
evidentials 39, 46, 59
evolution 88, 90–1, 95–6, 103–4
evolutionary history 96, 102, 104–5
expected accuracy 148–9, 173
expected payoff 88, 90, 154, 157, 161 88, 90–1, 95, 102–4
  maximizaton of 104
expected value 151, 159, 181–2, 194
external world 83, 108, 119, 127
externalism 63–5, 75, 76, 81, 82
  content 75
  epistemic 63
  inferential externalism 81–3
  see also internalism

Fader, P. S. 106
Feldman, R. 5, 11, 30, 64, 76, 85, 109, 138
Field, H. 114, 138
Foley, R. 5, 30, 76–7, 85
foundationalism 63, 67, 72–3, 75–6, 79–81, 84–6, 113, 119, 133
  classical 67, 80–1
  moderate 113, 133, 137
  modest 81
framing effects 94, 95, 100, 102
Frege, G. 39, 41
Frege-Geach Problem 53, 55
Fumerton, Richard 18, 30, 64, 75, 81–2, 85–6, 138
function 4, 35–6, 41, 46, 48–9, 51–2, 58, 145, 148–155, 157–163, 196–7
  credence eliciting 150–2, 157, 192, 194, 199
  eliminative 52
  distributive 52
  non-credence eliciting 181, 183, 184, 185, 186, 189, 194
functional composition 49

Gajewski, J. 60–3
Garber, D. 28–30
Genesove, D. 106
Gibbard, A. 165, 166, 172–4, 179–181, 186, 189
Gigerenzer, G. 104–6
Gillies, A. S. 33, 53, 56, 59, 60–1
Glimcher, P. W. 89, 106
Goldman, A. 5, 30, 63, 67, 81, 86

Goldstein, D. G. 106
Groenendijk, J. 46, 49, 52, 61
Groeneveld, W. 60
guidance value 144, 150, 152, 154–7, 159–163, 172, 179, 189, 202–3
  actual 156, 157, 162

Hacking, I. 5, 30
Hacquard, V. 61
Hammond, P. 147, 163
Hansson, S. O. 4
Hardie, B. G. S. 106
Harel, D. 47, 61
Hastie, R. 106
Hawthorne, James 4
Hawthorne, John 60, 108, 116, 123, 138–9
Heim, I. 46, 61
Hellman, G. 174, 178
Hintikka, J. 35, 61
homologous cognitive mechanisms 102
homomorphism 48
Horwich, P. 4, 30, 146, 161, 163
Howson, C. 174, 176, 178
Huemer, M. 69–70, 86, 108, 138
Hume, D. 66, 86

Iatridou, S. 40, 43, 61
ideally rational agent (IRA) 3, 4, 7, 8, 12–13, 16, 20, 23–8
inference 29, 33, 38, 39, 40, 71, 73, 82–4
information state 46–7, 49, 50–1, 53–4, 57
  absurd 48
  minimal 48
integration 13, 15, 20, 24, 28
intentional state 64, 69, 71, 73–7, 79
internalism 63–8, 81–3
  inferential 66, 81–2
  internal state 64–7
see also externalism
isomorphism 48

Jackson, F. 32, 39, 43, 118, 138–9
Jacobson, K. 107
Jaynes, E. T. 176, 178
Jeffrey, R. C. 27, 175, 178, 180, 189
Jenkins, C. 114, 138
Johnson, E. J. 106
Joyce, J. M. 4, 145, 148, 150, 159–161, 163, 189
justification 10, 15, 16, 18, 64–73 75, 77–81, 85, 175, 108–118, 120, 123, 125–6, 130–133
  anti-skeptical 118, 131
  cogito-style independent 132
  coherence theory of 72
  empirical 113
  experiential 132
  immediate 108, 111–113, 131–3, 136–7
  independent 110–112, 114, 116–121, 127–8, 129–136
  inferential 65, 80, 82
  noninferential 65–6, 74, 78–9, 84, 108, 112
  perceptual 109, 111, 113–114, 116, 118, 121, 125, 128–135, 137
  propositional 109
  testimonial 132

Kacelnik, A. 96, 102, 106
Kahneman, D. 87, 91–6, 100, 106–7
Kamp, H. 46, 61
Kant, I. 41, 61
Karttunen, L. 38–40, 46, 61–2
Kelly, T. 11, 29–30

Keynesian epistemic probability 82, 83
Kim, J. 155, 163
Kitcher, P. 5, 30
Knetsch, J. L. 106
knowledge 18, 23, 32–4, 39, 44, 103
  animal 23
  reflective 23
Koons, R. 4
Kozen, D. 61
Kratzer, A. 35–6, 40, 62
Krebs, J. R. 89, 106
Kripke, S. 35, 62

Lakshminarayanan, V. 95, 100–1, 103, 106
language 32, 39, 47–8, 55, 73, 87
  intermediate 48–9, 53, 54, 55
  natural 33, 41, 47, 56
  propositional 47–8
Levi, I. 4, 30
Lewis, D. 46, 62, 146–7
Liberal view 112–115, 119, 122–3, 129–130
  see also conservative view
Liberalism 109, 111–115, 118, 119–120, 122, 128–9, 131–7
  strong 131–2
  see also conservatism
Liv, C. 106–107
Loewenstein, G. 105
Loewer, B. 148–9, 163
logic 4, 6, 8–9, 16, 19, 20, 23–6, 29, 47, 71
  deductive 4
  formal 4
  propositional 48
logical consistency 4, 6
logical entailment 9
logical error 16–17
logically omniscient being 14–15, 28
loss aversion 93–6, 98, 101–102, 104
Ludlow, P. 65, 86

MacFarlane, J. 33, 62
Macomber, J. 107
Maher, P. 4, 30, 148, 160, 163, 175, 178
Markie, P. 85, 86, 138
Marsh, B. 96, 102, 106
Martin, N. 61, 65, 86
Matthewson, L. 40, 62
Mayer, C. 106
McGrew, T. 75, 86
McKinsey, M. 121, 138, 139
mentalism 64, 65
mentalist internalism 68
might-statement 54, 55, 58
Modal:
  auxiliaries 34
  expressions 35, 53, 55, 59
  epistemically modalized sentences 32, 33, 40, 42, 44–5
  deontic 42
  epistemic 32–3, 35, 37, 39–44, 52–3, 55–6, 58
mental states 64–5, 71, 76
modality 32–5, 40–1, 56
  of judgment 41
Moore, G. E. 61, 108–111, 115–120
Muller-Lyer illusion 70
must-statement 54

Neta, R. 108, 120, 138
Nickel, B. 61
norm of gradational accuracy 148

Odean, T. 106
Okasha, S. 123, 129, 138

omniscient being 4, 21
optimal foraging theory 90

parentheticals 41, 44
Pargetter, R. 118, 138
Pascal, B. 45
Peacocke, C. 108, 113–114, 117, 126, 138–9
perception 22, 68, 73 , 109
perceptual belief 113, 118–119, 130–1, 136, 137
see also belief
perceptual evidence 110
see also evidence
Plantinga, A. 63, 72–3, 86
plausibility assessments 177
plausibility judgments 176–7
Pollock, J. 108, 139
possible worlds 33, 35, 43, 44, 56, 59
postfix notation 49
Potts, C. 32, 41, 62
pragmatics 45–46, 60
problem of criterion 70
Principle of Reflection 13
Pritchard, D. 116, 139
probability 82, 83, 84, 89, 90, 93, 158–9, 163, 168, 174, 177, 184, 185
axioms 191, 199, 201
distribution 176
judgments 176
theory 174, 175, 176, 177
propositions:
complex 40, 41
contingent propositions 16
prejacent 36, 45, 58, 59
prospect theory 94, 104
Pryor, J. 108, 109–110, 113, 117, 120, 122, 126, 131, 134, 135, 139

Quine, W. V. O. 63, 73, 86

Raiffa, H. 146, 163
Ramsey, F. 147, 156
rational 3, 5, 7, 9, 11,12, 14–15, 17–18, 20–8, 77–8, 82, 89, 91, 95, 102–5, 144, 145–7, 150–1, 153–5, 160–2, 166, 172–7
agent 4, 7, 20, 23–4, 26, 56, 89, 169, 180, 182, 200.
certainty 14–15, 17, 21
choice 88
desideratum 6
ideals 3, 4, 6, 8–9, 12, 19–20, 23–6
ideally 4, 7, 14, 22–6, 28
perfection 14, 16, 21
principles 20–3, 28
reflection 8
representational realist 71
reference dependence 94–6, 98, 102, 104
reference point 92, 94, 99–101
Reid, T. 74, 86
reliabilism 66, 80
report relation 182, 183, 184, 185, 186, 187, 188
Rocca, A. 107
Rullmann, H. 62
Russell, B. 69

SAM-qualifying 153–5, 159–60
Sandeberg, T. 74, 86
Santos, L. 87, 95, 101, 103, 106
Savage, L. J. 4, 30, 147, 152, 164
Schervish, M. J. 147, 150, 152, 155, 157, 158, 160–1, 164
Schiffer, S. 108, 113, 120, 123, 139
Seidenfeld, T. 161, 164
semantics:
approach to epistemic modals 33, 45

natural language 41
possible worlds 33, 35, 38, 40, 43, 44
pseudo-dynamic 47
pseudo-dynamic, update 49, 50
relativist 33, 58
static 33
update 50, 53
sensation 68, 71–2
Shah, N. 145, 164
Shuford, E. H. 152, 153–164
side value 172
Siegel, S. 110, 139
Silins, N. 116, 126–7, 139
Simons, M. 41, 44, 62
skeptical hypothesis 108, 110–111, 113–120, 123, 125–6, 127–8, 130–7
skepticism 63–4, 66–8, 82–5
Slingshot Argument 73
Slovic, P. 106
Smith, L. B. 103, 107
Sobel, J. H. 13, 30
Sosa, E. 23, 31
speech act:
modifiers 42
pragmatics 45
Spelke, E. 103, 107
Stalnaker, R. 45–6, 62
Stephenson, T. 33, 59, 62
Steup, M. 115, 120, 139
Stokhof, M. 46, 49, 52, 61
Sundell, T. 32, 37
Suomi, S. J. 106–7
Swanson, E. 33, 42, 62, 190, 192–9

Talbott, W. 4
Thaler, R. H. 94, 106, 107
Tiuryn, J. 61
Todd, P. M. 104, 106
Tooley, M. 69
truth: 10, 38, 40–1, 50–1
logical 4, 9, 12, 14, 18–19, 29
modalized, conditions 42
conditional 41–2, 44–5, 52
conditions for 33, 38, 42, 44–5, 55, 64
functional tautologies 29
immodesty 154–5
values 33, 40, 48
Tversky, A. 87, 91–6, 100, 106 107
two-dimensional proposals 44, 55

uncertainty 16, 47, 52, 56, 94
unmodalized claims 38
unmodalized proposition 41
unmodalized sentence 41–2
utility:
epistemic 165–175, 177, 199–201
epistemic, function 166, 171–2
expected, maximization 88–92, 102, 104, 147, 151, 155–6, 173
expected epistemic, maximization 169, 172, 200
Urbach, P. 174, 176, 178
utterance 32–3, 44, 46–7, 56
assertive 46

value functions 180–6, 189
credal 182–3, 185, 187–8, 192
symmetric 181
van Benthem, J. 50, 52, 60
van Cleve, J. 63
van der Does, J. 53, 60
Velleman, D. 143, 145, 161, 164
Veltman, F. 40, 46, 53, 56, 60, 62
Vogel, J. 3, 18, 31, 116, 139
von Fintel, K. 33, 40, 43, 60

Weatherson, B. 60, 62, 126, 139
Westergaard, G. C. 97, 106–7

White, R. 108, 123, 125–6, 129, 139
Willet's Taxonomy of evidentials 39
Willett, T. 63
Williamson, T. 7, 31, 32, 63, 64, 86, 115, 123, 139
Winkler, R. L. 181, 189
Wright, C. 110, 114, 116–117, 121–2, 138–9

Yalcin, S. 33, 61, 63

Zynda, L. 7, 14, 27, 31